MW00984137

THE
JAW-DROPPING
BEAUTY OF JESUS

"As a Jew who follows Jesus wholeheartedly, I always long for and love diving into Hebrews with Gospel-tinted glasses. Joshua and Gary have done a wonderful job bringing this mysterious and powerfully evangelistic book to light for this cultural moment, bringing this book of the Bible to life with a laser focus on one thing—the beauty and majesty of Jesus. This work is a gift to the believer and a captivating Gospel presentation to those we long to know Jesus, like my own Jewish family!"

—ZACH MEERKREEBS

Pastor-in-Residence at Asbury University

Author, Speaker

"There is no one better than Jesus! *The Jaw-Dropping Beauty of Jesus,* an expository devotional book by Joshua West and Gary Wilkerson, will evoke a strong response of honor and thanksgiving to our Lord. Jesus is the Capstone of God's amazing love story, the redemption and restoration of mankind. A must-read for fresh insights for those desiring to rekindle and recapture a sustained heart of true worship. I highly recommend this devotional."

—RON BROWN

Executive Director/CEO Teen Challenge of Southern California

International Conference Speaker for pastors and Christian leaders

"Since the day that I met Him, the moment He walked into my heart, I have been captivated by the beauty of Jesus. There are many good books on theology, hermeneutics, and biblical exposition. Here is a book on the beauty of Jesus. He is all-captivating. Masterfully, Gary and Joshua dig for the jewels of Hebrews and come forth with . . . Jesus—all-captivating, all-beautiful, all-surpassing Jesus."

—LEE SHIPP

First New Testament Church

"When I read the title of this book, if I didn't know the authors as I do, I would have thought the title was hype. It is not. The beauty of this book is that they share the all-sufficient and all-encompassing beauty of Jesus. It is like a diamond that sparkles in every facet of who Jesus is. Gary and Joshua have given us a study of Hebrews unlike anything I've ever read. Read it carefully and prayerfully and make personal application of the truths they share. I believe that long after you lay this book down, God will be speaking to you of what you have read."

—DON WILKERSON

Co-founder of Teen Challenge

"*The Jaw-Dropping Beauty of Jesus* is the commentary pastors and teachers of God's Word have been waiting for. This commentary/devotional on the book of Hebrews does not waste a single word. It brings the glorious truths of Hebrews into the present day with power and clarity. This remarkable commentary will not only assist pastors and teachers in crafting sermons and lessons but also edify and encourage individuals in their personal journey through Hebrews. So prepare to be inspired, equipped, and captivated by the jaw-dropping beauty of Christ."

—CHAD BURTON

Senior Pastor of Living Word Global Church, Irving, Texas

THE
JAW-DROPPING
BEAUTY OF JESUS

JOSHUA WEST AND GARY WILKERSON

FOREWORD BY JIM CYMBALA

Ambassador International
GREENVILLE, SOUTH CAROLINA & BELFAST, NORTHERN IRELAND

www.ambassador-international.com

THE JAW-DROPPING BEAUTY OF JESUS

©2024 by Joshua West and Gary Wilkerson
All rights reserved

ISBN: 978-1-64960-622-8, hardcover
ISBN: 978-1-64960-623-5, paperback
eISBN: 978-1-64960-673-0
Library of Congress Control Number: 2024939233

Cover Design by Hannah Linder Designs
Interior Typesetting by Dentelle Design
Edited by Katie Cruice Smith

No part of this publication may be reproduced, distributed, or transmitted in any form or by any means, including photocopying, recording, or other electronic or mechanical methods, without the prior written permission of the publisher, except in the case of brief quotations embodied in critical reviews and certain other noncommercial uses permitted by copyright law. For permission requests, contact the publisher using the information below.

Unless otherwise indicated, all Scriptural quotations are taken from the HOLY BIBLE, ENGLISH STANDARD VERSION, ESV. Copyright © 2008 by Crossway, a publishing ministry of Good News Publishers. All rights reserved.

Scripture marked KJV taken from the *King James Version* of the Bible. Public Domain.

Scripture marked NIV taken from the New International Version®, NIV® Copyright ©1973, 1978, 1984, 2011 by Biblica, Inc.® Used by permission. All rights reserved worldwide.

Ambassador International titles may be purchased in bulk for education, business, fundraising, or sales promotional use. For information, please email sales@emeraldhouse.com.

AMBASSADOR INTERNATIONAL
Emerald House
411 University Ridge, Suite B14
Greenville, SC 29601
United States
www.ambassador-international.com

AMBASSADOR BOOKS
The Mount
2 Woodstock Link
Belfast, BT6 8DD
Northern Ireland, United Kingdom
www.ambassadormedia.co.uk

The colophon is a trademark of Ambassador, a Christian publishing company.

JOSHUA WEST'S DEDICATION:

To my son Jameson: you have brought more joy to my life than I could have ever imagined. I pray that you walk with the Lord all of your days.

To all my brothers and sisters in Christ around the world who suffer persecution and reproach for the name of Jesus: you shine bright for the glory of God, and great is your reward in Heaven.

To my beautiful and brave wife, Kiara: words could never fully articulate the love and appreciation I have for you. Outside of salvation, you are the greatest grace and gift that God has blessed me with in this life.

GARY WILKERSON'S DEDICATION:

To my wife Kelly: I believe one of the great ways of living a loving, fruitful, successful and Godly life is to marry someone more loving, fruitful, successful and Godly. If I have attained any small measure of the above mentioned it is because my wife of forty-five years has shown me by example to live these attributes.

Kelly, you live like Jesus and love like Jesus more than anyone I have ever met. I am so glad God gave me you and to this love I will remain true. All good gifts come from above and you are such a special gift of love.

TABLE OF CONTENTS

FOREWORD

IT WAS MARTIN LUTHER WHO said that the key to rightly dividing the Word of God was to understand the difference between the Old Covenant versus the New Covenant revealed through Jesus Christ. How easy it is for people to slowly become "Old Testament Christians—a contradiction that makes spiritual growth impossible. Of course, the centerpiece of the New Covenant is the Person of Jesus Christ. It would be hard to argue that any sermon preached by Paul, Peter, or John had any other main subject except Jesus. No matter where they might begin, they would quickly get to Jesus, Who is the Image of the Invisible God and the only One in Whom salvation is found.

This is why *The Jaw-Dropping Beauty of Jesus* by Joshua West and Gary Wilkerson is so timely. We live in a day when sermons and books about Jesus Himself are actually declining. That's probably why more than 60 percent of Americans polled recently said they expected to end up in Heaven for eternity because they lived "good lives" here on earth!

Open both your mind and heart as you travel through the book of Hebrews with two gifted men of God. Their goal is to have us end up seeing as never before the jaw-dropping beauty of Jesus.

JIM CYMBALA

Senior Pastor, The Brooklyn Tabernacle

INTRODUCTION

THERE ARE MANY REASONS THAT people endeavor to write a book. But there are only a few sound reasons to write a Christian book: to teach sound doctrine; to correct, rebuke, and encourage those who are in the faith; to draw people to Christ and His Word; to make seemingly complicated teachings simple to understand, so they are practically applicable to daily life. I pray that all of these things will be true of this book. But the main reason that we wanted to write this particular book is to showcase the perfection, majesty, glory, and jaw-dropping beauty of Jesus Christ.

The book of Hebrews practically, precisely, and brilliantly does this. Hebrews is an academic and theologically deep and rich book. It has some hard-to-understand sections and, frankly, some very mysterious statements and concepts contained within it. It is one of those books that cause us to do one of a few things: skip past it altogether and pretend like it is not there, pull a verse or two out of it from time to time about faith or the power of Jesus, or humbly and studiously study to show ourselves "approved" (2 Tim. 2:15) as we dig into the richness of this God-ordained writing.

The book of Hebrews is an opportunity to understand the continuity of the Old and New Testament, as well as a unique lens through which we may gaze at the jaw-dropping beauty and excellence of Jesus. We do not need to dumb down the Bible or skip over its depths. We need to dive in headfirst and let the Bible teach us, grow us, and change us. If you, in fact, are in Christ, the same Spirit Who raised Christ from the dead and the same Spirit Who divinely inspired the writing of the book of Hebrews lives inside of you; and He is the Helper meant to lead us into all truth.

Displayed across the backdrop of the Old Covenant, the Gospel and Person of Jesus shines beautifully and radiantly as an unignorable reminder that all things were made by Him and for Him. God purposely ordained all things to testify to the superiority of Christ. The imperfection of everything is made clear when contrasted with Christ.

The book of Hebrews makes clear to the believer the necessity of understanding the Old Testament, the Law, and the prophets—a stage set to bring maximum glory to the King of all kings and the Lord of all lords! It is my humble hope that this book will glorify Christ and help you see the biblical Jesus from the book of Hebrews and all the Old Testament books connected with it.

One of the reasons we are very excited to write this book is because we write in very different styles, and it is our hope that this fact will make the content of this book much more robust than it could be if just one of us had written it. We hope that this writing rides the line of being extremely readable but not shallow, challenging but not over-academic, and commentary-like but not wooden.

We live in an era in which many who call themselves Christians seem to despise words like "doctrine," usually because they imagine that there is a means of knowing and worshiping God free of rules and boundaries, a relationship that is accessible through their own set of terms. We do not want God to set rules and boundaries for us, but we have many for Him. We want to be "spiritual" but not religious, and we want a savior we don't have to bow down before as Lord. There is no such savior! There is only One Who is mighty to save, and we are able to know Him through the revelation of Scripture that God has preserved for us down through the ages.

It is our great hope that for some, this study of Hebrews will reveal to you the biblical Christ in all of His glory. Or for some of you, it will deepen your understanding, worship, and adoration of our Savior King. D. Martyn Lloyd Jones once said, "We cannot approach the Bible without considering it worship. The Bible is no ordinary book, it is God's book and all things concerning God require worship."[1]

This book will be imperfect as we are merely men—Christ-followers who have been called to teach and preach the Gospel and the full counsel of God by His Spirit and according to His Word and for His glory. There is only one perfect book, and that is the Bible. The goal of this book—as it is with all the books—is to point you toward Christ and His Word. It is our hope that this book would ignite a passion and a pang of hunger within you for the biblical Jesus and that from His Word, you will see His incomparable beauty.

We believe that Jesus is jaw-droppingly beautiful and that this beauty deserves to be shouted from the rooftops, announced to the nations, proclaimed to generations, and declared unashamedly in all churches. We have one drum to beat—Jesus is our All-in-all. We have one note to play—Christ is to be exalted above all things. We have a single message—Jesus reigns! We are less interested in writing a book and far more interested in heralding the joyful news of a most wonderful, glorious, unique, powerful, majestic, stately, holy, awesome, precious, loving, beautiful, imposing, exquisite, above all, one-of-a-kind, Name-above-all-names—Jesus the Christ.

Jesus is lovely above all things. Yet His beauty constantly grows on our hearts, and our minds are ever-increasingly wrapped up with His loveliness as we continue to know Him better. This loveliness is not to be confused with romanticism. His loveliness is wrapped in power, His beauty in vigor, and His splendor matched by His superiority. Be careful; the beauty of Jesus, once gazed upon, will addict you, mesmerize you, consume you, and never let you go. You will go from the glory of Jesus to the greater glory of Jesus.

---

1   Martyn Lloyd Jones, *Romans: An Exposition of Chapter 12: Christian Conduct* (Carlisle: Banner of Truth Trust, 2000).

If this is of little interest to you, we pray you will read this book and, in doing so, will drop your jaw. If you already find the pursuit of Jesus as the foremost passion in your life, we pray these chapters will add fuel to the fire in your bones.

One good thing about writing a book about the beauty of Jesus is that there is an unending reservoir of content, as if thousands had gathered from the first century and every generation from then until now and said, "We will write of His beauty all the days of our lives." If we wrote tens of millions of volumes, we would find ourselves yet at the introductory stages, the kindergarten of the knowledge of His beauty. Yet we are not surrendered to the notion that nothing of profit can be said. We believe that each word spoken of His loveliness will have its intended impact. We have endeavored to fill these pages with words spoken of His loveliness.

We hope this book not only drops your jaw but that it also drops you to your knees in adoration of Jesus. We trust we have honored Christ in such a way as to have Him become more exalted in your life. We believe that nothing this world has to offer compares with the wonderful glory of Jesus. Read and be ready to encounter Jesus.

He is the radiance of the glory of God and the exact imprint of his nature,

and upholds the universe by the word of his power. After making purification for sins,

he sat down at the right hand of the Majesty on high.

HEBREWS 1:3

CHAPTER 1
JESUS IS THE FINAL WORD

BY: JOSHUA WEST

Long ago, at many times and in many ways, God spoke to our fathers by the prophets,
but in these last days he has spoken to us by his Son, whom he appointed the heir of all things,
through whom also he created the world. He is the radiance of the glory of God and the exact
imprint of his nature, and he upholds the universe by the word of his power. After making
purification for sins, he sat down at the right hand of the Majesty on high, having become as
much superior to angels as the name he has inherited is more excellent than theirs.

HEBREWS 1:1-4

THERE IS NO WAY THAT we could ever overstate or exaggerate the beauty, majesty, and wondrous brilliance of Jesus. "All things were created through him and for him" (Col. 1:16). The purpose of everything in creation is to magnify and give testimony to His worthiness of worship and His supremacy in all things. This is why the sun rises and sets each day. This is why flowers bloom. This is why our planet rotates around the sun, and this is why blood circulates through our veins and air flows in and out of our lungs. All things in creation were made to bring glory to God. And God the Father has given all power, authority, and dominion to His Son Jesus Christ. John 3:35 says, "The Father loves the Son and has given all things into his hand."

Everything in all of creation was created for the glory of Christ, and the Bible is no exception. Although the Hero of the story does not make His entrance for thousands of years and thirty-nine books into the Bible, everything that comes before is in support of His entrance into the world. The entire Bible is about Jesus. From Genesis to Revelation, the words of Scripture either directly or indirectly point to the surpassing worth and beauty of Christ.

The entire Old Testament is a stage that was set to usher in the coming of the King above all kings and the Lord of all Lords. One of the greatest questions answered by the coming of Christ in the New Testament is this: "How can a fallen and sinful people be reconciled to a just and holy God?" This question is definitively answered in the Gospels, as we see the life, death, and resurrection of Jesus and the exclusive means of salvation that He secured on the cross for all who, by faith, would believe in Him alone for salvation.

In the epistles, the Gospel message is explained and applied in the context of the Church and the life of the believer, serving as pillars built on the firm foundation of the apostles and the prophets of which Christ Himself is the Chief Cornerstone (Eph. 2:20). In the book of Romans, we find the clearest and most detailed explanation of the Gospel message—its need, power, and purpose as we see the depravity of man; the holiness of God; the inability of the law to save; and the all-sufficiency of the Gospel work of Christ on the cross. But it is in the book of Hebrews that we see the greatest display of the jaw-dropping beauty of Jesus most clearly as His eternal superiority in all things is magnified against the backdrop of the Old Covenant.

The overarching theme of the book of Hebrews is that Jesus Christ is better than anything in all of creation, and this includes all Old Testament types and shadows that were merely meant as placeholders and markers to point to the person of Christ. Jesus is better, superior, and greater than the angels, Abraham, Moses, and all the prophets, priests, and kings throughout the history of Israel. He is the all-sufficient Sacrifice for sin; and He is our Prophet, Priest, and King now and forever, amen.

The book of Hebrews is a mysterious and powerful book, although it is unclear who authored it. It is clear that it was viewed as sacred Scripture by first- and second-century disciples. There is no book in the New Testament that explains in such depth the meaning and purpose of the practices and ceremonies of temple worship and the sacrificial system under the Old Covenant. The book of Hebrews also sheds great light on the progressive nature of how God chooses to speak and reveal Himself to humanity over the course of time. Also, like most of the New Testament epistles, there is a warning about the danger of falling away and encouragement for the true believer to persevere in the faith.

Ultimately, the point of Hebrews is to show that the final reality of the New Covenant as revealed in Jesus Christ far exceeds the temporary foreshadowing of the Old Covenant. This is revealed to us in a few ways:

1. Jesus has brought final and ultimate salvation from sin that the Old Covenant could not bring. The author of Hebrews spends a great deal of time expanding on the reality that since the One Who is bringing the New Covenant is superior in every possible way, what He is bringing is superior in every possible way as well.

2. Jesus is a Savior Who brings us into a greater rest and a greater Promised Land than Moses or Joshua did.

3. Jesus permanently and eternally fulfills the roles of those who were chosen in the past to lead God's people. Jesus is our final Prophet, our permanent Priest, and our eternal King. He is the Anointed One!

4. The book of Hebrews instructs us that as faithful men and women have always done from the beginning of time and throughout the ages, we, too, must live by faith, looking and living toward a future reward and a future kingdom that, to some degree, is

unseen in this life. But ultimately, everything in this life will be overtaken and outshined by the beauty and reward of Christ that will never fade and will never pass away.

It is so very important that we make sure right from the start that our view of God is in the right perspective. We are so far beneath the holy perfection of God that we cannot help underestimating and misunderstanding Him. He is so far beyond our understanding and outside of our reach that it is ridiculous. We are tiny specks of dust compared to God. God is unreachable and unknowable to us. We are completely unable to interact with God outside of His will to know us. This is what makes the first verse of Hebrews so profound; it says that God spoke to us. What an amazing statement: "God has spoken." God has spoken, but we must be mindful of the means by which He chose to speak. God has revealed Himself to us in the way He has chosen, and you had better believe that there is a purpose in it. There is nothing that God does that is not thoughtful, deliberate, and perfect. God has revealed Himself to us through the person of Jesus Christ, according to the Scripture.

Hebrews 1:1 tells us that God has spoken in the past through the fathers and the prophets, and this is referring to the Old Testament and the Old Covenant. In the Old Testament, God set aside the Hebrews as a chosen people for His holy purposes. And from within that chosen people, He set aside imperfect but faithful men through whom He gave us His perfect and sacred Word. God's Word is very important to Him, so it should be very important to us.

In the past, God's Word was given to us through men like Moses, Joshua, King David, and the prophets who were set aside as the very mouthpiece of God to the people of Israel—men like Isaiah, Jeremiah, and Daniel. But all throughout the Old Testament, Christ is pointed to, as the sum of creation groans in anticipation of His appearing. Deuteronomy 18:14-19 says:

For these nations, which you are about to dispossess, listen to fortune-tellers and to diviners. But as for you, the Lord your God has not allowed you to do this. "The Lord your God will raise up for you a prophet like me from among you, from your brothers—it is to him you shall listen—just as you desired of the Lord your God at Horeb on the day of the assembly, when you said, 'Let me not hear again the voice of the Lord my God or see this great fire any more, lest I die.' And the Lord said to me, 'They are right in what they have spoken. I will raise up for them a prophet like you from among their brothers. And I will put my words in his mouth, and he shall speak to them all that I command him. And whoever will not listen to my words that he shall speak in my name, I myself will require it of him."

This Scripture foretells a greater Prophet than Moses, Whose message will be superior to the message he brought; and Hebrews 1:2 tells us that this is referring to Jesus. Here is what we must see: Christ is God's final Word, and there is no need for another one. Jesus is the Fulfillment of Old Testament prophecy; He is the Answer to all things because He Himself is the origin of all things. Jesus isn't just another messenger or apostle or merely a good teacher or just another prophet.

This is one thing that makes the religion of Islam not only wrong but demonic. It represents Jesus as a mere prophet among many others, a prophet the Quran says will one day bow down before Muhammad. The opposite of this is true. Not only will Muhammad bow before Jesus; but every being ever created, all of the angels in Heaven, all the demons in Hell, and every person ever created will also bow down at the feet of Jesus. There are none above Him, but there is also no one beside Him.

"Therefore, God has highly exalted him and bestowed on him the name that is above every name, so that at the name of Jesus every knee should bow, in heaven and on earth and under the earth, and every tongue confess that Jesus Christ is Lord, to the glory of God the Father" (Phil. 2:9-11).

THE BEAUTY OF THE WORD MADE FLESH

Right from the beginning, the author of Hebrews wants to make one thing very clear: every Old Testament prophet, priest, king, ordinance, rite, and ritual were a mere shadow that is swallowed up like a raindrop in the ocean when compared to the Person of Christ. This is a theme that permeates the entirety of the New Testament. The Gospel of John also makes it clear that Christ is God; that it was through Him the world was created; and that He is worthy of all worship, honor, and praise. "In the beginning was the Word, and the Word was with God, and the Word was God. He was in the beginning with God. All things were made through him, and without him was not any thing made that was made. In him was life, and the life was the light of men. The light shines in the darkness, and the darkness has not overcome it" (John 1:1-5).

Hebrews 1:1-4 makes it very clear that God the Father has appointed Jesus as the Heir of all things, and that affirms Him as the second Person of the Trinity by attributing the creation of the world to Him. Verse three says, "He is the radiance of the glory of God and the exact imprint of His nature." Do you want to know God? Look at the person of Jesus. He is the exact Imprint of His nature. The apostle Paul also uses this same language when writing to the church in Colossae:

> He is the image of the invisible God, the firstborn of all creation. For by him all things were created, in heaven and on earth, visible and invisible, whether thrones or dominions or rulers or authorities—all things were created through him and for him. And he is before all things, and in him, all things hold together. And he is the head of the body, the church. He is the beginning, the firstborn from the dead, that in everything he might be preeminent. For in him all the fullness of God was pleased to dwell, and through him to reconcile to himself all things, whether on earth or in heaven, making peace by the blood of his cross (Col. 1:15-20).

In just the first four verses of Hebrews chapter one, we see the preeminent and sovereign power of Christ as God; but in the same breath, we also see the beauty of His compassion and love for us as it states His purpose in coming to earth, which was to make purification for our sins.

It goes on from here to compare the superiority of the glory of Christ and how He outshines that of the angels in every way; but in the midst of glorifying Christ, it includes the purification He made for our sins on the cross. One of the most strikingly beautiful characteristics of Jesus is His compassion toward humanity and His willingness to leave Heaven to walk among His creation in order that He might die to save them.

Hundreds, if not thousands, of hymns and songs have been written contrasting the infinite majesty of Christ and the finite wretchedness of sinful man and asking the same question King David did in Psalm 8: "What is man that you are mindful of him?" (v. 8). It is in the person of Christ that we clearly see God's heart toward man. He stepped down from the perfection of Heaven, took on flesh, walked among those He created, lived a perfect life, died a brutal death on our behalf, and rose from the dead so that we could be restored to God. This is the beauty of Christ, and this is the love of God.

The idea that the all-powerful and infinite God would become like His creation in order to save them and have eternal fellowship with them is a thought that should be pondered and reflected upon often because it reveals the love of God and His heart toward humanity. But this should not be our starting point; our starting point should be on Who God is and what He has revealed to us through the entirety of the Scripture. It was intentional on God's part that He revealed Himself progressively over thousands of years before the coming of Christ. There is nothing about God's plan that does not serve a purpose. God the Father ushered in the coming of His Son at the perfect moment in history, so that all things might be accomplished according to His will and that Christ might receive the maximum glory He is due.

Paul wrote to the Romans, "For while we were still weak, at the right time Christ died for the ungodly" (Rom. 5:6). And to the Galatians, he wrote, "But when the fullness of time had come, God sent forth his Son, born of woman, born under the law, to redeem those who were under the law, so that we might receive adoption as sons" (Gal. 4:4-5).

Christ is the Anchor Who holds us steady in every storm. He is the Author of our salvation. He is the Sacrifice made for the purification of our sins; and He is due all praise, worship, glory, and honor—not simply for what He did for us on the cross but because of Who He is—the unrivaled and un-disputed King of the universe.

"Looking to Jesus, the founder and perfector of our faith, who for the joy that was set before him endured the cross, despising the shame, and is seated at the right hand of the throne of God" (Heb. 12:2). All things in this life, in the universe, and in eternity are meant to magnify the jaw-dropping beauty of Jesus and to bear witness to His majesty and supremacy in all things.

THE ANCHOR OF SCRIPTURE

The Centerpiece of Christianity is Jesus Christ. But truthfully, He is the Center of all things because He is the eternal and infinite Creator. He is the Answer to all things because, like John chapter one tells us, He is the Origin of all things. He is the *logos,* the Word of God made flesh. We must be very clear that when we talk about Jesus, we are talking about Jesus as revealed in the Scripture. Many people call themselves Christians and invoke the name of Jesus, but they do this in ways that contradict Scripture. We must know the God of the Bible.

Jesus warns us that many will come in the name of Christ and will try and attribute things to Christ that have nothing to do with the biblical Jesus. He warns us that they will try to validate their false teachings about Jesus with signs and wonders, and these are meant to lead us astray. He says even the elect may be led astray. "'Then if anyone says to you, *Look, here is the Christ!*

or *There he is!* do not believe it. For false christs and false prophets will arise and perform great signs and wonders, so to lead astray, if possible, even the elect'" (Matt. 24:23-24).

So often today, false teaching about Jesus is accompanied by language about how wonderful Jesus is and how much they love Him. Many times, this is the excuse that is made when their teaching is exposed as unbiblical. People say, "How could they be wrong? They sound so sincere"; or "They say that they love Jesus so much." But when your description of the person, character, or teachings of Jesus do not line up with the revelation of Scripture, you are spreading a "false christ."

Here is my version of an analogy I heard my wife give once when she was teaching a women's Bible study. It would be like someone coming up to pay a compliment to me about my wife and saying how wonderful and beautiful she is and that they loved her so much. They said that they love her beautiful, short blonde hair and her slender and tall build and that her beautiful blue eyes sparkle like the sea. Although their comments were complimentary and nice, they are not describing my wife. My wife has long brown hair; she is short and curvy and has beautiful brown eyes.

What they are expressing affection for is not my wife. So no matter how sweet and complimentary their words are, they are clearly not directed at who my wife really is; so they are meaningless. Sadly, this is often true of Jesus also. When people sing songs of worship or preach messages that are sweet and sentimental about Jesus but have poor theology and do not accurately reflect what God's own Word says about Jesus—no matter how sweet—they are meaningless, pointless, blasphemous, and damaging. If you do not know Jesus as revealed in Scripture, you do not know Jesus. You can say you love Jesus all you want; but if that love is not rooted in biblical truth, you are deceived.

In a very real way, the author of Hebrews is telling Christians that they must hold fast and be anchored to Christ. To do this, they must be anchored to the unchanging promises of God's Word. As Hebrews 6:19 says, "We have this as a sure and steadfast anchor for the soul, a hope that enters into the inner place behind the curtain."

One of the most important truths that the book of Hebrews reveals is that Jesus is not a different God than the God of Abraham, Isaac, and Jacob. He is the Answer to all the questions asked in the Old Testament, the Culmination of things that were left undone, and the Fulfillment of all things. But even as believers, we have the tendency to drift; and when we drift, it is never toward God but always away from Him.

The devil, our flesh, and this fallen world are like an ocean current that is pulling us away from the Lord—away from the sureness of our salvation, away from the joy of our salvation, away from lives of obedience and holiness, and away from daily fellowship with God. This was true when the author of Hebrews penned his epistle, and it is true today. Often, it is not that we turn our backs on God all at once; instead, we drift off little by little like an unmanned or unanchored vessel drifting out to sea.

> Therefore we must pay much closer attention to what we have heard, lest we drift away from it. For since the message declared by angels proved to be reliable, and every transgression or disobedience received a just retribution, how shall we escape if we neglect such a great salvation? It was declared at first by the Lord, and it was attested to us by those who heard, while God also bore witness by signs and wonders and various miracles and by gifts of the Holy Spirit distributed according to his will (Heb. 2:1-4).

The Greek word *pararrhyéō*—which is translated into the two English words, "drift away"—means to float past or away from its intended destination due to the current of the water. This is describing something floating along with the current or a sea vessel that is unmanned and is going in whatever direction the waves, wind, or current is taking it. The author of Hebrews is warning

Christians that just like an unmanned or unanchored sea vessel, their lives will drift if not intentionally anchored to something that is strong and secure.

How do we avoid this? The author of Hebrews tells us that as well—by paying careful attention to what we have heard. And what is that? Well, to this first-century audience, it is the words of the Old Testament, the Law, and the prophets and the apostles' testimonies of the Gospel of Jesus Christ. But to us, it is the entirety of inspired Scripture. We are blessed to have the Old and New Testaments to inform our faith and direct our steps. We must be anchored to Christ and to His unchanging Word. God never changes, and His Word never changes. It is never outdated, and will never pass away, just like the Savior it reveals—Jesus Christ.

"Jesus Christ is the same yesterday and today and forever. Do not be led away by diverse and strange teachings, for it is good for the heart to be strengthened by grace, not by foods, which have not benefited those devoted to them" (Heb. 13:8-9). This beautiful truth not only should anchor our lives as our primary source of knowledge and direction for our lives; but it also should bring us comfort knowing that Jesus Himself and His sacred Word are dependable, unchanging, and unbreakable. In an ever-changing world that is full of uncertainty, we can be at peace when we are anchored to Christ, knowing that His Word is dependable.

This is a great comfort to those of us in Christ, but it is also a warning. Jesus is God's final Word and the greatest blessing given in the history of the world; but we must remember that apart from the atoning work of Christ on the cross, we are under the law. In the past, those who never even saw Christ were judged by the witness and message of angels and prophets and the law of Moses. How much more will God judge those who had access to the full revelation of God's Word and the Gospel of Jesus Christ?

"How shall we escape if we neglect such a great salvation? It was declared at first by the Lord, and it was attested to us by those who heard, while God also bore witness by signs and wonders and various miracles and by gifts of the Holy Spirit distributed according to his will" (Heb. 2:3-4).

Under the law of Moses, someone could be condemned to death based on the witness testimony of two or three imperfect witnesses. A question posed by the author of Hebrews more than once throughout the epistle is this: if this was the standard imposed on those who did not have the revelation of Christ, how much more severe will judgment be for those who have access to the full revelation of Christ and the full revelation of His Word? If we neglect the salvation afforded to us through Christ in the Gospel, we will not escape; and we will be subject to the full measure of God's wrath.

Jesus became flesh—not only to save us but also to be a High Priest who could identify with us. We have a great Savior; and through Him, we have such a "great salvation" in terms of what it provides for us but also in its grandeur and essence of power. In light of the standard of moral perfection that is demanded by the law of God and our complete inability to live up to it, we should be overwhelmed with thanksgiving and praise for the salvation Christ secured for us on the cross.

So in light of this, how could we ignore or neglect this unearned gift of God's saving grace? All throughout the book of Hebrews, its author uses the Old Covenant and the Law to showcase how infinitely better the New Covenant is and the superiority of the One Who brought it. Think about this in terms of a court of law. The author of Hebrews is basically saying if imperfect witnesses can be used to convict, how much more will a perfect Witness?

God the Father is a Witness to the Deity of the Son. He uses the entirety of the Old Testament to expose how desperately we need salvation. We needed a better covenant, a better Priest, a better Sacrifice, a better King, a better Rest, and a better Savior. Jesus comes and answers every question, fulfills every prophecy, and offers forgiveness for our sins past, present, and future, as well as a place as a son or daughter in the eternal family of God. So why wouldn't we want to accept all of this? It is simply because to have all the benefits of

Christ the Savior and Christ our Sacrifice, we must bow down and surrender to Christ as Lord and King. This is the offensiveness of the cross.

It is the narrow singularity and exclusivity of Jesus as the only Way to God that causes so much offense among humankind. To the Jews of the first century, it was offensive that Jesus claimed to be God and the long-awaited Messiah foretold in the Old Testament. He claimed to be greater than the patriarchs Abraham and Moses. To the Greeks, it was offensive that Jesus claimed to be the only true God among the pantheon of Greco/Roman gods. To modern man, it is offensive that Christians hold up the Gospel of Jesus Christ as the only remedy for the death brought on by our sin. It is offensive that in a world of technological innovation and scientific and medical breakthroughs, we are still subject to the wrath and judgment of a holy God.

Matthew 7:13-14 says, "'Enter by the narrow gate. For the gate is wide and the way is easy that leads to destruction, and those who enter by it are many. For the gate is narrow and the way is hard that leads to life, and those who find it are few.'" It seems that the very same thing that makes Jesus beautiful to the redeemed is the exact thing that makes Him offensive to the world at large. It is His preeminence in all things, His holy perfection, His worthiness of worship, His glory, His majesty, and His supremacy. This is what makes His sacrifice so beautiful, special, and precious to those of us who are being saved. But this is also an indictment against those who reject His Lordship, thus rejecting the great salvation that He came to earth to bring.

It seems that the author of Hebrews intends to magnify the glory, supremacy, and all-sufficiency of Christ to the point that we are overwhelmed and left without excuse. He also seems to want us to see everything in life through the lens of Christ. This is the preeminence and supremacy of Christ put on display. Jesus is God, the Creator, Savior, the King of kings, and Lord of lords. Jesus is Lord if you accept it or not. Jesus is the Centerpiece of the universe past, present, and future if you acknowledge it or not. His beauty is undeniable, and His majesty is indescribable. His love is insurmountable, and He is worthy of all worship and all praise forever and ever amen.

Author Richard Sibbes wrote:

> Here is a sea indeed if we should enter into it, to see the love of God, which is the most beautiful and amiable grace of all: the love of God in Christ, and the love of Christ towards us. Christ was never more lovely to His church than when He was most deformed for His church; 'there was no form nor beauty in him,' Isa. 53:2 when He hung upon the cross. Oh! There was a beauty to a guilty soul, to see his surety enduring the wrath of God, overcoming all his enemies, and nailing the law to his cross. And that should endear Christ to us above all things. He should be the dearer to us, the more vile and base He was made for us, and He should be most lovely in our eyes, when He was least lovely in His own, and when He was deformed when our sins were upon Him.
>
> We should consider those times especially. The world is most offended at that, that a Christian most joys in. 'God forbid that I should joy in anything but in the cross of Christ,' Gal. 6:14, saith St Paul. So we should joy in and love that, especially in Christ."[2]

The author of Hebrews spends the last nine verses of chapter one establishing the superiority of Jesus to the angels, explaining that not only will we spend eternity worshiping Jesus but also will all of creation, including the angels. This is a verification of the Deity of Christ. Over the next several chapters, we will see Jesus magnified as superior to every patriarch, every king, every temple ordinance, every sacrifice, and every priest. One by one, the imperfection of all created things will be drowned out in the shining and unique perfection that is Christ!

The author of Hebrew's message to His first-century audience in chapter one of the epistle is as true today as it was then. We must hold fast to the

---

2   Richard Sibbes, "A Breathing After God," in *The Complete Works of Richard Sibbes*, ed. Alexander Balloch Grosart, Vol. 2 (Edinburgh: James Nichol, 1862), 231.

Anchor of Christ as revealed to us in the Scripture, lest we drift away with the wind and waves of this fallen world. And we know we can depend on this because Christ is the Rock of Ages. He is steady, unchanging, and all-powerful. He is the Source of life and salvation, and He has been granted all authority and power in Heaven and earth. He is seated at the righthand of the throne of God. And in light of all of this, we see that we will, by grace, be co-heirs of this inheritance that rightfully belongs to Christ—not because of anything we have done but in spite of all we have done—simply because of the grace and goodness of God, revealed to us in the Person of Christ.

> For to which of the angels did God ever say, "You are my Son, today I have begotten you"? Or again, "I will be to him a father, and he shall be to me a son"? And again, when he brings the firstborn into the world, he says, "Let all God's angels worship him."
>
> Of the angels, he says, "He makes his angels winds, and his ministers a flame of fire." But of the Son he says, "Your throne, O God, is forever and ever, the scepter of uprightness is the scepter of your kingdom. You have loved righteousness and hated wickedness; therefore God, your God, has anointed you with the oil of gladness beyond your companions." And "You, Lord, laid the foundation of the earth in the beginning, and the heavens are the work of your hands; they will perish, but you remain; they will all wear out like a garment, like a robe you will roll them up, like a garment they will be changed. But you are the same, and your years have no end." And to which of the angels has he ever said, "Sit at my right hand until I make your enemies a footstool for your feet"? Are they not all ministering spirits sent out to serve for the sake of those who are to inherit salvation? (Heb. 1:5-14).

CHAPTER 2
JESUS SPEAKS

BY: GARY WILKERSON

By the word of the Lord the heavens were made and by the breath of his mouth all their

host. He gathers the waters of the sea as a heap; he puts the deeps in storehouses.

Let all the earth fear the Lord; let all the inhabitants of the world stand in awe of him!

For he spoke, and it came to be; he commanded, and it stood firm.

PSALM 33:6-9

JESUS SPEAKS TO NOTHINGNESS, AND it bursts with abounding substance. Void becomes fullness. Emptiness now sprawls with newly created forms. He splits the darkness with light, flinging stars, planets, and moons across the vast expanses. Oceans separate from lands; living organisms spring to life—all by the power of His word. Even man and woman, though formed from the dust of the newly created earth, were breathed upon by God yet were part of Him speaking life into creation. "By him all things were created" (Col. 1:16). And all things were created by His word.

Jesus still speaks. He says to our darkness of soul, "'Let there be light'" (Gen. 1:3). He says to our downcast heart, "Let there be joy." He speaks life into our dreariness, dullness, and deadness of spirit. He speaks to our depravity and says, "Let there be redemption." He sees our hearts drifting, our minds dulling, and our soul decaying; and He cries out, "Come alive!" He speaks to marriages, "Be restored"; to addicted young adults, "Be free"; to prodigals, "Come home!" His voice commands evil to flee, sin to be quelled, and sickness to be healed.

And He has more to say. He will one day soon say to the devil, "Be cast into the pit for eternity." He will say to His sons and daughters, "Welcome into my kingdom. 'Well done good and faithful servant'" (Matt. 25:23). He will say to His Father, "All things I have conquered, and now I give all these kingdoms to You."

The book of Hebrews celebrates this incredible wonder. "Long ago, at many times and in many ways, God spoke to our fathers by the prophets" (Heb. 1:1). God is a speaking God. How marvelous it must have been to hear a mighty prophet of God thunder truth from Heaven. How awesome to have the voice of an angel speak words of hope or of direction in a time of need. How overwhelming to see the words of God written on tablets of stone. Every single one of these words of prophets and law written long ago are the very words of God. All of these words are inspired and infallible. When we see this shift from old to new, it in no way demeans nor diminishes them. Yet now God has spoken something new; something better is about to take place. Jesus has become the ultimate Spokesman from Heaven. It is as if Jesus is a Prism that gathered all the induvial bands of light and shone them into one pure beam.

The next sentence reveals a greater and better way of God speaking to us—not just through created things, not through visitation from angels, not through prophets, but from the man Christ Jesus—fully God and yet one of us. The Son of God came to us, spoke to us, and still speaks to us as fully Man. John the beloved speaks of Jesus that "which we have heard, which we have seen with our eyes, which we looked upon and have touched with our hands . . . this is the message we have heard from him" (I John 1:1-5). The oft unspoken glory of the incarnation is that we have God as fully Man speaking to us. He is speaking in a form to which we can clearly relate.

JESUS HAS SPOKEN

We believe Jesus still speaks today. When the Word of God is preached and a sinner is saved, it is because the Holy Spirit has made the words of Jesus in the Gospel come alive in the present time. We believe Jesus will speak. There is much to be fulfilled in prophecy, and it will be so by the word of His power. We cannot diminish the need to understand that Jesus speaks. Yet what we must come to know is that Hebrews 1:2 does not say Jesus speaks; it says He has spoken. It is not present tense, nor future tense. It is past tense. This dramatically tells us everything we need to know. He has spoken and, by His spoken word, "granted to us all things that pertain to life and godliness, through the knowledge of him" (2 Peter 1:3). We must be careful in these last days not to run after prophetic words or angelic visitations; we are to run after the words of Jesus. If He wills, God, in His Sovereignty, can give prophetic words or even have angels among us without us knowing (Heb. 13:2). But it is a sad situation in the Church today, particularly in the hyper-charismatic Church, that people seem to want a prophetic word or an angelic word more than the Word of God. They seem to love the sensational more than the substantial. Jesus has spoken; and the Word of God is our first, primary, and utmost source of life.

Jesus speaks again and again. More than any other book in Scripture, Hebrews speaks of just how very much Jesus speaks. It speaks of Jesus speaking; it quotes the Holy Spirit speaking; and it tells of what the Father speaks about the Son. This book clearly reveals that God loves to speak. He wants us to know Him, and He is making Himself known through His Son.

As seen in the following verses, Hebrews is full of either Jesus speaking, the Holy Spirit speaking about Him, or the Father speaking of Jesus:

- 1:5—"Did God ever say, 'You are my son'?"
- 1:5—"Or again, 'I will be to him a father.'"
- 1:6—"And again . . . he says, 'Let all the angels worship him.'"

- 1:7—"Of the angels he says, 'He makes his angels winds.'"
- 1:8—"Of the Son he says, 'Your throne, O God.'"
- 1:10—"And 'You, Lord, laid the foundation.'"
- 1:13—And to which of the angels has he ever said, 'Sit at my right hand.'"
- 2:6—"It has been testified, 'What is man?'"
- 2:11—"He is not ashamed to call them brothers."
- 2:12—"Saying, 'I will tell.'"
- 2:13—"And again, 'I will put my trust in him.'"
- 2:13—"And again, 'Behold, I and the children God has given me.'"
- 3:7—"The Holy Spirit says, 'Today if you hear his voice.'"
- 3:10—"And said, 'They always go astray.'"
- 4:3—"As he has said, 'As I swore in my wrath.'"
- 4:5—"Again in this passage he said, 'They shall not enter my rest.'"
- 5:5—"Who said to him, "You are my Son.'"
- 5:6—"As he says also . . . 'You are a priest forever.'"
- 6:14—"Saying, 'Surely I will bless you.'"
- 7:17—"For it is witnessed of him, 'You are a priest forever.'"
- 8:8—"When he says, 'Behold, the days are coming.'"
- 10:5—"When Christ came into the world, he said, 'Sacrifices and offering you have not desired.'"
- 10:7—"Then I said, 'Behold, I have come to do your will.'"
- 10:8—"When he said, 'You have neither desired nor taken pleasure in sacrifices.'"
- 10:9—"Then he added, 'Behold, I have come to do your will.'"
- 10:15-16—"For after saying, 'This is the covenant that I will make with them.'"
- 10:17—"Then he adds, 'I will remember their sins and their lawless deeds on more.'"

- 12:5—"Have you forgotten the exhortation . . . 'My son, do not regard lightly the discipline.'"
- 12:26—His voice shook . . . 'Yet once more I will shake not only the earth but also the heavens.'"

Hebrews 12:24 summarizes all these words by saying that Jesus "speaks a better word" and then tells of the significance of His words, warning us not to refuse Him. In thirteen chapters, we have revealed to us that God is more than willing to speak to us and that He loves speaking to us through His Son. At least thirty times in thirteen chapters, we have God speaking of the Son, about the Son, or through the Son. How glorious that we have a Mediator in Christ Jesus, Who is speaking to us through His Word and the Spirit today.

WHEN JESUS SPEAKS

Not only does Jesus speak a better word; but Jesus, as the One Who speaks it, is also what gives the word its greater glory and authority. I could say to you, "'Yet once more I will shake . . . the earth'" (Heb. 12:26) with my little authority or ability, and my words would hold little account. They could be easily dismissed. But when the Son of God speaks these words, Who He is gives authority to His words.

If Joe the plumber got up on a stage and said, "Let us 'remember the poor,'" (Gal. 2:10), it would be true, right, and good. But if Mother Teresa got up on that same stage and spoke to the same crowd and said, "Let us 'remember the poor,'" it would hold far more weight and authority. Many in the crowd would be swayed and never forget her words because of who she is. When Hebrews starts off by saying that God is now speaking through His Son and not just angels or prophets, He is sending us a Voice of greater authority. We should much more heed these words because of Who is speaking. When Jesus speaks, it is more than words; the Bible tells us it "is living and active, sharper than any two-edged sword" (Heb. 4:12). There may be other swords, but Jesus is doubled-edged and far sharper.

When we know Jesus, we recognize His uniqueness and stand-alone authority. Having our eyes opened to Who He is, we gladly follow Him. We become His sheep. As the great Shepherd, Jesus could have limited what He speaks to us as commands. He could say to His sheep, "Eat what I provide. Drink from the river I lead you to. Draw close when wolves come." And He did say these types of things to us. But this Great Shepherd does more than give commands; He says, "'My sheep hear my voice'" (John 10:27).

It is great that Jesus has spoken in these last days, but He has done us another great favor. He has allowed us to hear His voice. The whole book of Hebrews warns us not to be among those who are dull, not paying close attention, neglectful, uncaring, unheedful, not striving to enter, not holding fast, unskilled in hearing the Word, lacking powers of discernment, and neglectful in constant practice in hearing the Word. Jesus' voice speaks, yet He calls us to be His sheep so that we would know His voice.

In Hebrews 5:11, the writer tells us he has much more to say; but the listeners had become dull of hearing. How tragic that we might miss so much more that could be said of Jesus and the glorious revelation of Who this Man Christ Jesus is in His fullness—not because He is unwilling to reveal the great depths of His wonder but because we are not ready to hear it. We hear a bit and feel it is enough and grow dull to what more we could have. I want as much of Jesus made known to me as humanly possible. Imagine having the desire for Jesus to speak more into your life, but you not ready or able to hear it. What wonders would you be missing, what delights unknown, what knowledge of the infinite and holy God unattained? This is why Hebrews 2:1 tells us that "we must pay *much* closer attention" (emphasis mine). There is more to see of what Jesus has spoken. You can have as much of Jesus as you want. He is more than willing to speak beyond your wildest dreams. When the Bible speaks of

God doing more than we think or imagine, it is not limited to Him changing our external circumstances or meeting our physical needs; it speaks, as well, of the depths and height of greater revelation of Who He is.

To receive the "much more" that Jesus longs to reveal, we need to be the opposite of the dull, neglectful, and unskilled who miss the opportunity for a greater awakening to all that Christ would reveal. We need to be lively, alert, bright, focused, invigorated, stirred, passionate, and stimulated when we open the Word of God and come to the Holy Spirit for quickening of spirit that we might hear all that Heaven would open to a hungry heart.

The Word we have given to us today speaks to us about the unique and altogether otherness of Jesus. God speaks of angels, prophets, and the Law. In the phrase in Hebrews 1:8, "But of the Son he says," the Bible is showing the uniqueness of Christ. God will say many wonderful things about various subjects and entities, but it is only of the Son that He holds his highest delights and accolades. We should be the same. We can appreciate many fine things and extend our compliments to many people; but of the Son, we feel, think, and say higher, more exalted things—things exclusive to Jesus. The Bible says that "out of the abundance of the heart the mouth speaks" (Matt. 12:34). Do we speak out of our heart the glories of the exclusive nature of Christ? Or do we too often hold equal to Christ lesser things our heart desires? I say of my wife, she is beautiful; of my children, they bring such wonderful joy; but I hold the highest praise for Jesus. Nothing compares to Him. I speak high praise of many things; but only of the Son will I say, "He is exalted above all things. He alone is worthy of our highest praise."

Joshua and I wrote this book not so you would have more information about Jesus but that you would fall to your knees in wonder at the jaw-dropping beauty of Jesus. We write to encourage you to lay aside every weight, including that which hinders you from hearing. Lay aside the weight of spiritual anemia, dispassionate pursuit, and trifling attempts to dig into the depths of the Word of Jesus. If you have lost the fervent love for the words of Jesus, you can right now simply ask Him to restore a love for His Word.

We are hoping to ignite a zeal for the Word of the Lord. There is so much more He has to say to you. All you need is "ears to hear" (Matt. 11:15).

CHAPTER 3

THE INCOMPARABLE GREATNESS OF CHRIST

BY: GARY WILKERSON

Great is the LORD, and greatly to be praised, and his greatness is unsearchable.

PSALM 145:3

A SMALL HOUSE CHURCH HUDDLED together, sharing the reports of their extremely difficult week. One family had their home and all their possessions plundered. One of their leaders had been taken away from his wife and children at night, shackled in chains, and led off to a dark, cold prison. This little church was facing fierce persecution not only from Rome, the city in which they lived, but also from the Jews in the city that rejected and scorned them. These saints in Rome were Jews who believed in Jesus as their Savior, causing them to be the scourge of both Romans and Jews.

Some in this house church were new—just checking things out, tasting the Word, getting some enlightenment but not yet all in. Others were dedicated—devoted but now in great fear, ready to abandon their faith, reject Christ, and return to a lesser difficult life of Judaism. And then the core of them—rock solid, unshakable, unflappable—were ready to die for their faith. These few would not abandon the Lord—not because they were better, bolder, or braver in themselves but because they had come to trust in Christ above all else, to desire Him more than anything the world could ever offer, having placed their hope in Christ. Because of this, they could cry out even to their last breath, "[We] will not be shaken" (Psalm 16:8).

How could they have this faith? They had a vision of something better, something far worthier than their other interests, far more magnificent than their possessions, of greater joy than their comfort, far more unbelievable than their greatest desire. They grasped the incomparable greatness of Christ; they were undone by the grandeur of the infinite supremacy of Jesus.

The letter this house church received spoke to all those who were gathered. To the onlookers who were tasting but not trusting came a grave and sober warning. They told them that to experience Christ's truth, see His Holy Spirit at work, sit and hear the Word week after week, and then reject without ever truly embracing it would bring judgment. They would become worse than if they had never heard. They were in danger of apostasy, of trampling the precious blood of Jesus under their feet (Heb. 6:4-8).

This letter was less a warning and more an awakening for those who had been truly born again but were wavering. It was a call to remember how much better Christ is than anything they had ever experienced, known, owned, or lived for. To these, the author says, "Hold on. Don't go back but rather strive all the more to enter fully into the better and more beautiful things of the Gospel" (see Heb. 2:1; 10:35-39).

And to the faithful, the writer reminds them of the saints who went before them, who received the rewards, promises, and inheritance. They were reminded that by enduring such hardships, struggles, and sufferings, they could joyfully, not just dutifully, accept the plundering of their property. Their knowing the betterness of Jesus made all other things seem dull. They could be included in Moses' great affirmation that choosing rather to be mistreated with the people of God is far better than to enjoy the fleeting pleasure of sin (see Heb. 10:32-34; 11:1-40).

What would be the clarion cry that would be sufficient to buoy the buffeted believers? What would be the message to awaken the dull? What could be said to those onlookers who had settled in among them without ever truly receiving the Gospel who now were ready to give it all up? What one thing could possibly awaken the unbelievers, stir the passions of those drifting away, and be dulled by the temptation to throw in the towel? What could the inspired writer say to stir up the continued course of the most faithful among them? This is quite a task for a single letter to such a suffering church.

Yet the author was given by the Holy Spirit such a word. It was not "try harder." It was not "others have it worse than you, so buckle up." It was not like many messages in the Church today: "try harder; believe more; you can do it." No, rather, it was a single word. That word was, "Better!" Jesus is better than the prophets, better than the mighty angels, better than Moses and the Law, better than the previous covenant, and better than the old priesthood. He is the better Word, the better Law, the better Covenant, the better High Priest. His betterness is mentioned more than a dozen times in multiple ways with implicit passion and clarity.

To those who were among them but not of them (1 John 2:19-21) came the most fearful warnings. The warning to these worldly-minded onlookers, who wandered in and never came into true fullness of faith, spoke of their apostasy. In their wickedness, they were trampling the blood of Jesus. They held to the false view that the things of the world were better than Christ. To them, Christ was interesting and alluring but not worthy of utmost devotion. To the taste-tester who had not come to fullness of faith, the message is clear. There is a better way than remaining on the peripheral. The world was threatening them with confiscation of their goods, the loss of their livelihoods, and diminishing of social standing; but if they were to disengage without truly coming to faith, the warning of God is far more awe-striking and dangerous (Heb. 10:26-31). It would have been better if they had never known the message of this church in Rome. Now they would be judged as those who had heard and never entered.

To those who were tempted to go back due to the persistent persecution, those who were on the cusp of giving up, weary of well-doing and staying faithful, the message is that there is a better course than going back. There is a better reward for remaining faithful, a better promise of things to come. They had true faith but were beginning to weary, causing them to become dulled in passion. They also had a warning: "we must pay much closer attention to what we have heard, lest we drift away from it" (Heb. 2:1). They were not unbelievers; they were people of faith, who needed a godly nudge to persist in the right direction. Their encouragement was to look to Jesus.

The message to those who stood the test and endured the trial with an unshakable, joyful faith was, "What you have and what you will have is far better than anything your fathers ever experience; and what you have is far better than any generation. What you will receive is far better than anything this world, in all its so-called glory, could ever offer" (see Heb. 11:40). God has provided something better for them.

How could the word "better" make such a difference? It seems such a nice word but not a world-changing word. It may be a kind word but not a kingdom-shaking word. It seems to speak of improvement, like making a better automobile or improving the team with the new quarterback. Such improvement would not be sufficient for the life-and-death needs of this congregation. It is nice to have something that is better, but what we need would seem to be far beyond merely better.

This is where our language fails us. The Hebrew word for "better" is much better than our meaning of better! When this book speaks of better, it speaks in a high and lofty tone. It speaks of what is far beyond, what is almost incomprehensible, and what is incomparable.

The Greek word for "better" can be translated as superior, more excellent, even the dominion of planting God's flag upon enemy territory.

THE INCOMPARABLE BETTERNESS OF CHRIST

When Hebrews uses the word "better"—which it does some thirty times—it is not used in the way we are accustomed to today. It is not speaking of a thing higher on a scale than other comparable items. It is not that I am good at basketball or that a top college player is better. Morally, it is not that Hitler is on the bottom of the measurable scale, a thief is higher than a good person, or Billy Graham is near the top of the scale. According to Hebrews, being better is not Jesus being on the top of the scale in comparison to anyone. The meaning behind this oft-repeated phrase in this book is that Jesus Christ is better in such a fashion that He would not even be on any scale. He is other than. All things on any scale are finite, but Jesus is infinite. Nothing measures up to Him because He is unlike all things created. Many preachers or writers are far better than I, but Jesus as a Preacher is not on the same measuring table. He is of another sort. His level is so far beyond anything we could measure that it is immeasurable. The finite cannot fully comprehend the infinite, let alone the finite measure the infinite. "His ways [are] past finding out" (Rom. 11:33 KJV). "His greatness is unsearchable" (Psalm 145:3 KJV).

The implications for us are astonishing and better (immeasurably more) than we could possibly think or imagine. In other words, His betterness is impossible to fully grasp. Yet the Hebrew writer, caring so much for this church in troubled times, goes to great lengths to attempt such a feat.

The Hebrews begin a brilliant journey of the comprehension of the incomparable greatness of Christ by extolling the great truth that He is better than any scale, category, or order; better than anything created, anything existing, anything in thought, emotion, or anything the human mind can even partially grasp. To think of Jesus on a scale only above another is to minimize His grandeur. Even to say Jesus is rare is too small a thing; He is far more than rare. Christ is sole, unshared in singularity of glory. He is the One and Only, exclusively exceptionally superior. God speaks of how clearly holy

He is: "'To whom will you liken me and make me equal, and compare me, that we may be alike?'" (Isa. 46:5).

JESUS' WORD IS BETTER THAN THE PROPHET'S WORDS

Who would not know that Jesus' word is better than that of all the previous prophets? It is easy to say this in our culture and time; but at the time Hebrews was written, the prophets held the place of the highest esteem. These great men and women of God spoke as they were inspired by God. No one else had the inspiration that was theirs. The Jewish believers, many new in their faith, were raised on the words of the prophets. And rightly so, the wonderful words of the prophets made up their Holy Scriptures and gave the only true revelation of God. So for them to hear that Jesus was greater than the prophets meant that what Jesus speaks is greater than the Torah, greater than the major and minor prophets, greater than any word heretofore given.

Jesus' word is not merely better than the prophets; it is completely other than. It is of a different sort. We do understand the prophets spoke and wrote what we hold to be the infallible, inspired Word of God. Yet the prophets spoke for God, and Jesus is God. How amazing that the prophets wrote the infallible Word of God; yet Jesus' words are the capstone, culmination, and fulfillment of all previous words. The prophets predicted what Jesus fulfills. Both speak the Word of God, but there is no near comparison between the prophets and Jesus. One is human, though inspired by God; and the Other is Divine, speaking as God. One is finite, created, and dependent; the Other is infinite, uncreated, and independent, needing nothing from any other source. Jesus' word ends mankind's search for a better word.

God spoke profoundly and powerfully through our spiritual fathers and through the prophets. Prophets were often the soul of the nation and the guiding force morally, spiritually, and politically. They thundered warning, gave needed comfort, and led through spiritual insight. They foretold of things to come. The people of Israel could not do without the Word of God through the prophets. Who could forget Nathan pointing a finger in the face of King David for his sin? Who could neglect to see Jeremiah with fire shut up in his bones or Ezekiel seeing dry bones coming together and breathing with life? Who could forget Isaiah, who saw the Lord "high and lifted up; and the train of his robe filled the temple" (Isa. 6:1)? As powerful as these words were, they were not a match for the word that Jesus was to bring.

Dozens of prophets spoke thousands of prophetic words; yet combined, all the prophets and all their prophecies paled in comparison to what this one man, Christ Jesus, was to tell the world. That is why the end times prophecy says that "the testimony of Jesus is the spirit of prophecy" (Rev. 19:10).

Jesus is not simply better than any one of the prophets; He is more excellent, greater than, and superior to all of them put together. Some list up to eighty-eight prophets, but the following is a shortened list:

- Moses
- Elijah
- Micaiah
- Elisha
- Jonah
- Hosea
- Amos
- Isaiah
- Micah
- Oded
- Nahum
- Zephaniah
- Jeremiah
- Huldah (the Prophetess)
- Habakkuk
- Ezekiel

- Obadiah
- Joel
- Haggai
- Zechariah
- Malachi*

His word was better because of Who He is—"the radiance of the glory of God" (Heb. 1:3). No prophet could claim such a high honor. He is the exact imprint of God's nature now visible to mankind. No prophet could be anywhere near the exact imprint. He upholds the universe by the word of His power. Prophets of old could barely hold up the nation. And though Jesus is exalted high above all else, He was still willing to make purification for our sins. This sinless Son paid for our sin.

The Son inherits all things; the prophets are only a part of the inheritance. The Son created all things; the prophets are created by Him. The spotless Son, perfect and sinless, took the penalty for our sins, including the sins of the prophets. Prophets spoke of the One to come Who would "[take] away the sin of the world" (John 1:29). Jesus did not just speak about it; He did it. Prophets spoke the word; Jesus is the Word (John 1:1).

JESUS' SUPREMACY IS GREATER THAN THE ANGEL'S SERVANTHOOD

Reading this insight today seems strange, even unimportant. After all, who of us worship angels today? To understand the powerful significance of this admonition, we must look at the first-century Hebrew church. To them, the prophets brought the very words of God and gave them the instructions by which they live. And it was the angels who often spoke those messages to the prophets. Angels destroyed armies and fought off Satan; the appearance of a single angel would make the bravest cower in fear. Angels today are seen as distant entities, who fly around invisible, possibly doing some good but to which we are uncertain of the actual effect. We wonder if they may have helped us avoid that traffic collision or stood between us and that man who headed in our direction to possibly rob us. But again, the early church had a much higher reverence for angels. They were even in danger of being disqualified by insisting on the worship of angels (Col. 2:18).

Even John the beloved, in his old age and after many years of worshipping Christ, was tempted to worship angels. "I, John, am the one who heard and saw these things. And when I heard and saw them, I fell down to worship at the feet of the angel who showed them to me, but he said to me, 'You must not do that! I am a fellow servant with you and your brothers the prophets, and with those who keep the words of this book. Worship God'" (Rev. 22:8-9).

Angels, brothers, and prophets are all serving us in our walk with God, but none can compare with the glorious splendor of Jesus Christ. He stands alone, incomparable, outstanding, and overwhelmingly amazing. To a church that was holding prophets and angels in comparison with Christ, Christ may have been more; yet they were holding other entities to be comparable to Christ. That is why this letter strongly admonishes and restricts the esteem of these compared with that of Jesus.

Hebrews 1:5 says it so clearly, "To which of the angels did God ever say?" This sentence is repeated in verse thirteen: "And to which of the angels has he ever said?"

God never said any of the glorious things He says about His Son about the angels. No angel is a son; no angel is to be worshiped; yet all the angels are to worship Him. "Of the Son he says, 'Your throne, O God, is forever and ever, the scepter of uprightness is the scepter of your kingdom.' . . . God, your God, has anointed you with the oil of gladness beyond your companions'" (Heb. 1:8-9). Angels and prophets may be anointed and have joy, but Jesus is declared as one with a greater anointing and greater joy! And to place a capstone upon these declarations, He says, "'Sit at my right hand until I make your enemies a footstool for your feet'" (Heb. 1:13). These can only be said of the Son, Christ Jesus. No other name holds this place of highest glory and esteem.

I find this question of "did He say" personally applicable in my walk with Jesus today. I may not worship prophets nor angels, but can I not ask myself this same question with a modern twist? To which of the (fill in the blank) did He ever say . . . To which of the financial blessings, to which of the career advancements, to which of the blessed lives, to which of the ministry successes, to which of the personal comforts, to which of the (fill in the blanks in your life) did He say . . .

What things today do we have the propensity to unknowingly worship in comparison with Jesus? You can tell what you worship by assessing what you think of most often; what you hope to receive most passionately; and where you spend your time, energy, and money.

JESUS IS WORTHY OF MORE GLORY THAN MOSES

Moses was trusted by God with the communication of the whole law, civil codes, and ceremonial rules. Moses led out millions of slaves from the most nefarious of evil kingdoms. Moses was the great deliverer. Gandhi, Martin Luther King, Jr., and a dozen others would not have delivered so many people as Moses did. Moses was the pinnacle of Jewish honor and glory. There were none like him—that is, until Jesus, Who not only compares but surpasses. Moses was faithful over God's house, but it was Jesus Who built God's house. And the Builder is greater than the house itself. This is saying all things created are the "house." The prophets are the house; the angels are the house; and Moses is the house. But Jesus is worthy of more glory because He built all these as parts of God's house.

This is so encouraging for us today because we are God's house, created by Jesus; and Christ "is faithful" over His house. He created us, knows us intimately, and charted our course long before we were born. And He faithfully oversees the outcomes of our designed destiny. Just as Israel learned they could trust Moses for their deliverance from slavery, we can more so trust Jesus. We can give more glory to Jesus for an even greater deliverance. Moses' great work was under the oversight of the Builder. Every event in our lives that brings freedom, salvation, deliverance, sanctification, satisfaction, blessings, and joy is part of the work the Christ Jesus has faithfully brought forth.

JESUS, THE FINAL, PERFECT HIGH PRIEST

As grateful as we may be for Jesus being better than the prophets, angels, and Moses, we have a more wonderful praise in Christ—that He became for us a greater High Priest. We have a better Word, a better Deliverer; but without a better High Priest, none of these other "betters" would be complete. We could have the law, the servanthood of angels, and the great word of the prophets; but we would not be able to keep that law. We would fall into disobedience to the prophets and the "message declared by angels" (Heb. 2:2). We would be yet in our sin; we would have an inferior priest, who would be able to "deal gently with the ignorant and wayward since he himself is beset with weakness" (Heb. 5:2). But that priest could not free us from our sin because he must deal with his own sin. Jesus was perfect, spotless, and sinless; thus, His sacrifice could be offered on behalf of those in sin.

The old priesthood was led by imperfect men, giving imperfect gifts with a less-than-perfect result. Jesus sacrificed a perfect gift of such worth it is of lasting, eternal value and effect. The former priests went once a year into the Holy of Holies and then out to the same weaknesses, while Jesus, after having sacrificed, sat down. This phrase is used often in Hebrews, and it signifies that it is finished. The priest must remain standing for he remains in need of further sacrifice. Jesus could sit down knowing no further sacrifice will need to be offered. He accomplished forgiveness once for all who believe.

This mean we have a perfect High Priest, Who does not need to sacrifice for His own sins. Therefore, He, in His perfection, can take our place. This has been called substitutionary atonement. He took our sin; we take on His righteousness. He has the fullness of supply to pay our debt. No other mediator could suffice, only Jesus! And being that the sacrifice was perfect, it will be lasting and eternal. There is no more need to pay for our sins; they are marked fully paid. Having "made" (past tense) purification for our sin, it is finished. The following verses indicate this:

- "Securing an eternal redemption" (Heb. 9:12).
- "He . . . once for all . . . put away sin" (Heb. 9:26).
- "By a single offering he has perfected for all time" (Heb. 10:14).

This is such an overriding, central theme of this life-altering letter. The letter itself clearly says so: "now the point in what we are saying is this" (Heb. 8:1). Rarely a book of the Bible tells us so pointedly that this is the main point. So, we should take heed and pay closer attention to get the main point settled in our understanding. And what is this main point? "We have such a high priest" (Heb. 8:1). For generations, humanity has needed such a High Priest, and this whole letter has this as its main point. Here and now, we have such a High Priest. We have what we have been looking for. We now have what the prophets spoke about, what the angels longed to look into, and what Moses considered greater wealth than the treasures of Egypt.

Right now, those who put their trust in the finished work of our great High Priest have not only a cleansing of sins but also a cleansing that is once and for all time, a work of eternal effect only possible by an eternal Son "securing an eternal redemption" (Heb 9:12). It makes me want to shout, "See how much Jesus is greater than—far greater than anything we can own, need, want, or do! Jesus is the Great I Am!" This main "point in what we are saying" is our single greatest cause of joy, hope, and exaltation of Christ. When I think of what he has done for me, all I want to do is say thank You.

JESUS THE PROCURER OF A BETTER COVENANT

Whole volumes filling great libraries could be written concerning the glory of this better covenant. We could spend one hundred lifetimes and never come to know the fullness of the wonder and greatness of this New Covenant. So what is said in these next few paragraphs will be only a glimpse into this vast truth. Yet even a little said is sufficient to see Jesus in His magnificence.

To talk of a better covenant means there was a previous covenant; and good as it might have been, a new one has come—and it is better. The previous one was based on performing all that was commanded in the law. This covenant said that God would bless us and be with us if we kept all His law and commands. Deuteronomy 28 speaks of the vast blessings, and chapter twenty-nine speaks of the dreadful curses of disobedience. The great problem with this covenant was not the goodness of the covenant but that we were unable to keep it. "For if that first covenant had been faultless, there would have been no occasion to look for a second" (Heb. 8:7).

Was the fault in the covenant that God gave? No, the fault lies in people, not the covenant—in our inability to keep it. "For he finds fault with *them*" (Heb. 8:8, emphasis mine). Why then would God craft a covenant that none would be able to keep in their own power? The phrase "in their own power" is the key to realizing the impact of the new, better covenant in your life. The old covenant was good in that it taught us we were unable in our own power; it shut every mouth, quelled every boast, and left us with a desperate realization of our total need for another Source of power. Jesus is the better Source.

This better covenant would not be like the one made with our fathers. This one is not a call to external obedience that has no power to accomplish the call. This one is put into our minds, written in our hearts. This one puts the full force, power, and ability of Jesus' perfect ability to be obedient within us. This covenant is not asking us to see the law and change to do it. It is changing us, so we can do it.

This is not to say that we will be now living in sinless perfection; otherwise, this covenant spoken of in Hebrews 8 would not conclude with the words, "I will be merciful toward their iniquities, and I will remember their sins no more" (v. 12). Hallelujah, we have the power to keep it, the power to be acceptable, receiving mercy even when we do not keep it perfectly. Some may say this could lead us toward a lazy, lackadaisical view toward sin, thinking since we will be forgiven and given mercy, we can go out and freely sin. But this does not take into account a better truth: we now have a new law written on our hearts. Those living under the power of this better covenant would never even begin to think like that; to do so would signify that person is not living under this New Covenant.

One of the best ways to understand this covenant it to look at three possible positions. These are "you should"; "you can"; and a third better way we will show in a moment.

The first is "you should." This view is that you should try harder to obey and work at keeping the law. This is the "bootstrap" lifestyle that is not only futile and exhausting but is dishonoring of the work Jesus has done for us. It is a fleshly ambition to be enough and do enough to be acceptable. We clean ourselves up and then come to God and say, "Look how acceptable I am to You." But "you should" never works. Yes, you should, but you do not. So, you need something more—or, actually, Someone more. And when you live under "you should" and then do not, you redouble your efforts, promise better performance, and increase your commitment to work harder for God. You tell Him you will read twice as much and pray more than ever. But sadly, these are fleshly attempts to do it on your own. These lack the power to accomplish God's will.

The second is more popular in our generation. Our parents often lived under the "you should" mentality. Today, we believe we have progressed beyond that. Now, we believe better in ourselves and attempt to thrive in a "you can" culture. Psychology, education, family, and even the Church all echo the same sentiments: "You are wonderful; you are so good; you can do whatever you set your mind to." So, we take this worldly view and place it in our religious life. We hear sermon after sermon of how we can do it—how we can reach our best life, our greatest destiny. All we must do is believe more in ourselves and then, with the power of our words, create our own best futures. This "best life" is filled with fleshly desire, craving everything we could ever want. Of course, it is not called "fleshly desire"; it is called fulfillment, and God has become the Chaplain of our desires, rather than the great Judge and the great Deliverer of our sinfulness.

I believe this "you can" is more dangerous than the "you should"; for most often, those living under the "you should" become disillusioned and become inclined to give it up and look to God for help found in a better covenant. But those living under the delusion of "you can" are buoyed up by so-called preachers who are just selling false hope. And the people love it so, clamoring for a voice that tickles their ears, telling them of the abilities that lie within, just waiting to be opened by "faith"—albeit quite a false faith. This is more a faith in self rather than a Savior.

There is a better way found in the better covenant. It is jettisoning the "you should" and abandoning the "you cans." It is not "you should, nor you can"; it is found in "He did!" The problem with the first two is that they both begin with "you." The power of the new is that it begins with *Him*. The better covenant has removed the "you" from the source of supply and power and "looking unto Jesus the author and finisher of our faith" (Heb. 12:2). He is not only the Beginning of a new way in this new covenant; but He is also the Finisher, the Completer, and the Accomplisher of the covenant. "Accomplisher" means that He gives the law, but He also then gives the power to complete it. That power does not reside in "you" alone but only in you through *Him*.

JESUS THE GREAT PROVIDER

Hebrews 11 tells us of how Jesus provided a greater faith for men and women throughout history. This chapter ends by telling us God has "provided something better for us" (Heb. 11:40). We have a better word from a better prophet. We have a Son better and more powerful than all the angels in Heaven combined. We have the Builder of the house in Jesus. And we have a better covenant. Yet might I suggest one thing more, one thing greater than all these listed? This one thing is Christ Himself. The better Thing provided is not a thing at all but a Person. It is the Man Christ Jesus, Who provided the Word, the power, the priesthood, the covenant, and the accomplishment. Allow Jesus to be your All-in-all. He is all-sufficient, all-powerful, all-knowing, all-loving, all-merciful, all-wonderful, and better than all. All glory goes to Jesus. He reigns forever and ever. Jesus is better than anything, anyone, anything imaginable, anything created. Jesus is above, over, and better than all!

Can you relate to those in this Roman house church who took part in the meetings, heard the Word, and saw the power of the Holy Spirit but never truly believed on the Lord in a saving manner? This happens in the Bible Belt. There are people who belong to a church for social connections and to look good in the community, but their hearts have been growing colder and colder. Take heed to the warnings of this letter before it is too late.

Others may see themselves as those growing weary of the struggle. Possibly, you have been praying for relief from some difficulty. And yet as the struggle remains, you feel like giving up; you wonder if God will ever bring a breakthrough. God's Word is telling you to hold on. You are not following God so your troubles cease—though He is able and willing. You are His because He has won your heart, forgiven your sins, and made Himself known to you. He is too good to leave!

And for those who willingly give their all joyfully, the encouragement here is that it is worth it all. You have chosen the better part. Your reward in Heaven is great. And here in the land of the living, your life is counted as joy, even in trials and tribulations. Jesus is the greater for you. You have come to know how surpassingly wonderful is the incomparable greatness of Christ.

CHAPTER 4

ENTERING GOD'S REST

BY: JOSHUA WEST

Since therefore it remains for some to enter it, and those who formerly received the good news failed to enter because of disobedience, again he appoints a certain day, "Today," saying through David so long afterward, in the words already quoted, "Today, if you hear his voice, do not harden your hearts."

HEBREWS 4:6-7

CHAPTER THREE OF HEBREWS ENDS with a warning to the first-century Christians to whom it was being written. The author wanted them to be aware that the Israelites did not get to enter God's rest in the Promised Land because of their unbelief and disobedience. Or it may be better said that their unbelief led to disobedience. All disobedience is rooted in unbelief, which is ultimately rooted in pride. The original sin of the devil was pride, and the original sin of humanity was rooted in unbelief.

In Genesis 2:15-17, we read, "The Lord God took the man and put him in the garden of Eden to work it and keep it. And the LORD God commanded the man, saying, 'You may surely eat of every tree of the garden, but the tree of the knowledge of good and evil you shall not eat, for the day that you eat of it you shall surely die.'"

Of course, we know that the devil came in the form of a serpent and got Eve and her husband Adam to question the word of God. Their unbelief in God's word caused them to sin; and eventually, their sin caused them to die. This also brought sin into the world and a curse that caused everyone born after them to inherit sin and death. As Romans 6:23 says, "For the wages of sin is death, but the free gift of God is eternal life in Christ Jesus our Lord."

All disobedience to God is rooted in unbelief. Human sin was born in unbelief—namely unbelief in the word of God. And unbelief is what keeps humankind from God's saving grace today. Here is a deep and powerful truth that we must understand—while it is true that sin separates us from God, all sin is born in unbelief. From the Garden of Eden to man's ultimate rejection of God's saving grace in the Gospel of Jesus Christ, and everything in between, it is unbelief that will keep us from entering God's eternal rest. Hebrews 11:6 tells us, "And without faith, it is impossible to please him, for whoever would draw near to God must believe that he exists and that he rewards those who seek him."

The payment for sin is death; but in Christ, we have eternal life and rest if we, by faith, believe in Him. True faith in Christ is abandoning our hope in this world and the things of this world and living as sojourners and foreigners as we walk through this life. Our works do not save us; salvation is a free gift given to us by God. But true faith has action as evidence that we trust in Christ alone. We obey because we believe.

FEAR OF THE LORD

In the fourth chapter, the writer of Hebrews uses the story of the Israelites entering the peace and rest of the Promised Land in the Old Testament as a foreshadowing and example of the true and eternal Promised Land that is waiting for those who have been saved through the Gospel of Jesus Christ and who, by faith, live in eager expectation of the fulfillment of what God has promised. Verse one says, "Therefore, while the promise of entering his rest still stands, let us fear lest any of you have failed to reach it."

But sadly, most of them died in the wilderness because they did not have faith in what God had promised. Through His servant Moses, God had led the Israelites out of Egypt and had kept them, provided for them, and guided them. When they got to Canaan, which was the land God had promised to them, they sent in twelve spies to survey the land and the people who dwelled in it. But when the spies came out, ten of them said that the people were giants and that they could not defeat them. But two of the spies, Joshua and Caleb, trusted in the promise of God and wanted to go in and take the land.

Because of the unbelief of most of the Israelites, God swore that "'they shall not enter my rest'" (Heb. 3:11). Because of this, that generation of people wandered in the wilderness for forty years, and they died there. From that generation of people, only Joshua and Caleb were able to enter the Promised Land. The Israelites' unbelief and lack of faith in the word of the Lord caused them to not receive the blessed inheritance God had promised to His people.

One great evidence of unbelief is the lack of fear of the Lord. These men who did not want to go into the Promised Land proved that they did not fear the Lord or trust Him. They feared man more than God. This is still a great reason for disobedience to God today. We fear man, the opinions of man, the power of man, and the rejection of man more than we do that of the Sovereign and eternal God of the universe; and this is evidence of unbelief and the lack of saving faith.

Proverbs 9:10 says, "The fear of the Lord is the beginning of wisdom, and the knowledge of the Holy One is insight." If you do not have fear and reverence for God, it shows that you do not really know Him. You then disobey Him without repentance or fear of consequence. Speaking about the wrath and severity of God is not a scare tactic; it is merely an unchangeable reality, just like all of the attributes and characteristics of God.

Hebrews 4:1 admonishes, "Therefore while the promise of entering his rest still stands, let us fear lest any of you should seem to have failed to reach it." The story of the Israelites is an example that unbelief will keep us from the Promised Land of Heaven and spending eternity with Christ. The author of Hebrews wants his first-century audience, as well as us, to understand that if we let unbelief keep us from repentance and obedience, we will suffer eternal loss. Jesus is the only Way! Listen to what the apostle Paul says about this in Romans 11:17-23:

> But if some of the branches were broken off, and you, although a wild olive shoot, were grafted in among the others and now share in the nourishing root of the olive tree, do not be arrogant toward the branches. If you are, remember it is not you who support the root, but the root that supports you. Then you will say, "Branches were broken off so that I might be grafted in." That is true. They were broken off because of their unbelief, but you stand fast through faith. So do not become proud, but fear. For if God did not spare the natural branches, neither will he spare you. Note then the kindness and severity of God: severity toward those who have fallen, but God's kindness to you, provided you continue in his kindness. Otherwise, you too will be cut off. And even they, if they do not continue in their unbelief, will be grafted in, for God has the power to graft them in again.

THE BEAUTY OF THE GOSPEL

In verse two of Hebrews 4, we read, "For good news came to us just as to them, but the message they heard did not benefit them, because they were not united by faith with those who listened." This is the purpose of the witness testimony of the apostles and prophets—that we might be united with their message and, because of this, be united with them in the salvation promised by God to all who believe. There is only one way, one message, one Savior, one Spirit, and one God!

What makes the Gospel of Jesus Christ so beautiful is the very thing that makes Christ Himself so jaw-droppingly beautiful; it is the uniqueness and exclusivity of both. In the dark reality of the world and every fallen thing in it, we see Jesus—a bright and shining Light in the darkness, a blinding Light so bright that it outshines everything around it. To ignore the beautiful light of Christ, you must intentionally close your eyes; but even then, it is impossible to completely ignore it.

This, too, is the beauty of the Gospel of Jesus Christ. Just like the promise made to the Israelites about the Promised Land, God has also made a promise to us: "Everyone who calls on the name of the Lord will be saved'" (Rom. 10:13). The author of Hebrews is telling this first-century group of Christians that just like the Israelites, the message of the glorious Gospel of Christ is of no benefit to us if we do not respond to it by faith. Our actions and obedience are the evidence of our belief in the promise.

Salvation is promised in the Word of God; and when we respond by faith, it is for the glory of God. Saying that there are other ways is an indictment against the reliability and trustworthiness of God's Word, and God does not like His character being called into question. This is why God, through Christ, joyfully forgives repentant sinners but will harshly judge unbelief. It is impossible to please God without faith.

A caution to young Christians: do not confuse doubt with unbelief. We all have doubts and stumbling blocks. Unbelief is characterized by a life of unrepentant disobedience; and faith is characterized by a life of obedience, humility, and repentance. This is evidence of regeneration in your life—not that you will never doubt, stumble, or fall; but when you do, your faith is in the atoning work of Christ alone, and you get up and keep moving forward, knowing you are justified in Christ and because of Christ. He is sanctifying you, changing you, and keeping you; and He will finish the work He started in you.

Philippians 1:6 reminds us, "And I am sure of this, that he who began a good work in you will bring it to completion at the day of Jesus Christ." The evidence of our faith is the obedience of a surrendered life to Christ. The Gospel is only beautiful and good news to sinners who see God for Who He truly is, who take Him at His word, and who see the desperate need they have for salvation and respond by faith in His promised deliverance. Remember, we are not only being delivered *from* something but also *to* something. The reward of salvation is not merely avoiding Hell and the penalty of our sins, which is the second death; it is eternal unity with Christ. Christ is the Way to salvation and the Truth of salvation, and He is the Treasure and Reward of those who are being saved. If we are seeking anything other than Christ, we are very deceived about what the Gospel truly is. If you believe that the treasure of the Gospel is money, worldly success, comfort, a great marriage, your children, or anything thing else, you do not have the all-surpassing beauty of Jesus in focus. It is not that all these things are not valuable; but when compared to the value of Christ, they seem like rubbish and, if necessary, worth sacrificing because of the all-surpassing worth of Christ.

> But whatever gain I had, I counted as loss for the sake of Christ. Indeed, I count everything as loss because of the surpassing worth of knowing Christ Jesus my Lord. For his sake I have suffered the loss of all things and count them as rubbish, in order that I may gain Christ and be found in him, not having a righteousness of my own that comes from law, but that which comes through faith in Christ, the righteousness from God that depends on faith (Phil. 3:7-10).

ENTERING GOD'S REST

"For we who have believed enter that rest, as he has said, 'As I swore in my wrath, They shall not enter my rest,' although his works were finished from the foundation of the world. For he has somewhere spoken of the seventh day in this way: 'And God rested on the seventh day from all his works.' And again in this passage, he said, 'They shall not enter my rest'" (Heb. 4:3-5).

In this section of Scripture, the author of Hebrews is quoting part of Psalm 95, which is a royal psalm of King David. Although the book of Psalms itself does not attribute this psalm to David, the author of Hebrews does under the inspiration of the Holy Spirit.

> Oh come, let us sing to the Lord; let us make a joyful noise to the rock of our salvation! Let us come into his presence with thanksgiving; let us make a joyful noise to him with songs of praise. For the Lord is a great God, and a great King above all gods. In his hand are the depths of the earth; the heights of the mountains are his also. The sea is his, for he made it, and his hands formed the dry land. Oh come, let us worship and bow down; let us kneel before the Lord, our Maker! For he is our God, and we are the people of his pasture, and the sheep of his hand. Today, if you hear his voice, do not harden your hearts, as at Meribah, as on the day at Massah in the wilderness, when your fathers put me to the test and put me to proof, though they had seen my work. For forty years I loathed that generation and said, "They are a people who go astray in their heart, and they have not known my ways." Therefore I swore in my wrath, "They shall not enter my rest" (Psalm 95:1-11).

The author of Hebrews is saying the same thing David is in Psalm 95, except in view of Christ. The generation of Israelites that died in the wilderness did so because they were being led by the same God Who created the earth and rested on the seventh day. The same God was the One Whose mighty hand created the sea and the dry land. The same God delivered them from the bondage of Egypt by His mighty hand, performed signs and wonders, and many miraculous works as He was leading them to the Promised Land and His promised rest. But still, they did not believe; so in His holy anger, He swore that they would never enter His rest.

Now, let us think about this in view of the atoning work of Christ on the cross. Remember, we have "a better word"; we have a better Moses, a better Deliverer. And now, the author of Hebrews is telling us that in Christ, and for eternity, we have a better rest. "Better," is one way to say it, but I prefer the term "supreme" because there is nothing better than what we have in Christ.

Hebrews 4:6-7 says, "Since therefore it remains for some to enter it, and those who formerly received the good news failed to enter because of disobedience, again he appoints a certain day, 'Today,' saying through David so long afterward, in the words already quoted, 'Today, if you hear his voice, do not harden your hearts.'"

In Psalm 95, David prophetically says the same thing that the author of Hebrews is saying. David is looking forward to Christ as He uses language like "the rock of our salvation." This beautiful and powerful Christological language is a foreshadowing of what the author of Hebrews is saying to us today. As long as there is a "today," there is time to respond to the voice of the Lord. He is telling us not to harden our hearts when we hear the call to repentance. The prophets preached repentance; John the Baptist preached repentance; Jesus preached repentance; the apostles preached repentance. Every true man of God throughout Church history has preached repentance; and today, the true saving Gospel of Jesus Christ is still a message of grace and repentance.

So the idea that we should preach something that attracts or entices people rather than the true Gospel is preposterous. The call is not for the messenger to change his message; the call is for the hearer not to harden their heart.

"For he says, 'In a favorable time I listened to you, and in a day of salvation I have helped you.' Behold, now is the favorable time; behold, now is the day of salvation" (2 Cor. 6:2). We must live our lives with the awareness that there is no promised day called tomorrow. Today is the time to respond to the grace and mercy of Christ in humility, repentance, and surrender. We must also remember that have the responsibility to warn others of the coming day of judgment as we reach out and offer the grace of God in the Gospel. The Old Covenant and the Jewish religious system were merely placeholders, types, and shadows of the permanency and eternity of the New Covenant.

STRIVING FROM A PLACE OF REST

In the Bible, we see language used that seems to be telling us to rest in the promises of God and that salvation is not of works. Hebrews 4:11 encourages, "Let us therefore strive to enter that rest, so that no one may fall by the same sort of disobedience."

But then we also see language that is telling us to "press on toward the goal" (Phil. 3:14) and "strive to enter through the narrow door" (Luke 13:24); and this can be confusing, especially if you are not well-read in the context of these statements. But thinking that these concepts are contradictions is a simple theological category error.

A very simple way to explain this is with the statement, "We strive from a place of rest." We are at rest in our salvation. We did not earn it; we do not deserve it; we are not maintaining it. We are at rest and also reborn because of what Christ has done—not because of anything we have done. We are saved because of our faith in Christ alone. But because we have been saved, we strive toward salvation—not to earn it but as evidence we have received it.

The apostle Paul makes this same distinction in his letter to the Philippian church: "Not that I have already obtained this or am already perfect, but I press on to make it my own, because Christ Jesus has made me his own" (Phil. 3:12). Paul strives toward Christ because his faith is in Christ, but he is pressing toward Christ—not in the hope that he might be accepted by Him but because Christ has already claimed him. We press toward God and strive to obey God because He has accepted us. As Christians, we are at rest in the fact that God loves us, has forgiven us, and, in the end, will glorify us.

We are at peace in this life, no matter what trial or tragedy may come upon us because we have already died to this world and crucified the passions and pleasures of this life and now bear evidence or fruit that we have been reborn in Christ. "But the fruit of the Spirit is love, joy, peace, patience, kindness, goodness, faithfulness, gentleness, and self-control; against such things, there is no law. And those who belong to Christ Jesus have crucified the flesh with its passions and desires" (Gal. 5:22-24).

Now, this does not mean that we have arrived at the fullness of God's rest and peace. We are still in a fallen world with sinful bodies and minds that are being renewed but are still corrupt to some degree. That is why we look forward to the day when we behold our beautiful and precious Savior face to face, and then He will make us like Him.

Hebrews 4:8-10 tells us, "For if Joshua had given them rest, God would not have spoken of another day later on. So then, there remains a Sabbath rest for the people of God, for whoever has entered God's rest has also rested from his works as God did from his." So it is because we are living for and looking toward this day and this eternal rest that we strive forward in obedience as children longing to bring pleasure and glory to our Father. There is a Sabbath rest for God's people beyond the rest we engage in at the end of every week. The author of Hebrews is encouraging true believers to keep their focus on the eternal Promised Land in which they will find rest from the fiery trials they are currently facing.

This letter was written to Christians who were facing extreme persecution for their faith. They were imprisoned, killed, stripped of their possessions, and endured all kinds of suffering. With that in mind, we should examine the genuineness of our own faith. Can suffering break your faith? If so, your faith is in something other than Christ.

Remember what we discussed earlier; disobedience is born in unbelief. Unbelief in God's Word is the root of every problem in the world. The opposite of unbelief is faith; and biblically, we are talking about saving faith. These two terms, "faith" and "unbelief," are not talking about temporal things, situations in your life, or your ups and downs as a person. It is talking about the difference between those who will inherit eternal life and rest in Christ and those who will be subject to the righteous wrath of God. True faith produces a changed life and obedience.

SAVING FAITH IN THE WORD OF GOD

In Hebrews 4:12-13, we see the power of the word of God: "For the word of God is living and active, sharper than any two-edged sword, piercing to the division of soul and of spirit, of joints and of marrow, and discerning the thoughts and intentions of the heart. And no creature is hidden from his sight, but all are naked and exposed to the eyes of him to whom we must give account."

All life and creation find their origin in the word of the Lord! The Word of God is unbreakable, unchanging, life-giving, eternal, all-powerful, and unfailing. To be aligned with the God of the universe is to be aligned and in complete agreement with His Word. From the Word of the Lord, we learn to fear God, come to know God, find the promises of God, and learn the way of salvation; but it is also from the Word of God, we are given faith.

Romans 10:17 says, "So faith comes from hearing, and hearing through the word of Christ." The Scripture also tells us that Christ Himself is the Word (John 1:1). So Christ is undivorceable from the perfection of His word. Neither is the Spirit, Who inspired its writing. Nor is the God Who revealed it in the Old Testament. We must come to the Word of God in reverence of God. It should humble us, train us, and changes us; correct, rebuke, and encourage us; and conform us to the very image of Christ.

The author of Hebrews is using the same imagery Paul uses in Ephesians 6, as he talks about the sharp precision of God's Word. But in the immediate context of this verse in Hebrews 4, the author is using it to convey the immediacy of a need to respond to the call for repentance from sin and unbelief, as we surrender our life to Christ by faith in Him alone. J.C. Ryle once said, "Of all the gambling in the world, there is none so reckless as that of the man who lives unprepared to meet God, and yet puts off repentance."

In his commentary on Hebrews, John MacArthur says, "The need for God's rest is urgent. A person should diligently, with intense purpose and concern, secure it. It is not that he can work his way to salvation, but that he should diligently seek to enter God's rest by faith—lest he, like the Israelites in the wilderness, lose their opportunity."[3]

We must remember that while it is true that the Word of God is a book of grace, love, comfort, and salvation, it is also a book of wrath, judgment, and condemnation. All of humanity will be judged by the Word of the Lord. Everyone's thoughts, intentions, and heart are known to God. While many people are deceived by this, we are often blind to our own hearts, our own intentions, and our own thoughts. The wise man will fear and tremble at the Word of the Lord. He will also use it to find out Who God is, what He demands, and how to be saved and to expose the condition of his own heart.

There is no true rest outside of God in this life and especially in the life to come. "Faith comes from hearing, and hearing through the word of Christ" (Rom. 10:17). It is urgent and of paramount importance. It is of eternal importance. "Now is the day of salvation" (2 Cor. 6:2 KJV). When you hear His voice, do not harden your heart. God has spoken to us. We want more, or something different, or something better; but everything we need for "life and godliness" (2 Peter 1:3) and salvation is in the Scripture. The person searching for something other than the word of Christ as revealed in His Word has hardened their heart to the true voice of God.

We must have the highest esteem for the Word of the Lord and the prophetic voice of God in the witness and testimony of Jesus Christ as revealed in Scripture. God has spoken definitively and authoritatively in the person of Jesus Christ as revealed in Scripture. We are laid bare and left without excuse by the precision of His all-sufficient word.

---

3   John MacArthur, *The MacArthur New Testament Commentary: Volume 27 Hebrews* (Chicago: Moody Publishers, 2016).

God is speaking through His final word of Jesus Christ; and today, if you hear His voice, do not harden your heart as the Israelites did in the rebellion because, like them, you will not enter into God's rest. Yesterday is gone; tomorrow is not promised; and today is "the day of salvation" (2 Cor. 6:2 KJV). Do not harden your heart to His voice; do not harden your heart to His Word; and let the Spirit of God use His Word to lay your life bare and to let him till the soil of your heart. Jesus is the great High Priest, and He will not turn away from a repentant and humble heart.

Christ came so that we might find permanent and all-satisfying rest in Him. As humans, we spend a great deal of time looking for joy, peace, and satisfaction in places and things that were never meant to satisfy our hearts. All of these things can be found in the same place salvation is found—in Christ alone. Jesus said, "'Come to me, all you who are weary and burdened, and I will give you rest. Take my yoke upon you and learn from me, for I am gentle and humble in heart, and you will find rest for your souls. For my yoke is easy and my burden is light'" (Matt. 11:28-30 NIV).

God is not hiding from us; He "'came to seek and to save the lost'" (Luke 19:10 NIV). He came for sinners who are also "gentle and humble in heart" and who are willing to take the yoke of Christ on themselves. The reason we are tired, weak, and weary is that we are carrying the burden of being the lord of our own life. We must lay down control of our lives and surrender to the Lordship of Christ. In Him alone will we find true joy, satisfaction, and rest.

CHAPTER 5

JESUS OUR GREAT HIGH PRIEST

BY: JOSHUA WEST

Since then we have a great high priest who has passed through the heavens, Jesus,
the Son of God, let us hold fast to our confession. For we do not have a high priest who
is unable to sympathize with our weaknesses, but one who in every respect has been
tempted as we are, yet without sin. Let us then with confidence draw near to the throne
of grace, that we may receive mercy and find grace to help in time of need.

HEBREWS 4:14-16

THE BEAUTIFUL, INTIMATE, AND PERSONAL description we see here in these
three powerful verses is a much-needed ending to chapter four of the book
of Hebrews. The other thirteen verses of this chapter are filled with heavy
warnings of the consequences of hardening our hearts toward the rest and
salvation God has provided to us through Jesus Christ. But the author of
Hebrews ends on a positive note that is directed to those who are in Christ.

The world of the Jewish Old Covenant religious and sacrificial system
seems not merely like another world but, instead, like another universe when
compared to our modern world in the West. It is tempting to brush past or
rush through these things, but we cannot. It is imperative as Christians that
we understand these things so that we can understand the grandeur and glory
of Christ as our High Priest. Jesus is our great High Priest; and to understand

the gravity of this, we have to do a little work in the Old Testament to help us perceive this statement the way that a first-century Hebrew would have.

If you want to take a more extensive look into this subject than we will in this book, I suggest that you read Leviticus 8-10 and 16. This will serve you well in deepening your understanding of Christ Jesus as our eternal Priest.

Leviticus 8:12-13 shows us how the priesthood was established: "And he poured some of the anointing oil on Aaron's head and anointed him to consecrate him. And Moses brought Aaron's sons and clothed them with coats and tied sashes around their waists and bound caps on them, as the Lord commanded Moses." Under the Old Covenant and the Law, God set up the tabernacle and the sacrificial system as a placeholder until the Messiah came. God commanded Moses to anoint Aaron and his sons as the priests of the tabernacle; and going forward for the Jewish people, all priests would be their descendants. All priests in the history of Israel would come from the line of Aaron. The priests of the Old Covenant were anointed with oil, which signified they were set apart for God's holy purposes; and they lived under special guidelines, since they oversaw the temple ordinances and even wore special clothing. Their many duties and responsibilities included animal sacrifice for the remission of the people's sins.

Something that is very important for us to remember is that these ordinances were not man-made or man-imposed. The work of the priesthood was instituted by God Himself so that we could see and understand some very important things. Here are three things that we really need to grasp as we study the Old Covenant temple ordinance of animal sacrifice:

1. We must be very conscious of the fact that the punishment for sin is death.
2. "Without the shedding of blood there is no forgiveness of sin" (Heb. 9:22).
3. And in light of this, we see that forgiveness is very costly.

Only the priests could go into the inner parts of the tabernacle, where the sacrifices were performed. They were the ones responsible for offering these sacrifices to God. The purpose of the priesthood was to serve as a mediator between God and man; and from among the priests, there was one man selected every year to be the high priest.

The tabernacle was divided into three parts: the outer court, the inner court, and the Holy of holies. But only the high priest was allowed to enter the Holy of Holies, and that was only once a year. Inside the Holy of Holies was the ark of the covenant, which is the mercy seat of God. This was where the presence of God dwelled on earth; and anyone who entered the Holy of Holies, other than the high priest, would be struck dead because God is holy and cannot be in the presence of sinful man. In a very real way, the people were separated from the mercy of God because of the holiness of God and the sinfulness of man.

But this system was never meant to be the permanent solution—it could not be—because the priests were fallen humans as well; so they, too, needed sacrifices to be made for their sins. These sacrifices had to be made over and over again, year after year. This was not a permanent solution to the problem of sin; it was merely a placeholder and a type and shadow until a better and permanent sacrifice for sin could be made.

> For every high priest chosen from among men is appointed to act on behalf of men in relation to God, to offer gifts and sacrifices for sins. He can deal gently with the ignorant and wayward since he himself is beset with weakness. Because of this, he is obligated to offer sacrifice for his own sins just as he does for those of the people. And no one takes this honor for himself, but only when called by God, just as Aaron was (Heb. 5:1-4).

Since these priests were fallen and sinful like the rest of the people, they also had to offer sacrifices for their own sins, as well as the sin of the people.

This should have made them sympathetic and caring; but in most cases, they were not. The high priest was not self-appointed or voted in; he was chosen from among the people by God, so there was no reason for him to be boastful or to view himself as less sinful than the people. All the priests, just like all the people, were needy and desperate for a Savior.

Romans 3:23 says, "For all have sinned and fall short of the glory of God." We needed a better Sacrifice and a better Priest. We see that by the time Jesus walked the earth, not only was the priesthood imperfect but it was also legalistic and corrupt. They used the fact that they sat in the seat of Moses and were over the temple as a power to be leveraged, rather than viewing their position as they should have—as servants and mediators between God and man. It is in the deficiency of the Jewish priesthood that we can clearly see the need for Christ. Listen as Jesus rebukes the Jewish leaders of His day:

> Then Jesus said to the crowds and to his disciples, "The scribes and the Pharisees sit on Moses' seat, so do and observe whatever they tell you, but not the works they do. For they preach, but do not practice. They tie up heavy burdens, hard to bear, and lay them on people's shoulders, but they themselves are not willing to move them with their finger. They do all their deeds to be seen by others. For they make their phylacteries broad and their fringes long, and they love the place of honor at feasts and the best seats in the synagogues and greetings in the marketplaces and being called rabbi by others (Matt. 23:1-7).

Jesus' words of rebuke exposed the corruption and hypocrisy of the Jewish leaders of His day, but the problem went much deeper than the insincerity of the current leadership. We needed a better Priest, a perfect One, Who would shepherd the people and be a true Mediator between God and man. The priests should have shepherded the people and helped them draw close to God; but instead of doing this, they often used their earthly power and prominence to their advantage and imposed a legalistic, works-based system on the people that no one could live up to, not even the priest themselves.

They laid unbearable burdens on the backs of the people and heaped condemnation and judgment on them, not realizing that they were storing up condemnation for themselves; and this was made very clear in their rejection of Jesus as the Messiah. They should have been better than anyone at being able to recognize Christ. They were supposedly awaiting the King of the Jews to arrive; but when He did, they rejected Him because they did not truly love God or know God. Because of that, they did not fear Him.

> "But woe to you, scribes and Pharisees, hypocrites! For you shut the kingdom of heaven in people's faces. For you neither enter yourselves nor allow those who enter to go in. Woe to you, scribes and Pharisees, hypocrites! For you travel across sea and land to make a single proselyte, and when he becomes a proselyte, you make him twice as much a child of hell as yourselves . . . Woe to you, scribes and Pharisees, hypocrites! For you tithe mint and dill and cumin, and have neglected the weightier matters of the law: justice and mercy and faithfulness. These you ought to have done without neglecting the others" (Matt. 23:13-15, 23).

This hypocrisy and corruption were not anything new. In the Old Testament, we see the prophet Ezekiel rebuking the priesthood as well for being self-serving and wicked:

> The word of the LORD came to me: "Son of man, prophesy against the shepherds of Israel; prophesy, and say to them, even to the shepherds, Thus says the LORD God: Ah, shepherds of Israel who have been feeding yourselves! Should not shepherds feed the sheep? You eat the fat, you clothe yourselves with the wool, you slaughter the fat ones, but you do not feed the sheep. The weak you have not strengthened, the sick you have not

healed, the injured you have not bound up, the strayed you have not brought back, the lost you have not sought, and with force and harshness you have ruled them" (Ezek. 34:1-4).

Although not all of the priests were wicked, even the godly ones were still lacking because they themselves were sinful and in need of a Mediator to make sacrifices on their behalf. They were not qualified to do the work of the true and eternal Priest, Who is Christ. They were appointed by God to be a placeholder but also, in their deficiency, to magnify the glory, perfection, and superiority of Jesus in all things.

THE PERFECT SACRIFICE, OUR BEAUTIFUL HIGH PRIEST

In Hebrews 4:14, we see that we no longer need a high priest because the perfect High Priest has already interceded for us: "Since then we have a great high priest who has passed through the heavens, Jesus, the Son of God, let us hold fast to our confession." Unlike the priests and shepherds of Israel who rejected Him and their duty as instruments of reconciliation between God and men, Jesus fulfilled the duties left derelict by all who came before Him. He did come to strengthen the weak, heal the sick, bind up the injured, bring back the stray, and seek and save lost sheep. Jesus left the beauty and majesty of Heaven—not unwillingly, or begrudgingly, but because He loved us. We were "the joy that was set before Him" (Heb. 12:2). This is another deep and beautiful truth that should keep us anchored in our confession of faith and give us comfort in times of despair. We must fix our eyes on Jesus, our great High Priest, and hold fast to our faith because He endured the cross for us and is now making intercession for us.

Hebrews 12:2 reminds us to be "looking to Jesus, the founder and perfecter of our faith, who for the joy set before him endured the cross, despising the shame, and is seated at the right hand of the throne of God." When we talk about Jesus as our great High Priest, we first and foremost are referring to the perfection of His sacrifice. Under the Old Covenant, the priest had to repeat their sacrifices, over and over, year after year, because the blood of bulls and goats cannot truly atone for the sin of human beings. And no human blood could either because all who are born of woman have been conceived of the sin-infected seed of man. This is why Jesus was born of a virgin.

Christ was the perfect, sinless Sacrifice, Whose value is worth more than every created being ever born put together. He made our atonement when He suffered and died in our place. His perfection made atonement that never needs to be repeated, nor could it be. He was our substitutionary Sacrifice in death; and in the resurrection, He is our Intercessor, our great and beautiful High Priest forever. Christ ensured the sufficiency of the sacrifice by becoming the sacrifice Himself.

"For we do not have a high priest who is unable to sympathize with our weakness, but one who in every respect has been tempted as we are, yet without sin. Let us then with confidence draw near to the throne of grace that we may receive mercy and find grace to help in time of need" (Heb. 4:15-16). Christ Jesus is fully Man and fully God. Through His divinity, He was able to rise from the dead and become our High Priest, but it is in His humanity that He is a sympathetic High Priest. Both of these qualities distinguish Him from the priests of Israel under the Old Covenant—His Divine perfection and His deep and caring love, a love that made Him willing to lay down His life.

John 15:13 tells us of this love: "Greater love has no one than this, that someone lay down his life for his friends." In stark opposition to the imperfect and corrupt priests of Israel, Christ was sympathetic and caring "to the point of death, even death on a cross" (Phil. 2:8). The greatest display of meditation is the fact that God Himself took on human flesh in the likeness of His creation in order to reconcile man to Himself. The place of honor given to the Son was not self-appointed but was given to Him by the Father.

As we read in Hebrews 5:5-6, "So also Christ did not exalt himself to be made a high priest, but was appointed by him who said to him, 'You are my

Son, today I have begotten you'; as he says in another place, 'You are a priest forever, after the order of Melchizedek.'"

Although Jesus is the second Person of the eternal Godhead, there is an order in the Godhead. The Father sent the Son, and the Son willingly came. It is hard for us to understand the perfection of the unity of God's will; but the Father, Son, and Holy Spirit are in complete unity at all times. We see the beautiful character of God displayed for us in the Son and His willingness to come and be the perfect Sacrifice and Priest that no one else in the universe was qualified to be.

Verses one through four of chapter five list the qualifications of the high priest, and verses five through ten explain how Jesus fulfills these and goes even beyond what is required. Jesus was chosen by God and sent by God the Father. In verses five and six, the author of Hebrews quotes Psalm 2:7 and Psalm 110:4 and attributes them to Christ: "'You are my Son, today I have begotten you'" (Psalm 2:7), and "'You are a priest forever after the order of Melchizedek'" (Psalm 110:4). Melchizedek will be discussed further in a later chapter; but briefly, he is a priest mentioned in the Bible (Gen. 14:18), who is not from the line of Aaron as the other high priests were.

Because Christ is our great High Priest, we are never alone; and we need not ever be ashamed. It is so easy to gravitate to parts of Jesus' character as we neglect others. This is much of the problem of the modern American Church. We must take all of Christ or none of Him. He suffered, and so will we; He was persecuted, and so shall we be; and He rose to victory and eternal life, and so shall we if, in fact, we belong to Him.

Many, if not most, in the Church today have a sad lack of understanding of the Old Testament, a lack of understanding of the continuity between the Old and New Testament, and a misunderstanding of how God relates to humanity in the Old and New Testament. The God of Abraham, Isaac, and Jacob is the very same God Who walked with Peter, James, and John. Jesus is the Image of the invisible God; He is the exact Imprint of His nature. So many today have an uninformed and distorted view of God in the Old Testament, so they have a very shallow view of Him and what He did for us in the New Testament. I am not saying that all Christians should be academic biblical scholars, but I am saying that we should seek biblical understanding of the entire Bible as if it is the most important issue in the world because it is.

Second Timothy 2:15 encourages, "Do your best to present yourself to God as one approved, a worker who has no need to be ashamed, rightly handling the word of truth." Many pastors and Bible teachers should be ashamed because they are not humble and careful tacticians of the whole counsel of God's Word. It is very important that we understand the Old Testament because all Scripture is inspired by God (2 Tim. 3:16). Often the reason we do not have the confidence to boldly approach the throne of God for mercy and grace in our time of need is that we do not understand the depth of the meaning of the priesthood of Christ. All of God's Word is for all of God's people because we are indwelled by the Holy Spirit, Who will lead us into all truth.

THE SYMPATHETIC AND SUFFERING SAVIOR

Although Jesus is God, He became a Man, making Him fully God and fully Man. But because of His human nature, He can sympathize with the plight of mankind in a unique and personal way. He knows our pain and our struggles; He endured temptation at every turn but never sinned. Christ's willingness to become like His creation is something to be pondered, meditated on, and forever grateful for.

Jesus also sets for us a beautiful example of prayer and supplication. "In the days of his flesh, Jesus offered up prayers and supplications with loud cries and tears, to him who was able to save him from death, and he was heard because of his reverence" (Heb. 5:7). But we must not gloss over these prayers as if it was only for the sake of setting an example. These are genuine and heartfelt prayers, as Christ cried out in His flesh to His Father in Heaven.

In the death of Christ, the veil that separated us from God was forever torn in half, making a way for us to boldly approach the throne of grace.

We must never minimize the human pain and suffering of Christ any more than we do His Divine nature. We have a Savior Who can sympathize with us; and knowing this, we can trust that He understands our pain, struggles, and despair. What makes this aspect of Jesus our High Priest so utterly beautiful is that He did so willingly.

We must also rightly understand that when it says, "Jesus offered up prayers and supplications with loud cries and tears, to him who was able to save him from death," He was not trying to be delivered from the cross. The entire reason Jesus came to earth was to die on the cross; the meaning of this statement is that Jesus was praying to the only One Who could make sure that he would not stay in the grave.

The text tells us that Jesus was heard because of the reverence of His prayer. Reverence is a great expression of love and obedience. Jesus' love toward the Father is expressed in the way he approached Him. Although we have the right to approach God now because of what Christ did for us on the cross, this must always be expressed in obedient reverence. This is evidence we truly know God and that we honestly understand the gravity of what Christ has done for us.

"Although he was a son, he learned obedience through what he suffered. And being made perfect, he became the source of eternal salvation to all who obey him, being designated by God a high priest after the order of Melchizedek" (Heb. 5:8-10). We may believe that the Son of God should have been able to face the cross without anguish because He knew that God would raise Him up, but there is really no way for us to understand what Christ was truly facing. Having been born in sin into a fallen world as created beings, we have a hard time grasping the idea of bearing the sin of the world. A sinless Being is something simply beyond our comprehension. Jesus drank the full measure of the wrath and judgment of God that was stored up for us all at one time.

The wording "he learned obedience through what he suffered" might seem perplexing to us because the idea of "learning" implies that there is something God does not know. But this is not saying that Christ learned something He did not know or understand, as much as it is saying He experienced something. He put obedience to practice through His experience as a human. John Owen said it well in his commentary on the book of Hebrews: "One special kind of obedience is intended here, namely a submission to great, hard, and terrible things, accompanied by patience and quiet endurance, and faith for deliverance from them. This Christ could not have experience of, except by suffering the things he had to pass through, exercising God's grace in them all."[4]

There is something we must not miss here: although Christ is our great Example in all things, His life was not merely symbolic. Often, people who do not like the substitutionary aspect of Jesus suffering and dying on our behalf try and minimize what the cross truly accomplished or the bloody means by which it was accomplished; but we must focus on every painful, gory, and meaningful depth of the substitutionary atonement of Christ's death on the cross. Jesus suffered and died to satisfy the wrath of God, and any other view of this is heresy. To reject this is to reject Christ.

> Beloved, do not believe every spirit, but test the spirits to see whether they are from God, for many false prophets have gone into the world. By this you know the Spirit of God: every spirit that confesses that Jesus Christ has come in the flesh is from God, and every spirit that does not confess Jesus is not from God. This is the spirit of antichrist, which you heard was coming and now is in the world already (1 John 4:1-3).

The suffering and death of the fully Human Christ is the only atonement for our sins. Without the punishment, suffering, and death of Christ in the flesh, we would still be liable for our sins and subject to the rightful wrath

---

4   John Owen, *An Exposition of the Epistle to the Hebrews* (Carlisle: Banner of Truth Trust, 1991).

and condemnation of God that is stored up for all humanity. This was always the plan of God for humanity. The Old Testament is filled with prophecy that was fulfilled by and through Christ. Jesus is the suffering Messiah foretold in the book of Isaiah:

> Who has believed what he has heard from us? And to whom has the arm of the Lord been revealed? For he grew up before him like a young plant, and like a root out of dry ground; he had no form or majesty that we should look at him, and no beauty that we should desire him. He was despised and rejected by men, a man of sorrows and acquainted with grief; and as one from whom men hide their faces he was despised, and we esteemed him not. Surely he has borne our griefs and carried our sorrows; yet we esteemed him stricken, smitten by God, and afflicted. But he was pierced for our transgressions; he was crushed for our iniquities; upon him was the chastisement that brought us peace, and with his wounds we are healed (Isa. 53:1-5).

DRAWING CLOSE TO GOD

One of the most amazing differences between all false gods and false religions and the one true God is that instead of telling us that we have to work our way to God, He drew near to us. The reality is no one could ever work their way to God; so in the most beautiful act of love in the history of the world, God condescended to our level, became like us, and laid down His life for us.

"Have this mind among yourselves, which is yours in Christ Jesus, who, though he was in the form of God, did not count equity with God a thing to be grasped, but emptied himself, by taking the form of a servant, being born in the likeness of men. And being found in human form, he humbled himself by becoming obedient to the point of death, even death on a cross" (Phil. 2:5-8).

God drew close to us so that we could draw close to Him. If we are in Christ, we can confidently draw near to God to receive grace and mercy in our time of need. Our ultimate need was initially the forgiveness of our sins, but this mercy and grace extend into every area of our lives. He saved us; He is advocating for us and interceding for us; and through His mighty hand, we will be preserved until the end. Jesus is our great High Priest! He is superior to every prophet, priest, and king in the history of Israel and the history of the world. "At the name of Jesus every knee should bow . . . and every tongue confess that Jesus Christ is Lord" (Phil. 2:10-11). But the ultimate reason Christ came and died was so that we might freely and boldly approach the mercy seat of God and benefit from His amazing and unmerited grace. "Let us then with confidence draw near to the throne of grace, that we may receive mercy and find grace to help in time of need" (Heb. 4:16).

Christ became a man, lived a perfect life, died on the cross, and rose from the dead on our behalf; and because of this, He can sympathize with our struggles and our weakness. The author of Hebrews says that because of Christ's work, we can now "draw near to the throne of [God]" to seek mercy and grace in our time of need. Christ is the true Priest and Mediator Who permanently bridged the gap between us and God. We can draw near to God; this is the glory of the Gospel and the greatest news in the history of the world. But we must remember that as our Mediator Christ's work on the cross not only tore the veil of the Holy of Holies that separated us from the mercy and grace of God, but He also continues to advocate for us. He is saving us, sustaining us, conforming us to His image, and will finish the work he began in us. He is loving, caring, sympathetic, and patient with us. We are His, and He is ours now—to the end of the age and forever. Our High Priest will never fail us!

CHAPTER 6

THE FOUNDATION OF GOD'S PROMISE IN CHRIST

BY: JOSHUA WEST

"Therefore let us leave the elementary doctrine of Christ and go on to maturity, not laying again a foundation of repentance from dead works and faith toward God."

HEBREWS 6:1

THE PROMISE OF CHRIST AS our High Priest is a beautiful and powerful promise, but those who will benefit from Christ's work of obedience to the Father are those who are not merely "hearer[s] of the word," but by faith are "doers of the word" (James 1:22). The theological concept of faith permeates the entire book of Hebrews; but so does the evidence of saving faith, which is obedience to God.

Christ also understood obedience. "Although he was a son, he learned obedience through what he suffered. And being made perfect, he became the source of eternal salvation to all who obey him" (Heb. 5:8-9).

On the heels of the author's glorious representation of Christ as our sympathetic and great High Priest, where he plums the depths of God's eternal promises to His children, he now shifts his tone and warns his audience of the danger of having a superficial faith. In the last section of

Hebrews 5, he contrasts the depths of the reality of true and saving faith with that of having a false faith, which seems to have caused many of them to fall away. The author of Hebrews concludes this is evidenced by their lack of obedience and ability to live out their faith. "About this we have much to say, and it is hard explain, since you have become dull of hearing" (Heb. 5:11). The writer of Hebrews has just begun to uncover the deep riches of the priestly office of Christ for them, but he says that it is hard to explain this beautiful truth to some of them because they apparently have become "dull of hearing." He uses this seemingly sarcastic statement to rebuke them. He seems to be saying that if they understood the richness of these promises, they would live in obedience to God's commandments.

The author takes this even further: "For though by this time you ought to be teachers, you need someone to teach you again the basic principles of the oracles of God. You need milk, not solid food, for everyone who lives on milk is unskilled in the word of righteousness, since he is a child. But solid food is for the mature, for those who have their powers of discernment trained by constant practice to distinguish good from evil" (Heb. 5:12-14).

Being able to walk out a simple life of obedience to God is the milk, the most basic evidence that you truly belong to Christ. This refers to the basic fundamentals of the faith. We must take God's Word at face value and strive to walk it out with consistency. This does not mean we are striving to be justified by God or working to gain His acceptance but rather evidence that He has opened our eyes and that we are, by faith, now living for Him because He is living in us. It is normal for a brand-new believer to struggle with the simple things of the faith, but apparently, many of the people this letter is directed to seem to have been Christians for some time. Therefore, the writer of Hebrews rebukes them by saying, "By now you should be teachers but instead you can't even feed yourself."

There is grace for the new believer who is new to the Word of God and following Christ, as well as the mature believer who is struggling; but

Hebrew's author is saying that if you are still acting like a new believer after years of following Christ, maybe you are not truly reborn. In his second letter to the church at Corinth, the apostle Paul makes the same analysis of the Corinthians and urges the believers who seem to still be walking according to the flesh to examine themselves to see if they are truly in the faith. "Examine yourselves, to see whether you are in the faith. Test yourselves. Or do you not realize this about yourselves, that Jesus Christ is in you?—unless indeed you fail to meet the test" (2 Cor. 13:5).

Those who are truly in Christ have been saved by Christ, justified by Him, and in the process of being conformed to His image through the renewing of their minds by the washing of God's Word, which is the process of sanctification. If your love of the world is not decreasing as the love of God increases in you to the point you strive now to obey what God commands in His Word, hating the sin that you once loved, you might not be in Christ. God transforms those He saves, and a good tree will bear good fruit. Those who are connected to the Vine, Who is Christ (John 15:1), will bear much fruit. As Christians, we walk by faith and take God at His Word.

Milk is what you feed a baby because they cannot feed themselves. But if there truly is life there, a baby will grow; and it will not be long before they are able to eat solid food and eventually feed themselves. To mature and grow in the faith means that you can discern the difference between right and wrong and good and evil and are able to walk out it out consistently. Remember what we discussed in chapter three: all sin is rooted in unbelief.

CHRIST OUR FOUNDATION

"Therefore let us leave the elementary doctrine of Christ and go on to maturity, not laying again a foundation of repentance from dead works and faith toward God, and of instruction about washings, the laying on of hands, the resurrection of the dead, and eternal judgment. And this we will do if God permits" (Heb. 6:1-3). Let's be clear, this is not saying that the doctrine of Christ is elementary, nor is it saying that we need not repent of our sins anymore. It is saying that a true believer should not have to be convinced over and over again of the necessity of repentance. A foundation need only be laid once; and if it needs to be laid again, it means it was not laid properly the first time. Like any good pastor or minister, the author of Hebrews understands that he is writing to true believers and false converts alike, so the tone is often encouraging and rebuking at the same time.

The Gospel according to Jesus as laid out in Matthew 7 tells us that Christ Himself is that Foundation; and if your life is not built on the Jesus of the Bible, it will not endure the storms of this life. This is what Jesus is talking about when he tells us that the Gospel road is narrow and hard. The way to life is exclusively found in Christ. Jesus is not a sage, a good man, or merely a wise teacher. He is God in the flesh, our only Means of salvation and our only Hope. To view Him as anything less than Lord of lords is blasphemy.

Matthew 7:13-14 encourages us to "'enter by the narrow gate. For the gate is wide and the way easy that leads to destruction, and those who enter by it are many. For the gate is narrow and the way is hard that leads to life, and those who find it are few.'"

The people to whom the letter of Hebrews was written were in the middle of great persecution and trial, and the author is conveying a sobering truth to them; if you fall away from Christ, it is because you never knew Him. Dead works and faith in God are not enough; it must be true faith in Christ. Outward works and expressions of faith are not enough to sustain us or save us. We must be born again of the Spirit of God "by grace . . . through faith" (Eph. 2:8) in Christ alone. You must know Christ and be "known" by Him in regeneration. This is the narrow and exclusive way of life, and those who are alive in Christ will bear fruit. A mere profession of faith in Christ is not enough. So, every healthy tree bears good fruit, but the diseased tree bears bad fruit.

> A healthy tree cannot bear bad fruit, nor can a diseased tree bear good fruit . . . "Not everyone who says to me, 'Lord, Lord' will enter the kingdom of heaven, but the one who does the will of my Father who is in heaven. On that day many will say to me, 'Lord, Lord, did we not prophesy in your name, and cast out demons in your name, and do many mighty works in your name?' And then I will declare to them, 'I never knew you; depart from me, you workers of lawlessness'" (Matt. 7:18, 21-23).

Those who have saving faith in Christ will build their lives on His words, the words of sacred Scripture; and they will not be put to shame. It will not be in vain; and even if you lose your life in this world, you will have eternal life.

In Matthew 7:24-25, Jesus tells us about the ones who hear His words: "'Everyone then who hears these words of mine and does them will be like a wise man who built his house on the rock. And the rain fell, and the floods came, and the winds blew and beat on that house, but it did not fall, because it had been founded on the rock.'"

There is no way around it if you are still struggling with discerning the most basic elements of right and wrong and good and evil. It may be evidence that although the house of your life might have some "Christian"-looking construction materials on the outside of it, something may be wrong with your foundation. If your life is built on the solid Rock of Jesus Christ, your life will be characterized by the Gospel; and there will be evidence of it. Here are some of those evidences:

1. The greatest desire of your life will be to do the will of the Father.
2. Although in practice, you will fall short of perfection, you will be able to discern good from evil and right from wrong.

3. You will feel conviction when you do fall short, which is evidence of Christ's nature living in you.

4. You will hunger and thirst to be righteous, and God promises you will be satisfied (Matt. 5:6).

The author of Hebrews wants those reading this letter—but especially his Jewish readers—to understand that the message of repentance is foundational to following Jesus. It was the message of all the prophets, John the Baptist, the apostles, and Jesus Himself.

We read in Matthew 4:17, "From that time Jesus began to preach, saying, 'Repent, for the kingdom of heaven is at hand.'" The heart of repentance toward God is something essential for salvation. The author of Hebrews wants to make sure that his Jewish audience also understands that the sacrifices of bulls and goats under the Old Covenant had to be repeated because they were merely placeholders until the true sacrifice could come. Since the fulfillment has come, there is no longer any need for these types and shadows that pointed to Jesus. So if you reject Christ, there is no forgiveness for sin; even if you repent, these are dead works and dead faith. There is no fellowship with God, and there is no life outside of Christ. As Jesus proclaimed in John 14:6, "I am the way, and the truth, and the life. No one comes to the Father except through me.'"

THOSE WHO HAVE BEEN ENLIGHTENED

"For it is impossible, in the case of those who have once been enlightened, who have tasted the heavenly gift, and have shared in the Holy Spirit, and have tasted the goodness of the word of God and the powers of the age to come, and then have fallen away, to restore them again to repentance, since they are crucifying once again the Son of God to their own harm and holding Him up to contempt" (Heb. 6:4-6).

This section of the Scripture has been the point of much contention and confusion; but when viewed in the context of the entire book of Hebrews and the entire teaching of the Bible, it really is quite clear. This is not to say that you can lose your salvation. The term "enlightened" does not have any of the New Testament language typically associated with justification, salvation, or regeneration. Many false converts appear to have the same characteristics as true believers, seemingly enlightened, but how could anyone truly perceive the Gospel and then turn their back on it?

They encountered the Gospel, lived and professed Christ, shared in the benefits of the Holy Spirit with the community of God, and tasted the goodness of the Word of God and the powers of the age to come but did not truly have saving faith because saving faith will endure to the end. What a shame it is to be so seemingly close to the things of God—the saving grace of God—and even have benefited from them on some level in this life but still not be transformed.

It is impossible for someone to find repentance who already believes that they are right with God, and it is also impossible for someone to find forgiveness of their sins apart from Christ. If you have tasted the things of God and truly and ultimately reject them, there is no hope for you. The author of Hebrews says to believe this is possible is like crucifying the Son of God once again and holding his finished work of the cross in contempt. He gives an analogy in verses seven and eight that explains what he means: "For the land that has drunk the rain that often falls on it, and produces a crop useful to those for whose sake it is cultivated, receives a blessing from God. But if it bears thorns and thistles, it is worthless and near to being cursed, and its end is to be burned."

This will be the fate of those who seem to follow Christ but prove they do not have saving faith by ultimately rejecting Him. Any branch that is broken and dead is reserved for fire. But the same is true for the branch that bears thorns and thistles; in the end, they will be pruned from the vine, and their fate is the same as the broken branch. As John 15:6 warns, "'If anyone does not abide in me he is thrown away like a branch and withers; and the branches are gathered, thrown into the fire, and burned.'"

It is also important to establish that this is not saying that God will ever refuse the truly repentant. God will never refuse a truly contrite and repentant heart. But like Jesus said, "'A good tree will bear good fruit'" (Matt. 7:17). And the only ones who will enter the kingdom of Heaven are those who are reborn and do the will of the Father, and these people are one and the same. Those who truly repent and put their hope and faith in Christ will be saved.

The point the author of Hebrews is trying to make is that if a person confesses faith in Christ, benefits from the goodness of the preached Word of God, experiences the work of the Spirit to some degree and the promises of the age to come, and still falls away, there really is not anything that can be done for them. Our faith in this life is tethered to the promise of the age to come; if you reject this, it means you do not have saving faith. Hebrews 11:6 tells us, "And without faith it is impossible to please him, for whoever would draw near to God must believe that he exists and that he rewards those who seek him."

Spurgeon makes the same estimation of these verses in Hebrews 6: "If all the processes of grace fail in the case of any professors, what is to be done with them? If the grace of God does not enable them to overcome the world, if the blood of Christ does not purge them from sin, what more can be done?"

Here is something to ponder. If you can live in open and unrepentant sin for long periods of time and not be worried about the state of your soul because you believe that you are "saved" due to a prayer you prayed at some point or some sort of external work of your life, you are in a very dangerous place. These are the same people Jesus speaks about in Matthew 7, who said, "Lord, Lord" but will not enter the kingdom of Heaven. If you claim to see and perceive the holiness of God, the sinfulness of man, and the amazing grace of God in the Gospel but can walk away from it, there is no hope for you. A lifestyle of sin without conviction might be evidence of dead works. How can you see and perceive the glorious treasure of Christ and

His glorious Gospel and not fall on your knees before the throne of God to receive mercy and grace?

Matthew 13:44 says, "'The kingdom of heaven is like treasure hidden in a field, which a man found and covered up. Then in his joy he goes and sells all that he has and buys that field.'" Once the value of the treasure is seen and perceived, it can never be forgotten. Remember, true salvation is taking God at His Word by faith; but those who truly do are reborn, and I do not see any evidence in the Scripture that those who are truly reborn can ever be un-reborn. A great example of this is Saul of Tarsus, who would later become known as the apostle Paul. He was a Pharisee and a great persecutor of the Church; but when He encountered Christ on the Damascus Road, He was changed forever to the point that He spent the rest of His life preaching Christ. He was persecuted for Christ, whipped and beaten for Christ, many times imprisoned for Christ, and died as a martyr for the sake of Christ.

It almost seems like he had found "a treasure in a field" and, perceiving the value of it, sold and gave up everything to gain it. This is the kingdom of Heaven; this is the beauty of Jesus; this is what true salvation looks like. Listen to how Paul describes the jaw-dropping beauty of Jesus in his letter to the Philippian church. He wrote this letter while in prison for preaching the Gospel of Christ. Listen to how he compares the beauty and worth of Jesus to everything else in this world:

> But whatever gain I had, I counted as loss . . . because of the surpassing worth of knowing Christ Jesus my Lord. For his sake I have suffered the loss of all things and count them as rubbish, in order that I may gain Christ and be found in him, not having a righteousness of my own that comes from the law, but that which comes through faith in Christ, the righteousness from God that depends on faith—that I may know him and the power of his resurrection, and may share his sufferings, becoming like him in his death, that by any means possible I may attain the resurrection from the dead (Phil. 3:7-11).

Those who truly have saving faith in Christ will gladly suffer for Christ and with Christ because, by faith, they know they are obtaining resurrection from the dead. So, they will live for Christ and, if necessary, die for Christ because they have already died to this world. If you are truly born again and truly have saving faith, nothing will ever compare to the surpassing worth and beauty of the One Who saves you. If anything in this world can take away your faith in Christ, it shows that you never really had saving faith; and you never really knew Christ. There are only two groups of people—"those who shrink back and are destroyed" and "those who have faith and preserve their souls" (Heb. 10:39).

We must deny the holiness of God and the sinfulness of man in order to reject the mercy and grace of God that Jesus secured for us in the Gospel. If we do not see Christ as a Treasure worth forsaking all things for, then we do not really see Christ! The foundation of a truly repentant lifestyle comes from truly perceiving that the Gospel should shape every part of your life. If you can reject the saving treasure that is Christ, you do not truly know Him in a saving way. Living a life of disregard or rejection toward Christ exposes that one or more things are true about your life:

1.   You do not really know the God of the Bible.
2.   You do not really know the depths of your sinfulness in light of a holy God.
3.   You do not understand the holiness of God or the depth of your sin and undervalue the worth of the grace of God and what Christ did for us on the cross.

If you really knew and believed in the God of the Bible, you would have reverent fear toward Him. As Proverbs 9:10 says, "The fear of the LORD is the beginning of wisdom, and the knowledge of the Holy One is insight."

We expose our lack of knowledge concerning God by the posture we take with God. The holy God of the Old Testament, Who created the world, flooded the world, raised up nations, and toppled kingdoms is the same God Who saved and delivered those who belong to Him and destroyed those who opposed Him. The God of vengeance, justice, and judgment is, in fact, the same God in the New Testament, Who so loved the world that He gave His only Son to save those who believe in Him. God is sovereign, and God is holy!

If we truly see God in holy perfection, unable to co-exist with sin, then we will see ourselves in light of God's perfection as the grievous sinners we truly are. This is what produces real repentance. The unrepentant do not have a clear view of these two things. The truly repentant person understands that they deserve the wrath, judgment, and condemnation of God because they see God for Who He truly is and see themselves for who they truly are.

Charles Spurgeon once said, "The truly regenerate man who understands the depth of his sinfulness and the degree to which a holy God detests sin,[sic] is not surprised such a God punishes sin with eternal damnation,[sic] he is surprised that God would save anyone, especially himself, being that he knows how sinful he truly is,[sic] this is the gift of grace."

To truly perceive and value the grace and mercy that God has given to us through the Gospel of Jesus Christ, we must first truly know and fear God, repent of our sins, and, by grace through faith, put our trust in Christ alone for our salvation. Those who fall away from the faith were never truly anchored in Christ and His unfailing and unchanging Word because those are two things that will never fail.

THE SURETY OF GOD'S PROMISE

> Though we speak in this way, yet in your case, beloved, we feel
> sure of better things—things that belong to salvation. For God
> is not unjust so as to overlook your work and the love that you

have shown for his name in serving the saints, as you still do. And we desire each one of you to show the same earnestness to have the full assurance of hope until the end, so that you may not be sluggish, but imitators of those who through faith and patience inherit the promises (Heb. 6:9-12).

After a very harsh rebuke and warning to those who would abandon the saving grace of Christ, the Hebrews author now appeals to them in a much more positive tone. Like all good pastoral exposition, he hopes to separate the sheep and the goats by rebuking false converts and exposing their unstable footing, while at the same time encouraging the true believer as they hold fast by faith to the promises of God. We know that he is talking exclusively to believers here because he uses a word reserved in the New Testament only for Christ's true sheep: "beloved," unlike those who were merely "enlightened" but not reborn or regenerated.

It is possible to experience enlightenment or have a revelation about God, to experience the blessings of God, to come close and taste the things of the Spirit, to have an emotional response, and to make a superficial declaration or profession without being reborn in the Spirit. This is what makes false converts hard to detect, but those who fall away without repentance show that they were never really born of the Spirit.

The author of Hebrews is saying that it is his great desire that all those who claim Christ would have the same earnestness to have the full assurance of hope that will keep them to the end, true saving faith. He is telling those that are unsure of their souls to be imitators of those who by faith and patience will inherit the promises of God—not that simply doing good works can save them but to follow the pattern of saving faith that is evident in all who truly have put their faith in the promises of God.

For when God made a promise to Abraham, since he had no one greater by whom to swear, he swore by himself, saying, "Surely

I will bless you and multiply you." And thus Abraham, having patiently waited, obtained the promise. For people swear by something greater than themselves, and in all their disputes an oath is final for confirmation. So when God desired to show more convincingly to the heirs of the promise the unchangeable character of his purpose, he guaranteed it with an oath, so that by two unchangeable things, in which it is impossible for God to lie, we who have fled for refuge might have strong encouragement to hold fast to the hope set before us (Heb. 6:13-18).

So, in reference to the promise of the saving grace of God found in the Gospel, the author of Hebrews appeals back to a promise every Hebrew would know about and understand—the promise God made to Abraham. He promised that He would bless and multiply him and make him a nation. But he does not want us to focus on the promise as much as he wants us to focus on the One Who made the promise. All roads lead back to the Gospel.

There are three things that we can always count on: God's person, God's purpose, and God's promise. To have saving faith in God is dependent on our trust that these things will never fail. The author of Hebrews uses one of the greatest examples in Jewish history to make his point—Abraham. Abraham knew he could believe in the promise God made to him because he trusted the person of God and the purpose of God. The author of Hebrews basically says it this way: because he knew the person of God, he could trust His purpose and His promise. These are two unchangeable things. God cannot lie!

The way we get to know the person of God, the purposes of God, and the promises of God is by looking deeply and intently at His Word. God kept his promise to Abraham against all human odds and human understanding; and the author of Hebrews wants those reading his letter to see that this is evidence that God keeps His promises, so He will also keep His promises to us. The promise of blessing and multiplying Abraham's descendants in the natural is merely a foreshadowing of the promise God made to Abraham because, ultimately, the Blessing of Abraham was Jesus Christ.

"Know then that it is those of faith who are the sons of Abraham. And the Scripture, foreseeing that God would justify the Gentiles by faith, preached the gospel beforehand to Abraham, saying, 'In you shall all the nations be blessed.' So then, those who are of faith are blessed along with Abraham, the man of faith" (Gal. 3:7-9).

All the promises of God to the believer are built on the solid foundation of Christ. He is the Word, and He is the Anchor. He is the Answer to all things because He is the Origin of all things and the Fulfillment of all things. Christ is the Promise and the Fulfillment of the promise. We who have fled and turned from our past and put our faith in Christ have a strong encouragement to hold fast to the hope set before us. "We have this as a sure and steadfast anchor of the soul, a hope that enters into the inner place behind the curtain, where Jesus has gone as a forerunner on our behalf, having become a high priest forever after the order of Melchizedek" (Heb. 6:19-20).

Your faith will not fail if it is truly anchored in the promises of God as revealed in the Scripture and in the God Who made the promises. Here is the place where many of us get off track—we either put our faith in the wrong place, or we stand on promises that God did not make to us. Typically, this is because we do not know and understand the Bible in context; we view the Bible the wrong way, or we confuse really wanting something with a promise from God. God did not promise He would give us anything that we want.

God gave Abraham great reason to put his faith in Him, His Person, His purpose, and His promise. But under the New Covenant, we, too, have all of these things; but we also have something else—His priesthood. We have Christ, our great and eternal High Priest, Who is our Mediator. He is the sure and steadfast Anchor for our souls. Like the high priests of the Old Covenant, He went behind the veil in the inner place, the Holy of Holies. But He is holy, so He had the right to go behind the veil because He is God. Jesus did what no priest before Him could do—permanently bridge the chasm between God and man, thus becoming our Forerunner. Jesus approached God as a permanent

Sacrifice for sin and thus became the ultimate and final Mediator between God and man, a role that He will never lay down. He is our Propitiation, Sacrifice, Fulfillment of the promise, and our great and eternal "high priest forever after the order of Melchizedek."

This is why we must know God's Word; and more importantly, we must know God from His Word because these are the true promises of God to us. It all points to one thing—not that God will part the Red Sea of your life, or that you will slay the Goliaths of your life, or that you will become great like Joseph if you go to prison. All of these fulfilled promises show us one thing: if God makes a promise, if it is God's will, if God has decreed it, it will come to pass. All whose lives are built on the solid Rock of Jesus Christ will stand and will not fail. The promise of God for all of His children is that He "'will never leave [us] nor forsake [us]'" (Heb. 13:5); through the cross, our sins are pardoned, and nothing will ever be able to separate us from the love of God; and we will forever be with Him in eternity.

The Bible was not meant to answer all of your questions because—as you will discover as you get to know God from His Word—some of your questions do not really even matter. The Bible answers the questions it wants to answer because God is Sovereign. We can depend on and trust in the purpose of God and believe in the promise of God because we truly know and trust the Person of God as revealed to us in the Person of Jesus Christ. Here are some promises for all of God's people that have been secured for us in Christ:

- "Jesus is the same yesterday and today and forever" (Heb. 13:8).
- "For 'everyone who calls on the name of the Lord will be saved'" (Rom. 10:13).
- "I give them eternal life, and they will never perish, and no one will snatch them out of my hand" (John 10:28).
- "Your word is a lamp to my feet and a light to my path" (Psalm 119:105).
- "'I will not leave you comfortless: I will come to you'" (John 14:18 KJV).

- "'I will never leave you nor forsake you'" (Heb. 13:5b).
- "But they who wait for the LORD shall renew their strength; they shall mount up with wings like eagles; they shall run and not be weary; they shall walk and not faint" (Isa. 40:31).
- "'But whoever drinks of the water that I will give him will never be thirsty again. The water that I will give him will become in him a spring of water welling up to eternal life'" (John 4:14).

CHAPTER 7

HOW GREAT

BY: GARY WILKERSON

Great is our Lord, and abundant in power; his understanding is beyond measure.

PSALM 147:5

MY WIFE AND I HAVE been reading through the book of Hebrews together almost every morning and evening. It takes us just over half an hour; and what we have discovered is a marvelous, majestic, and moving presentation of the jaw-dropping beauty of Jesus.

Jesus leaps off every page of this epistle to the Hebrews in all his wonder, glory, and supremacy. The more we consider Him in these pages, the more precious He becomes to us. It makes me realize that people who see Jesus' greatness only dimly will never be passionate, radical disciples of His. When we fix our eyes on Him, He grows larger and more prominent in our view of everything. By reading Hebrews, the brilliance of Jesus is illuminated.

If you long to know more of the greatness of Jesus; hunger for a move of God in your life; thirst for a closer, more intimate walk with the Lord; or desire a greater revelation of Christ, you will do well to spend much time in Hebrews. If, on the other hand, you seek helpful hints for a better life now and tips for attaining your desires, you should, instead, visit TED Talks or find a good self-help book (and there are many in the so-called Christian market). Yet for everyone who is not satisfied with temporal things, this chapter is written for you.

We behold Christ's jaw-dropping beauty in Hebrews 7, which describes Jesus through a strange and somewhat mystical view of a figure called Melchizedek. The chapter says this man has "neither beginning of days or end of life" (v. 3), as well as no mother and father. If that is not wild enough, Melchizedek is also called one "resembling the Son of God he continues a priest forever" (v. 3). Some scholars say he was an angel, while others say we do not know his genealogy. But most say, and I agree, that he was a pre-incarnate appearance of Christ. This means that Jesus appeared as a Man in the Old Testament (where Melchizedek is first mentioned) and was often called the Angel of the Lord.

Day after day, as my wife and I read through this letter, my eyes fixated on a single phrase in Hebrews 7:4: "See how great this man was." Melchizedek was great, but we know Jesus is far greater. Hebrews brings many great people to our attention, including Melchizedek; but by contrast, we are able to see how much greater Jesus was and is. He is always greater! And seeing His greatness is the key to entering a life of gratitude, praise, peace, joy, delight, and mission.

The first word of this phrase, "See," parallels other key ideas in Hebrews, marked by phrases such as "looking to Jesus" (Heb. 12:2) or "consider Jesus" (Hebrews 3:1). What makes Hebrews jaw-dropping is not just its rich theology, compelling history, ample encouragement, or vital warnings. What awes most is this thematic focus to see, look, consider, and fix our eyes on no one— no source, no power, no angel—nothing other than Jesus.

Contained in this "seeing" are precious promises. When we turn our gaze from anxious thoughts of daily problems and instead see Jesus—when our minds are less occupied with the cares of this world and more with Christ— everything changes. Our soul becomes settled, our heart warmed, our passion redirected, and our spirit lifted.

With Melchizedek, people could say, "See how great this man was." With Jesus, we see the greater One. He not only visited us on earth but was actually born among us as fully Man and fully God. With Him, we see the only human being who ever lived a perfect and righteous life. He did what no other had ever done nor could ever do: He completely obeyed and fulfilled the law of God. We could say of other men, "See how great this man was," a statement that would hold true of Noah, Abraham, Samuel, David, Elijah, and more. But none of these were the perfect, pure, spotless, holy, set-apart Son of God.

What was it about Jesus' greatness? What made Him more remarkable than any other? The obvious answer is, "He was God." But Hebrews' power is in detailing what His greatness accomplished for us. In chapter seven, we find three things that Jesus alone could accomplish, setting Him apart from other great people. These three things are:

1.   Perfection attained (Heb. 7:11).
2.   "The power of an indestructible life" (Heb. 7:16).
3.   Our greatest hope (Heb. 7:19).

PERFECTION ATTAINED

We first see how great this Man was in His claim as the only human in the world's six-thousand-year history to live a perfect life—and by all measures, He absolutely did. Jesus alone was pure and spotless, fulfilling the Father's desire that man would live perfectly holy before him. He also obeyed every word, command, and law of His Father. The Father could then say, "Here is one who has merited my favor, acceptance, and eternal reward."

The rest of us have failed miserably. We live in a world striving for perfection—in achievements, academics, career, attainment of homes and cars, family, health, and life. When hard realities come our way and we see our failures, shortcomings, and sin, we get angry either at ourselves or at others; and we fall into despair. We feel the weight of our failures whenever we are criticized and turn our pain into blaming others for ruffling our feathers. We may fall into self-hatred, rehashing again and again our failures; and we press on, trying harder, starting over, pursuing new schemes. We may try therapy, exploring early childhood causes that could explain our failures as adults.

Despite these endless, torturous cycles, most of us persist in the false idea that we can obtain perfection. In the end, no one escapes this life without a clear recognition of our failures. And our shortcomings are more than simply not measuring up to self-imposed standards. They are moral failures before a holy God. In fact, they are more than failures; they are sin. Our failures do more than let us and others down; they actually bring us under judgment. So much is said today in the pop-psychology world about how shame is the greatest negative in our lives. From a biblical standard, shame serves a purpose. It shows us our shortcomings, reveals our need for a Savior, and drives us to call upon God. Our approaches to human remedies never relieve our guilt and shame. Only God can free us.

How, then, does Jesus' perfection affect us? Can His perfection have any impact on our life? When we read Hebrews 7:11, "Now if perfection had been attainable through the Levitical priesthood (for under it the people received the law)," the meaning is clear: the Old Covenant priesthood could not make us perfectly clean, pure, holy, and acceptable before God. Those priestly sacrifices could only provide temporary relief from the cost of sin. It could never fully perfect the sinner.

Moreover, priests had to first make sacrifices for their own sins before they could perform rituals leading to atonement for the sins of the people. They were mere humans with their own imperfections to deal with.

For these reasons and others, Jesus' perfect life was as important as His sacrificial death. If He had sinned, His sacrifice would have lost its power to atone for us once and for all. Instead, His death served a dual nature. First, He could cleanse our sins; but just as importantly, He could impute to us—meaning, He could impart, pass on, or put into us—His own perfect righteousness. And in earning the right to be called holy, Jesus granted His perfections to us.

All told, Jesus allowed us to share in both His crucifixion and His resurrected life. On our own, we could never achieve the holy state that God requires. Jesus not only achieved that state but grafted us into it. This state is not what some call "sinless perfection" achievable in the here-and-now of our lives. Rather, our holy state is our standing—our position of acceptance before God—allowing us to be seen as holy before Him, just as Jesus is holy, as we see in the following verses:

- 1 Peter 2:22: "He committed no sin, neither was deceit found in his mouth." We stand before God as having committed no sin because our Savior, Jesus, wiped our sins away.

- 2 Corinthians 5:21: "For our sake he made him to be sin who knew no sin, so that in him we might become the righteousness of God." Jesus lived a perfect life and died for our sins—not for His own sake but for ours. This was so that our sins may be forgiven and that we may have Christ's own righteousness within us.

- Hebrews 7:26: "For it was indeed fitting that we should have such a high priest, holy, innocent, unstained, separated from sinners, and exalted above the heavens." Through Jesus's perfection, we are now holy, innocent, unstained, counted as separated from sinners and seated with Him in the heavenlies.

THE POWER OF AN INDESTRUCTIBLE LIFE

It brings us joy to know that Jesus lived a perfect life and that His perfection continues forever. Therefore, we can know His work is fully finished because what Christ has completed will never come to an end. Hebrews 7:16, 21 says, "Who has become a priest, not on the basis of a legal requirement concerning bodily descent, but by the power of an indestructible life . . . *'You [Jesus] are a priest forever.'"*

A political party may bring great changes to a nation; but then another party is installed, and negative changes undo all the good that was previously done. This kind of shift does not happen with Christ's work. The power of His indestructible life means that everything He accomplished will live on with Him through eternity.

The Old Testament speaks of good kings replaced by evil ones. Good priests were replaced by ungodly, wicked ones. These changes in kingship and priesthood brought about uncertainty, fear, and doubt because the good news of the day could become the horrors of tomorrow. Such uncertainty leads to anxiety, which is the great plague of the current generation. The only cure for anxiety is to know that Jesus' work was more than perfect; it was also lasting. Christ's words about marriage—"What therefore God has joined together, let no man separate'" (Matt. 19:6)—apply equally to God's covenant of grace upon us.

The joys we receive from Jesus bring an end to our anxieties because we can live in absolute assurance that He lives on. There will be no end to His kingdom, no end to the power of His blood, no end to the forgiveness of our sins, and no end to our full and certain acceptance before God.

And so we can draw near to God because "[Jesus] always lives to make intercession for them" (Heb. 7:25). "Them" refers to you and me; Jesus is making intercession for us. He lives with this purpose because "he holds his priesthood permanently" (Heb. 7:24). We have peace knowing He lives forever and that no power is able to end His reign of grace.

In this passage, intercession does not mean that Jesus is praying for us. Rather, it means He intercedes between one party and another. In short, His intercession here is between God and man. The image is of Jesus pleading our case before a Judge in the court of Heaven. Thanks to our Intercessor, we are able to stand before God *in Christ*, even though our sins are many. He intercedes for us, pleading our case; and because of His perfection, we are declared righteous, free from all guilt and punishment.

So whenever Satan accuses you of being unclean, you can answer, "I was once, but now Jesus has declared me clean." If self-doubt causes you to wonder if you are holy enough for God to accept you, accept that you are not holy enough on your own but that Jesus has made you totally acceptable before the Father. He stands before the Father as our Intercessor to declare us so.

OUR GREATEST HOPE

It is one thing to look at a man and declare how great he was. It is another thing to declare that that great man is our life's greatest hope. There are many great men who will never affect my life in any real measure. My favorite author might inspire me; a hero may spur me on; and I might even work out a bit more at the gym when I read about a man in great shape. None of these hold a candle to the Man who gives us our greatest hope.

Hebrews 7:18-19 speaks of this hope: "A former commandment is set aside because of its weakness and uselessness (for the law made nothing perfect); but on the other hand, *a better hope* is introduced, through which we draw near to God" (emphasis mine).

As good as the law and the commands are, their use for righteousness has been set aside by a new and better law. The law of Christ has come—not an external one but one written in our hearts. History has proved the hopelessness of trying to attain righteousness through the law. Now a new story has been written, revealing that righteousness comes through the one great Man, Christ Jesus. This is why we can fully announce, "How great this man was and is!"

Whereas hopelessness, despair, and despondency once reigned, we now have a better hope. This hope allows us to draw near to God—not with fear, hoping merely to be rescued, but with complete confidence to enter his presence boldly. We come in like children entering their father's office, knowing we are welcomed and even delighted in. This is what it means to "enter [God's] gates with thanksgiving" (Psalm 100:4). We enter, not wondering whether we will be cast out but full of joyful singing and praise. This joyful hope does not cause pride or nonchalance toward God's welcoming grace but comes from a grateful heart that understands how much Jesus did to make our acceptance possible.

If this amazing truth is not enough, another verse goes further. Hebrews 7:21 says, "But this one was made a priest with an *oath*" (emphasis mine). In His great love for us, Jesus made an oath that our hope will never be disappointed. He promises that His work—perfect, indestructible and forever fulfilling our greatest hope—will live on. It can never be destroyed.

These are just three of Hebrews' many great evidences that help us see how surpassingly great this one Man truly is. I fix my eyes on Him; I look to Him; and I consider Him above all else. In doing so, my heart leaps; my joy increases; and I am overwhelmed with gratitude. I pray the same for you as you read the pages of Hebrews 7—that as you look to Him, you find just how amazingly great this Man Jesus is.

CHAPTER 8

THE NEW COVENANT

BY: JOSHUA WEST

They serve a copy and shadow of the heavenly things. For when Moses was about to erect the tent, he was instructed by God, saying, "See that you make everything according to the pattern that was shown you on the mountain." But as it is, Christ has obtained a ministry that is as much more excellent than the old as the covenant he mediates is better, since it is enacted on better promises. For if that first covenant had been faultless, there would have been no occasion to look for a second.

HEBREWS 8:5-7

GOD IS A GOD OF covenant promises; and to rightly divide the Scripture, we must understand these covenants in proper context. Jesus did not come to fix a broken covenant; He came to be the fulfillment of the Law and the Deliverer of His people. He came to establish a new and better covenant. In chapter two, Gary wrote about the incomparable and supreme "betterness" of Christ. This does not mean that on a scale of one to ten, we are a two; and Jesus is a ten. It means that the perfection of Christ is so infinitely better, it is incalculable, immeasurable, and incomparable.

Understanding the power and beauty of the New Covenant is something every Christian should seek to deeply understand. As humans, we are bent and born for legalism. The idea of working hard to be justified is deep within our human nature. We so easily revert to it as we live out our Christian lives. But works-based righteousness is a millstone around our necks that is rooted in the pride of the devil. The Law of God is meant to show that we are not like God and that we desperately need God's mercy. Jesus makes this point when he compares the hearts of a proud and legalistic Pharisee and a humble and contrite tax collector.

> He also told this parable to some who trusted in themselves that they were righteous, and treated others with contempt: "Two men went up into the temple to pray, one a Pharisee and the other a tax collector. The Pharisee, standing by himself, prayed thus: 'God, I thank you that I am not like other men, extortioners, unjust, adulterers, or even like this tax collector. I fast twice a week; I give tithes of all that I get.' But the tax collector, standing far off, would not even lift up his eyes to heaven, but beat his breast, saying, 'God, be merciful to me, a sinner!' I tell you, this man went down to his house justified, rather than the other. For everyone who exalts himself will be humbled, but the one who humbles himself will be exalted" (Luke 18:9-14).

God cares about the heart above outward appearances (1 Sam. 16:7). The fruitful outworking of the Spirit in the life of the believer is merely an overflow and evidence of genuine inward working. Christianity is not a works-based religion; it is an evidence-based religion. Our outward expression is simply evidence of an inward fellowship with the living God. We will discuss this in greater detail in a later chapter.

There are many covenants discussed in the Bible that God made with people—the Noahic covenant and the Davidic covenant, to name two—but here we are going to discuss the three encompassing ones: the covenant of redemption, the covenant of works, and the covenant of grace.

The covenant of redemption is not a covenant made with men. This is a covenant made between the three members of the eternal Godhead before time began. In this, they agreed in perfect harmony to bring forth the necessary work of redemption so that God might have eternal fellowship with a remnant of His creation for all eternity. This was in place before God created the world, before Adam and Eve fell, and before there was any sin to be redeemed from. In God's sovereign foreknowledge, He knew the end from the beginning. It was always God's plan and purpose to magnify His Son through the cross and resurrection from the dead. Redemption is a work of the Trinity, just as all the works of the Lord are Trinitarian.

The Old Covenant, also known as the covenant of works, was merely types and shadows, placeholders that were always meant to be fulfilled and completely outshined by the holy perfection of Christ. Shadows do not have or hold form; they are simply products cast from approaching light. Once the light comes, the shadows disappear. Therefore, the One bringing the New Covenant is superior to the figures of the Old Covenant; the New Covenant He brings is also superior in every way. The most important thing to remember is the Old Covenant was never meant to bring salvation, only to magnify the One Who brought salvation. Salvation under the Old and New Covenant has always been the same. It is "counted as righteousness" (Rom. 4:3) to the person who believes in God and takes Him at His Word.

John Owen said, "Wherefore we must grant two distinct covenants, rather than a twofold administration of the same covenant merely, to be intended. We must, I say, do so, provided always that the way of reconciliation and salvation was the same under both."[5] We must see and understand that the New Covenant, the covenant of grace—or said more simply, the Gospel—was always God's plan. Jesus was destined to be the Lamb Who was slain and the resurrected Savior of His people before the foundations of the world were laid by the power of His words. Hebrews 8:1-2 says, "Now the point in what we are saying is this: we have such a high priest, one who is seated at the

---

5   John Owen, *Exposition of Hebrews, 3:7-5:14, vol. 4, Hebrews* (Seymour: Banner Publishing, republished 1992).

right hand of the throne of the Majesty in heaven, a minister in the holy places, in the true tent that the Lord set up, not man."

The main point of Hebrews 8, as well as the main point theologically of the book of Hebrews in general, is that of the revelation of Christ and the New Covenant. But for the sake of understanding the New Covenant in general, we must discuss two images that reveal the superiority of Christ in all things: Jesus seated at the right hand of God and Jesus ministering in the heavenly sanctuary.

It is true that Jesus is the King of all things "in heaven and on earth and under the earth" (Phil. 2:10). This is a detailed way of saying, "Jesus is the Ruler over all things." But while this is legally true in every way, not all things are currently acknowledging the kingdom of Christ or are surrendered to His Lordship. The reason that God's justice has been delayed is because of the mercy and kindness of God. It is the love and patience of God that held off His righteous judgment.

"The Lord is not slow to fulfill his promise as some count slowness, but is patient toward you, not wishing that any should perish, but that all should reach repentance. But the day of the Lord will come like a thief, and then the heavens will pass away with a roar, and the heavenly bodies will be burned up and dissolved, and the earth and the works that are done on it will be exposed" (2 Peter 3:9-10).

The New Covenant—or Gospel (which is how I will refer to the New Covenant or covenant of grace through the rest of this chapter)—is not a call to "do"; it is a call to repent and believe in what Christ has done on your behalf. This is the Good News that the book of Romans commands believers to spread everywhere.

THE MERCY SEAT OF CHRIST

Under the Old Covenant, the priests never sat; they ministered on their feet. This symbolized the perpetual need to continually make sacrifices on behalf of the people and on behalf of themselves. The Mercy

Seat of Christ was in the Holy of Holies, but it was separated from the people by a veil. No one could enter the holiest place, except for the high priest once a year; and the high priest had no right to sit because he was not the perfect and permanent high priest. The Holy of Holies was where the manifest presence of God resided on earth, and it was a place of fear and dread because of the sin of man. Sin separated us from being able to enjoy God's presence and to be able to commune with Him.

> For since the law has but a shadow of the good things to come instead of the true form of these realities, it can never, by the same sacrifices that are continually offered every year, make perfect those who draw near. Otherwise, would they not have ceased to be offered, since the worshipers, having once been cleansed, would no longer have any consciousness of sins? But in these sacrifices there is a reminder of sins every year. For it is impossible for the blood of bulls and goats to take away sins (Heb. 10:1-4).

Jesus offered His perfect sacrifice, which was Himself; but because it was sufficient, He sat down because the need for a sacrifice for sin had ceased. This is a further and deeper explanation of what Jesus meant on the cross when He said, "'It is finished'" (John 19:30). Nothing can ever be subtracted from it, nor will there ever be a need to add anything to it. Our salvation was eternally and completely secured on the cross.

All power, authority, and honor belong to Jesus; but unlike the Jewish leaders who sat in the seat of Moses during the time of Jesus' earthly ministry, He extends mercy to all who would bow before Him in this life. His death on the cross caused the veil that separated God and man to be ripped from top to bottom so that through the blood of Jesus, we might come into the presence of God to seek mercy and salvation.

As we read in Hebrews 4:15-16, "For we do not have a high priest who is unable to sympathize with our weaknesses, but one who in every respect has been tempted as we are, yet without sin. Let us then with confidence draw near to the throne of grace, that we may receive mercy and find grace to help in time of need."

Through the cross, we can now approach God with confidence because of what Christ did on our behalf. Hebrews 4 calls it "the throne of grace"—a place we can draw near to receive mercy and grace in our time of need. This, in fact, is one of the most beautiful aspects of the high priestly ministry of Jesus, He drew near to us so that we might be able to draw near to Him. For this, He gave us life; and now, through Him, we have abundant life forever.

Christ our King is just; and one day, His righteous wrath will be poured out. But although He is all-powerful and sovereign, He has chosen to show His ultimate supremacy in all things—not in His ability to crush His enemies but through showing mercy to those who would bow down and call Him Lord. Christ is seated at the right hand of God and has accomplished salvation and given as an unearned gift to those who are humble and contrite and who tremble at His Word—those who trust in the finished work of Jesus Christ, His atoning death on the cross, and His victorious resurrection.

The New Covenant is not a system of works or religious observances that we do to try and please God or a stairway to reach God. It is spiritual regeneration and salvation for all who put their trust in the finished work of Christ. "Thus says the LORD: 'Heaven is my throne, and the earth is my footstool; what is the house that you would build for me, and what is the place of my rest? All these things my hand has made, and so all these things came to be, declares the Lord. But this is the one to whom I will look: he who is humble and contrite in spirit and trembles at my word'" (Isa. 66:1-2). God looks upon those with favor and grace that know and fear Him, who are humble and contrite in spirit, and who tremble at His Word. Jesus is sitting at the right hand of God the Father interceding for these as a heavenly Minister, High Priest, and King.

THE HEAVENLY SANCTUARY OF CHRIST

A minister in the holy places, in the true tent that the Lord set up, not man. For every high priest is appointed to offer gifts and sacrifices; thus it is necessary for this priest also to have something to offer. Now if he were on earth, he would not be a priest at all, since there are priests who offer gifts according to the law. They serve a copy and shadow of the heavenly things. For when Moses was about to erect the tent, he was instructed by God, saying, "See that you make everything according to the pattern that was shown you on the mountain" (Heb. 8:2-5).

The Tent of Meeting, Solomon's temple, and King Herod's temples were always only "types and shadows" of the true temple. These were earthy shadows meant to reflect the true temple in Heaven. As impressive as Solomon's and Herod's temple might have been by human standards, they are nothing compared to the glory and majesty of the place God dwells in Heaven.

This is also true of the work done by Christ in His heavenly sanctuary. Human worship—as sincere as it is—has always been hindered by the stain of sin. So, since Christ died for the forgiveness of sin and is now sitting at the right hand of God, His ministry and intercession are also superior. Jesus is a ministering Priest; and His ministry is perfect, sanctifying, and life-giving. His resurrected life makes possible our worship, communion, confession, and forgiveness.

Remember, under the Old Covenant, no one could approach God; their sacrifices had to be made through a priest who acted as an intermediary. And before the priest could offer the sacrifice, he had to go through a set of rituals himself. Therefore, we do all things in the name of Jesus because He is our High Priest and Intermediary. Truly, "apart from [Him, we] can do nothing" (John 15:5). But through Him and in Him, "all things are possible" (Matt. 19:26).

This is what it means when the Scripture says that we are seated "with him in the heavenly places" (Eph. 2:6). Although not fully clear to us right now, we are positionally seated with Christ, not through or by anything that we have done but sheerly on the basis of grace.

THE BETTER COVENANT

"But as it is, Christ has obtained a ministry that is as much more excellent than the old as the covenant he mediates is better, since it is enacted on better promises. For if that first covenant had been faultless, there would have been no occasion to look for a second" (Heb. 8:6-7). Jesus is superior to the priests of the Old Covenant, the sacrifices of the Old Covenant, and the sanctuary of the Old Covenant in every way. It is in this evidence that we see that the New Covenant is also superior in every way. This New Covenant is not merely an improvement of the Old Covenant; it is also radically different. The Old Covenant was not a failed covenant; it was merely a backdrop meant to contrast the marvelous beauty of the New.

This is why it is so important that the cross is at the forefront of all we do. Apart from the cross, we would die in our sins. It is the enduring symbol of the greatest exchange in the history of humankind when Jesus traded His innocence for our guilt and traded His life for ours! As John Stott said, "The essential background to the cross, therefore, is a balanced understanding of the gravity of sin and the majesty of God. If we diminish either, we thereby diminish the cross."

The cross is the beauty and majesty of God. I have often heard people speak as if God were wrathful and harsh in the Old Testament but merciful and loving in the New Testament, but this is grossly untrue. In the Old Testament, we see the faithfulness, patience, and mercy of God as He dealt with the disobedience of Israel. It is in the New Testament that we see the greatest display of God's wrath and judgment in the entire Bible. It is only on Calvary's hill that we see the justice, wrath, mercy, and love of God all poured out in one place at one time. Jesus had the full measure of God's wrath and judgment poured out on Him, and this was so He could extend us mercy and grace because He loved us.

John 3:16-17 tells us, "'For God so loved the world, that he gave his only Son, that whoever believes in him should not perish but have eternal life. For God did not send his Son into the world to condemn the world, but in order that the world might be saved through him.'" Under the New Covenant, there will be granted eternal life and eternal damnation. These are permanent fates, and this is a permanent and eternal covenant. There is no other sacrifice; there is no other priest coming, no other prophets, and no other kings. Jesus is the Fulfillment of all things; and He alone is owed all worship, honor, and praise.

LAW AND GOSPEL

"Now we know that whatever the law says it speaks to those who are under the law, so that every mouth may be stopped, and the whole world may be held accountable to God. For by works of the law no human being will be justified in his sight, since through the law comes knowledge of sin" (Rom. 3:19-20). The Law was never meant to save us. The Law of God is the mirror that reveals the perfect character of God and shows us that we are not like God and are desperate and needy for grace. The Law is meant to plunge us toward Christ. The Law exposes our sins. It is a necessary companion to the Gospel. We must see the holy perfection of God and consider our own spiritual bankruptcy so that the gift of grace in the Gospel will shine beautifully like the midday sun.

The righteousness of God under the Old Covenant was seen through our inability to keep the Law. But like Paul says in Galatians 3:24-26, the Law was merely a schoolmaster meant to bring us to Christ. The Law could never save us because it was never *meant* to save us. There is nothing more crucial to New Covenant theology than understanding the distinction and purpose of the Law and the Gospel.

> But now the righteousness of God has been manifested apart from the law, although the Law and the Prophets bear witness to it—the righteousness of God through faith in Jesus Christ for all who believe. For there is no distinction: for all have sinned and fall short of the glory of God, and are justified by his grace as a gift, through the redemption that is in Christ Jesus, whom God put forward as a propitiation by his blood, to be received by faith. This was to show God's righteousness, because in his divine forbearance he had passed over former sins. It was to show his righteousness at the present time, so that he might be just and the justifier of the one who has faith in Jesus (Rom. 3:21-26).

In other words, the law is the diagnosis; and the Gospel is the cure. To see the cure as precious and necessary, we must first have a clear and compelling diagnosis. If left untreated, sin is fatal 100 percent of the time; and the Law shows us just how sinful we truly are. The Gospel is the solution. This is why the Gospel is the centerpiece of Christian theology. The cross is the most important event in history, and the book of Revelation tells us that we will sign songs about the Lamb of God and the blood He shed for all of eternity.

> For he finds fault with them when he says: "Behold, the days are coming, declares the Lord, when I will establish a new covenant with the house of Israel and with the house of Judah, not like the covenant that I made with their fathers on the day when I took them by the hand to bring them out of the land of Egypt. For they did not continue in my covenant, and so I showed no concern for them, declares the Lord. For this is the covenant that I will make with the house of Israel after those days, declares the Lord: I will put my laws into their minds, and write them on their hearts, and I will be their God, and they shall be my people. And they shall not teach, each one his neighbor and each one his brother, saying, 'Know the Lord,' or they shall all know me, from the least of them to the greatest. For I will be merciful toward their iniquities, and I will remember their sins no more" (Heb. 8:8-12).

This section of Hebrews 8 is a direct quote from Jeremiah 31. The author of Hebrews is basically saying, "Look what your own Scripture says about the New Covenant." They should have been looking for it and anxiously awaiting it like Abraham. Jesus rebuked the Pharisees for this same reason when He told them that they were not sons of Abraham because if they were, they would have rejoiced at His appearance as Abraham did (John 8:56)

Under the Old Covenant, the blessing of God was dependent on external obedience, but it was never enough to save because no one could obey perfectly. This was because our original father and mother had caused us to fall into sin. Adam and Eve brought sin into the world, and we have perpetuated and compounded it with our own sin. Adam brought sin into the world, and Jesus took on human flesh and lived the perfect life we were unable to. He overcame sin, died in our place, and rose from the dead taking mastery over death forever.

> Therefore, just as sin came into the world through one man, and death through sin, and so death spread to all men because all sinned—for sin indeed was in the world before the law was given, but sin is not counted where there is no law. Yet death reigned from Adam to Moses, even over those whose sinning was not like the transgression of Adam, who was a type of the one who was to come (Rom. 5:12-14).

Those who have salvation through the free gift of grace do not obey the law of God to become justified; those who have a regenerated heart through the miracle of God's saving grace obey because they have been justified. We obey God because we love God; we worship God because we love God; and we live in service of God because we love God. We love God, but this love is in response to His transforming love for us. "We love because he first loved us" (1 John 4:19).

> But God shows his love for us in that while we were still sinners, Christ died for us. Since, therefore, we have now been justified

by his blood, much more shall we be saved by him from the wrath of God. For if while we were enemies we were reconciled to God by the death of his Son, much more, now that we are reconciled, shall we be saved by his life. More than that, we also rejoice in God through our Lord Jesus Christ, through whom we have now received reconciliation (Rom. 5:8-11).

Under the Old Covenant, the Law of God was given externally, written on stone tablets, worn on wristbands or foreheads, and placed on doorposts as a reminder because they could not write it on their own hearts. But it was always meant to be in the hearts of God's creation. The people could not write it on their hearts because we needed new hearts.

> "Hear, O Israel: The LORD our God, the LORD is one. You shall love the LORD your God with all your heart and with all your soul and with all your might. And these words that I command you today shall be on your heart. You shall teach them diligently to your children, and shall talk of them when you sit in your house, and when you walk by the way, and when you lie down, and when you rise. You shall bind them as a sign on your hand, and they shall be as frontlets between your eyes. You shall write them on the doorposts of your house and on your gates (Deut. 6:4-9).

Under the New Covenant, true worship is internal, not merely external. This is the time when people from everywhere worship God "'in spirit and truth'" (John 4:24). This is the regenerating work of the Holy Spirit that causes the worship of the believer to be holy and acceptable to God. The greatest commandment given in the Bible is what the depravity of sin has made us incapable of doing—loving the Lord with all our heart, soul, and might. The Law of God is written on our hearts because we were created in the very image of God for the sole purpose of worshiping Him and bringing glory to His name. In our fallen state, the Law of God written on our hearts serves as an indictment of our guilt, so we suppress the truth of God because we are sinful.

It is through the true knowledge of the character of God as revealed in His Word that our eyes are opened to our spiritual poverty. We mourn over our sin; we meekly put our trust in Christ; and because of this, we hunger to be right with God (Matt. 5:3-6). No person in the history of the world has ever loved the Lord with all of their heart, mind, soul, and strength. This is evidenced by loving their neighbor as themselves (Mark 12:30-31). It is only through the New Covenant, as prophesied about in Ezekiel, that we truly can have a new heart that loves the Lord. And this is only because of the indwelling of the Holy Spirit. God saved us from God through God to fill us with God so that we might please God.

The Gospel of Jesus Christ is not for the remission of sins in a temporal sense. The atonement of Christ brings the total and permanent forgiveness of sins. It washes us clean to the uttermost. We do not have to be "re-saved" over and over again. It is precious and powerful!

Hebrews 8:13 says, "In speaking of a new covenant, he makes the first one obsolete. And what is becoming obsolete and growing old is ready to vanish away." We find the beautiful capstone and solidification of the New Covenant. Under the Old Covenant, sin could never be truly forgiven, just postponed, like paying interest on a debt that you could not pay off in a billion lifetimes. Puritan theologian John Owen said, ""The debt of sin could never be forgotten because it was never truly forgiven."[6]

Hebrews 8:12 is the fulfillment of Jeremiah's prophetic utterance: "'For I will forgive their iniquity, and I will remember their sin no more'" (Jer. 31:34). Christ not only wiped out the penalty of sin, but He also wiped out the memory of it. These words should set free every believer who has ever struggled with legalism. If you truly know the truth of Christ, it will set you free. "'So if the Son sets you free, you will be free indeed'" (John 8:36). This is not a license to sin; for the truly reborn man, this is a license to walk in Christ's freedom, to worship God, and to preach the Gospel as it truly is Good News.

---

6   Ibid.

"Behold, the days are coming, declares the LORD, when I will make a new covenant with the house of Israel and the house of Judah, not like the covenant that I made with their fathers on the day when I took them by the hand to bring them out of the land of Egypt, my covenant that they broke, though I was their husband, declares the Lord. For this is the covenant that I will make with the house of Israel after those days, declares the Lord: I will put my law within them, and I will write it on their hearts. And I will be their God, and they shall be my people. And no longer shall each one teach his neighbor and each his brother, saying, 'Know the Lord,' for they shall all know me, from the least of them to the greatest, declares the Lord. For I will forgive their iniquity, and I will remember their sin no more" (Jer. 31:31-34).

In the covenant of grace, we have the fulfillment of all things in Christ; nothing is left undone. By trusting in God, we are part of the salvation Christ afforded us that is sealed with an unbreakable covenant. Christ has washed our scarlet sins as white as snow and has freed us forever from the bondage of our pasts. To say that the blood of Christ is insufficient to forgive our sins—no matter what they are and no matter how grievous—is to trample underfoot the blood of the Lamb, which Hebrews 10 says is an outrage to the Spirit of grace.

Jesus is our better, permanent, and all-sufficient Sacrifice; and through His cross, we are "free indeed." I would encourage anyone who struggles with a legalistic/works-based understanding of salvation to dig even deeper than we do in this book so that you can come to a clear understanding of New Covenant theology and find freedom, joy, and surety in your salvation—not because of anything you could ever do but because of what Christ has done!

CHAPTER 9

BUT WHEN CHRIST

BY: GARY WILKERSON

But when Christ appeared as a high priest of the good things that have come.

HEBREWS 9:11

TWO GREAT THINGS COME FROM this one sentence in Hebrews 9. Christ appears, and good things come! "But when Christ"—these three simple words have changed history. And they can change your life profoundly.

We do not often speak of high priests in our culture today. It does not seem to have the same meaning as in this first-century church. For many generations, they attempted to keep the Law, tried to become right before God by relying on the works of the Law. When they failed, it was up to the high priest who brought sacrifices to release them from the penalty of sin. But it never quite worked out as they had hoped because:

- The priests were insufficient.
- The sacrifices were imperfect.
- The effect was temporary.
- The repetition was necessary.
- The conscience was left unpurified.

- The rituals were imposed, not enjoyed.
- The shadows were not the substance.
- It was all regulations.
- They had to perform ritual duties.
- The holy places were not yet opened.
- These practices were only copies of the heavenly things.
- The holy places were made with hands.
- They could not make perfect those who drew near.
- The was no possibility of its success.

The old temple, sacrifices, and priesthood served God's purpose but were imperfect due to man's inability to live in obedience. The work of the high priest and the temple sacrifices for sin were, at best, shadows of the good things to come. Christ appeared, then, at the perfect time as the final High Priest—all-sufficient, perfect, eternal, once-for-all-time, purifying, and thoroughly to be enjoyed. What joy knowing it is finished. By faith, there is no more sacrifice for my sin. Nothing out there in the future that would hopefully come and bring my troubled heart to rest. We can enter rest now. But when Christ became the final sacrifice, the announcement of "It is finished!" brought our weary souls to rest. We have found peace with God.

Jesus, as High Priest, is our Way through to the Holy of Holies, the entrance into God's presence. He provides acceptance into God's holy presence by the sacrifice, not of animals but by Jesus Himself. And by His priesthood, we come before God justified, righteous, holy, and acceptable.

These three words, "But when Christ," give us crystal clarity concerning what happens when Christ appears. He comes as the ultimate, perfect, and final High Priest. And we will see in this chapter how sufficient He is and why that is so essential to us, for He is the High Priest of *good things*. Often, life is full of troubling, heartbreaking trials. We find more than enough heartache and suffering. We lose a child; a marriage falls apart; the business collapses;

and depression and despair set in. We try and medicate it with substances and sins (which bring pleasure for a season); but soon, the medicating turns to sinful addiction, and we now have twice the problems and pains. Yet by faith, we receive a Priest Who acts on our behalf before God. And though we expect judgment, condemnation, and wrath, we find He comes as the High Priest of good things to come.

"All things work together for good" (Rom. 8:28) is a verse most of us know. But it cannot stand alone as a promise. It requires sufficient support. Not all things could work together for our good unless Jesus, as our High Priest, had done a work on our behalf that opened up all these good things for us. We do not receive good things because we are, by nature, good people. No, we are, by nature, sinners and deserving of no good thing from God. Our High Priest's work on the cross for us as our substitutionary Sacrifice met the conditions for the release of good things to come.

What are some of these good things? Our sins—past, present, and even future—are fully forgiven, never to condemn or haunt us with fear of wrath. Jesus paid for it all, but more good things were necessary. Having our sins forgiven is more than we could ever deserve. Still, it is not the totality of necessity for us to be justified and righteous and acceptable to a perfectly holy God. With our sins forgiven, it is as if we have a clean slate; it might be said we are at neutral—not having sin but not having perfect righteousness necessary to be made right with God.

Our need for righteousness to stand before God as acceptable was imputed to us by our High Priest's perfect, spotless, holy life. Jesus did what Adam nor any of his offspring have ever done—completely fulfilled all the law perfectly. All other priests failed and, therefore, were insufficient to pay the price for our sin because they had to spend equity on their own sin and needed to secure more by offering sacrifices. Not one drop of Jesus' blood was necessary for Himself. He needed no sacrifice because He had no sin. By thirty-three years of perfect obedience, He then added to His already perfect heavenly righteousness as God to His earthly, Adamic righteousness by obeying the law entirely for the first time since the Creation.

If this was not enough, He also ascended to the right hand of God and is seated there forever. This also is of his High Priestly work. No other priest was allowed to sit down. It would be considered irreverent and signaled that His work was finished. Jesus sat down, showing the sacrifice was sufficient and forever finished. We need no other source. We need not add our works of the Law. We need not promise increased devotion or higher levels of obedience to receive this finished work. The Law says, "Do." The cross says, "Finished." Jesus then invites us to be seated with Him. We no longer need to scurry about to produce proof of our righteousness, and Jesus has accomplished righteousness on our behalf.

Hebrews 10:11 says, "And every priest stands daily at his service, offering repeatedly the same sacrifices, which can never take away sins, But when Christ had offered for all time a single sacrifice for sins, he sat down at the right hand of God." So, what is He doing there, seated at the Father's right hand? Hebrews 7:25 tells us, "Consequently, he is able to save to the uttermost those who draw near to God through him, since he always lives to make intercession for them."

Imagine this. We long to draw near to God; but our sin, impure conscience, and unrighteousness not only excludes an audience with the Most High but demands a verdict of guilt and a sentence of death to be carried out. But this great High Priest is able to do what no other could—save to the uttermost. The word *uttermost* means "altogether, complete, for all time." So we long to draw near, knowing our only means of being able to come near to such a holy God is to be holy ourselves, something we have proven over and over that we are not. Then comes Jesus. He saves us to the uttermost, cleansing our sins and imputing His righteousness upon us. And to make the good things to come even more glorious, He declares us righteous before the Father.

Do you see this? We long to draw near, but our sin makes that impossible; Jesus deals with sin and gives us His righteousness to top it off. When we go before God, He declares to the Father, "Oh, this is Your son. He is forgiven; he is righteous, I declare this." "Just as David also speaks of the blessing of the one to whom God counts righteousness apart from works: 'Blessed are those whose lawless deeds are forgiven, and whose sins are covered; blessed is the man against whom the Lord will not count his sin'" (Rom. 4:6). Therefore, no one will be declared righteous in God's sight by the works of the Law; rather, through the Law, we become conscious of our sin.

But now, apart from the Law, the righteousness of God has been made known, to which the Law and the Prophets testify. This righteousness is given through faith in Jesus Christ to all who believe. There is no difference between Jew and Gentile (Gal. 3:28). No one is declared righteous in God's sight by the works of the Law. Only through the High Priestly work of Jesus are we forgiven, made righteous, and then declared to God righteous, justified, and acceptable in His presence.

This is what Hebrews 7:25 declares to us. Jesus "always lives to make intercession for them." This mediation is not that Jesus is saying prayers for us. It is Jesus advocating for us. It is Jesus taking our case before the Father and revealing His glorious work in us to Him. It is as if Jesus is our Lawyer, stating our case and having us declared innocent.

We deserved no grace or acquittal; but when Christ came, everything changed. We are addicted to sin—but when Christ. We are hopelessly lost—but when Christ. We are unrighteous—but when Christ. We are filled with worthless self-righteousness—but when Christ. We are downcast, discouraged, and depressed—but when Christ. We look for life in all the wrong places—but when Christ. We try to be acceptable to God through our works—but when Christ. Nothing we could do was sufficient—but when Christ. But when Christ appeared, all this changed!

Why would you fear; be downcast; keep trying the Law; and live under guilt, shame, and condemnation when Christ has appeared? We do not look at our own works. Hebrews 12:2 shows us where to place our hope: "Looking unto

Jesus, the founder and perfecter of our faith, who for the joy that was set before him endured the cross, despising the shame, and is seated at the right hand of the throne of God." There He is, speaking on our behalf, allowing us access by His enduring the cross. And having sat down, He tells God, "Let him in."

The author of this jaw-dropping book of Hebrews takes two chapters to unload all the depth and breadth of what transpires "when Christ." Chapters nine and ten compare the inadequacies and insufficiencies of the attempts of the former ways of covenanting with God. It is not that the former covenant was not useful or without merit. The Law showed us the exceeding sinfulness of our sin and the hopelessness of our human efforts. It pointed us to what would transpire "when Christ" Jesus did what we and the Law combined could not do.

These three words, "But when Christ," changed everything! The former priesthood, sacrifices, and rituals had glory. The first "came with such glory" (2 Cor. 3:7). Then comes the "but when Christ." So if that which "came with such glory . . . was being brought to an end, will not the ministry of the Spirit have even more glory?" (2 Cor. 3:7-8). Since our High Priest has sat down once and for all time, he has eternally made an unchangeable welcome of us before God. We can finally rid our consciences of guilt, shame, fear, and condemnation once and for all. We are as right before God now as we will ever be and as right as we need to be. This is glory. This is grace. This is what our High Priest has accomplished for us.

For a people living in darkness, with no hope offered by the Law, what a welcome word to hear that good things would come. But what exactly are these good things?

First and foremost, it is Christ Himself. Second Corinthians 4:6 says, "For God, who said, 'Let light shine out of darkness,' has shone in our hearts to give the light of the knowledge of the glory of God in the face of Jesus Christ." What could be a better good thing to come than in the hour of our darkness and hopeless despair? Jesus revealed the glory of God in His own face.

The greatest gift one could ever receive is this revelation that we see glory. We see God, and it is not distantly transcendent; it is in the face of a Man— the Man Christ Jesus. And this man would dispel the darkness; fulfill the Law; conquer sin, Satan, and death; and reconcile us to God by grace. Jesus Himself is the Best of the good things to come. Jesus came to give us this light of glory. Indeed, what He accomplished and what He has done for us merits our abundant joy and exaltation of worship, but all that He has done for us begins by being Who He is for us.

Secondly, from the fount of the face of Christ springs His work of cleansing of sin, imputation of righteousness, and the intercession at the right hand of God. Herein we find more of the good things to come that were released at the cross, resurrection, and ascension. This is what is described in this letter in Hebrews: that the good things to come were, in great part, better things—a better covenant, a better sacrifice, and a better High Priest were coming. And this was not only better but permanently better—no more ups and downs, ins and outs; this was it. It was finished. We need no longer live in anxiety and uncertainty. We no longer need to live with insecurity.

When Christ appeared, His finished work was:

- "Once for all" (Heb. 9:12)
- "By means of his own blood, thus securing an eternal redemption" (Heb. 9:12)
- "Purify[ing] our conscience from dead works" (Heb. 9:14)
- "Redeem[ing] . . . from the transgressions" (Heb. 9:15)
- A "better" sacrifice (Heb. 9:23)

"For Christ has entered . . . now to appear in the presence of God on our behalf . . . once for all . . . to put away sin" (Heb. 9:24, 26). If this does not make you rejoice, nothing will! This list is more important than our health, house, job, and any desire of our heart. Nothing compares to being made right with

God. Nothing is as good a thing as knowing we are eternally secured with the most incredible riches imaginable.

Does this not give you hope? When Christ appeared, He did away with the lesser first and established the second. This "second" causes our hearts to leap and our tongues to praise. The first was good, but it was a pencil drawing compared to a full-color Monet. Both are good, but one is more remarkable. Jesus was not just a good Teacher, Healer, and Prophet. He was the only One Who could secure our eternal life.

How can we be sure these "good things" have come to us? Hebrews answers this question and delivers us from all doubt. If you have ever questioned the assurance of your salvation or despaired you are not an heir of His great covenant or if your sins have caused you to believe Christ did not cleanse and free you, then you need a clear and better word. And a clear word is precisely what Hebrews delivers. When Jesus came, He did all these beautiful things. He then swore by oath that all these things would be accomplished. God is Truth. He never lies. He need not give us His oath as His Word is more than sufficient; yet in His love and tender kindness, He goes so far as to swear by an oath that when Christ appears, better things will come and will be sealed eternally. That is the grounds for all our hope.

CHAPTER 10

THE ASSURANCE OF SAVING FAITH

BY: JOSHUA WEST

Therefore, brothers, since we have confidence to enter the holy places by the blood

of Jesus, by the new and living way that he opened for us through the curtain, that is,

through his flesh, and since we have a great priest over the house of God,

let us draw near with a true heart in full assurance of faith, with our hearts sprinkled

clean from an evil conscience and our bodies washed with pure water. Let us hold fast

the confession of our hope without wavering, for he who promised is faithful."

HEBREWS 10:19-23

AS WE BEGIN TO VENTURE into Hebrews 10, it is important that we pause to discuss a few important details that will help us correctly and biblically interpret and apply this section of Scripture in a contextually sound manner. It is always important to read and interpret the Bible in a way that is in line with its context. We must understand each verse considering the surrounding verses, chapters, and book, as well as considering its cultural, historical, and geographical context. A very important hermeneutical question we should be asking is, "What was the author trying to communicate to the audience of His day?"

This is why all study and teaching of God's Word should be expository in nature. If you are using the Scripture as a garnish for your meal of words and ideas or your supposed personal revelation, you are misusing God's holy, sacred, and sufficient word for your own means and purposes. This seems to be done often when it comes to the book of Hebrews. Not many expositional sermons come from this section of Scripture but a lot of dipping in for a good faith Scripture, which is often used at the expense of the actual text.

While it is always important to read and apply the Bible in context, it is especially important in this portion of the book of Hebrews. To understand Hebrews 10-12, you must really understand them all together. This is a section of Scripture that is all about saving faith!

In the previous chapter, Gary magnificently dealt with the once-and-for-all sacrifice of Christ that has secured our salvation and given us eternal life, but let's look at a few verses here in chapter ten because this really is our foundation for understanding Hebrews 10-12.

> For since the law has but a shadow of the good things to come instead of the true form of these realities, it can never, by the same sacrifices that are continually offered every year, make perfect those who draw near. Otherwise, would they not have ceased to be offered, since the worshipers, having once been cleansed, would no longer have any consciousness of sins? But in these sacrifices there is a reminder of sins every year. For it is impossible for the blood of bulls and goats to take away sins. Consequently, when Christ came into the world, he said, "Sacrifices and offerings you have not desired, but a body have you prepared for me; in burnt offerings and sin offerings you have taken no pleasure. Then I said, 'Behold, I have come to do your will, O God, as it is written of me in the scroll of the book'" (Heb. 10:1-7).

Like the Old Covenant was merely a shadow of the good things to come, so were the sacrifices that were made year after year. These were meant to remind us of our sin because the payment had not yet been made. It was really like paying the interest on a debt that was used to push the debt into the future until a "paid in full" transaction could be made. This is why God does not require the continuation of the sacrificial system since Christ has come. There is no need to continue paying interest on a debt that has been satisfied and paid in full. This is what our faith is in—the finished work of Jesus Christ our Lord and Savior.

In verses five through seven, the author of Hebrews quotes Psalm 40:6-8 and then gives some commentary on it in light of the Gospel. "When he said above, 'You have neither desired nor taken pleasure in sacrifices and offerings and burnt offerings and sin offerings' (these are offered according to the law), then he added, 'Behold, I have come to do your will.' He does away with the first in order to establish the second. And by that will we have been sanctified through the offering of the body of Jesus Christ once for all" (Heb. 10:8-10).

The foundation of the surety of our salvation is laid in the sufficiency of the redemptive work Christ accomplished. This means the "first" is done away with in order to establish the "second." Christ fulfilled the ceremonial law and established Himself as the unwavering and unshakable Cornerstone upon which our faith is built. Here is something that must be said that I hope clears up confusion for someone who might be reading this book: you simply cannot be under both covenants at the same time. Either you are subject to the covenant of works, the letter of the Law, which the apostle Paul says is death; or you are under the covenant of grace by faith, in which you have life and freedom.

> And every priest stands daily at his service, offering repeatedly the same sacrifices, which can never take away sins. But when Christ had offered for all time a single sacrifice for sins, he sat down at the right hand of God, waiting from that time until his enemies should be made a footstool for his feet. For by a single offering he has perfected for all time those who are being sanctified. And the Holy Spirit also bears witness to us; for after saying, "This is the covenant that I will make with them after those days, declares the Lord: I will put my laws on their hearts, and write them on their minds," then he adds, "I will

remember their sins and their lawless deeds no more." Where there is forgiveness of these, there is no longer any offering for sin (Heb. 10:11-18).

Let's do a side-by-side comparison of the first system and the second system to examine the differences and effectiveness of the covenants.

THE OLD SYSTEM COULD NOT GIVE US ACCESS TO GOD

The shadows of the good things to come could not give us access to God because paying the interest on sin did not actually do anything to deal with the sin that separated us from God's presence. If sin did not really and truly separate man from God, then the cross was pointless.

> We ourselves are Jews by birth and not Gentile sinners; yet we know that a person is not justified by works of the law but through faith in Jesus Christ, so we also have believed in Christ Jesus, in order to be justified by faith in Christ and not by works of the law, because by works of the law, no one will be justified. But if, in our endeavor to be justified in Christ, we too were found to be sinners, is Christ then a servant of sin? Certainly not! For if I rebuild what I tore down, I prove myself to be a transgressor. For through the law I died to the law, so that I might live to God. I have been crucified with Christ. It is no longer I who live, but Christ who lives in me. And the life I now live in the flesh I live by faith in the Son of God, who loved me and gave himself for me. I do not nullify the grace of God, for if righteousness were through the law, then Christ died for no purpose (Gal. 2:15-21).

It is an either/or situation. We cannot have it both ways. Either man could be justified under the old system, by which we are saying that Christ died for nothing; or we are saying that the only means of salvation and justification is found in the crucifixion of Christ, which means under the Law, no one could ever be justified. Either Christ is the only Way or no way at all.

THE OLD SYSTEM COULD NOT REMOVE OUR SIN

The animal sacrifice of the Old Covenant was not able nor was it meant to cleanse us of our sins; it was merely meant to temporally cover them. The actual purpose was meant to magnify just how costly sin actually is. "The wages of sin is death" (Rom. 6:23). The death of precious life was a reminder of just how costly sin actually is. It was meant to remind us of condemnation and judgment, as it still should today. Becoming aware of the holiness of God makes us aware of the grievousness of sin, which is meant to beautifully magnify the value of God's grace. This magnifies the glory of Christ and the freedom that comes with not living under the condemnation that comes from living under the Law.

> There is therefore now no condemnation for those who are in Christ Jesus. For the law of the Spirit of life has set you free in Christ Jesus from the law of sin and death. For God has done what the law, weakened by the flesh, could not do. By sending his own Son in the likeness of sinful flesh and for sin, he condemned sin in the flesh, in order that the righteous requirement of the law might be fulfilled in us, who walk not according to the flesh but according to the Spirit (Rom. 8:1-4).

No one can hide from God and His righteous judgment and condemnation of sinners, but Romans 8:1 tells us that we can hide "in Him." This is the root and foundation of saving faith—to be "in Christ." Paul uses this term, directly and indirectly, dozens and dozens of times in his epistles. To be in Christ is not merely to have the penalty of your sin postponed and to have your sins covered but instead to have them "paid in full." Like the people saved from God's wrath by Noah's ark in the book of Genesis, we are saved from the wrath of God by putting our faith in Christ. In this, we are being saved from God by God. We will discuss this in greater detail in a later chapter.

EXTERNAL SACRIFICES COULD NOT DEAL WITH THE INTERNAL PROBLEM OF SIN

Even when the Old Covenant system was still relatively new, it was still clear that God looked at the heart and not external and outward appearances. Samuel reminds Saul in 1 Samuel 15:22 that "'to obey is better than sacrifice.'" To simply go through the motions of sacrifice without a heart that truly mourns the sin that caused the need for it in the first place is still missing the most important parts—a remorseful and repentant heart and faith in God.

This is why the Roman Catholic system of penance and confession to a priest is not only unbiblical but also anti-biblical—and so are all works-based systems that minimize the effect of Christ's once-and-for-all sacrifice. Even in the Old Testament, when the true heart of the sacrificial system was neglected, it displeased God to the point where He called it an abomination because it was done without what David said made sacrifices pleasing to God in Psalm 51: "The sacrifices of God are a broken spirit; a broken and contrite heart, O God, you will not despise" (v. 17).

It is because of faith in the Word of the Lord as they looked forward to a future Messiah that men were saved. Now, let's look at what makes the new system superior to that of the old.

THE NEW SYSTEM DISPLAYS GOD'S ETERNAL WILL AND PLAN

One important theological truth that must be established is that it was always God's plan to redeem mankind through the cross. It is superior because it was always God's purpose. The cross was not God's response to His first failed attempt at saving His people; it was the intended fulfillment all along. If you are one of those people who see a problem with the biblical truth that God is sovereign and that His plans are never thwarted by the enemy, by us, or by anything else, then the covenant of grace will never make sense to you.

Jesus' death was not merely symbolic; He paid our debt and satisfied God's justice by taking our judgment. There is now no condemnation looming over us because it has been taken care of in full. His obedience fulfilled the Law, and His sacrifice satisfied the righteous requirement of the Law.

A.W. Pink said:

> Salvation is by grace, by grace alone. Nevertheless, divine grace is not exercised at the expense of holiness. It never compromises with sin. It is also true that salvation is a free gift, but an empty hand must receive it and not a hand that still tightly grasps the world. Something more than believing is necessary to salvation. A heart that is steeled in rebellion against God cannot savingly believe. It must first be broken.[7]

THE NEW SYSTEM SANCTIFIES THOSE WHO BELIEVE

The new system does something the old could never do—it sanctifies the believer and makes Him holy in the sight of God. The word "holy"—when used in the context of people—is different than when it is used about the Person and character of God. God is completely holy, set apart unto Himself in moral perfection, and completely "other" from us. When used in regard to God's people, it means that we are set apart for God's holy use and purposes. But in the context of Hebrews 10, the author is not only saying that we are set apart for God's purposes; but because of the perfection of Christ's sacrifice, we, in fact, are holy in God's sight. He sees us through the perfection of Christ. And what is so amazing is that through sanctification, we are being permanently perfected into Christ's image. And upon death, this work will be complete and lacking nothing.

---

7   A.W. Pink, *Studies on Saving Faith* (San Francisco: Bottom of the Hill Publishing, 2016).

THE NEW SYSTEM TRULY AND PERMANENTLY REMOVES THE STAIN OF SIN

"'Come now, let us reason together, says the LORD: though your sins are like scarlet, they shall be as white as snow; though they are red like crimson, they shall become like wool'" (Isa. 1:18). Jesus came to take away our sins. He did not wink at it or ignore it. He paid for it in a legal and just way that gives us true freedom. To believe that you do not need Christ is foolish and really does make light of the value of His precious blood, but it is also trampling the blood of Christ to doubt its sufficiency to cleanse us. Both things are an indication of a lack of saving faith. At the completion of His priestly work as our Priest and sacrifice, it says that He sat down at the right hand of God because there will never be the need for a sacrifice again.

The Levitical priests always remained standing because their work was never done. But Christ, after he accomplished His work, sat down at the right hand of God because His work as a Sacrifice for sin is finished. The sacrifice of sin takes away the sin of all who believe in His name by faith—past, present, and future.

THE NEW SYSTEM PUT THE ENEMIES OF GOD UNDERNEATH HIS FEET

The old system did nothing in defeating the enemies of God. But with one swift blow, Christ once and for all defeated the devil and all who belong to the kingdom of darkness. What makes Jesus so amazing in this regard is that while those who are enemies of God are already defeated and scheduled for judgment, He is still extending a hand of grace to all who will repent and surrender to Christ. Usually, once the battle is over, those who are rebels are immediately judged; but Jesus has postponed judgment so that there is an opportunity for more to be saved.

Colossians 2:13-15 says, "And you, who were dead in your trespasses and the uncircumcision of your flesh, God made alive together with him, having forgiven us all our trespasses, by canceling the record of debt that stood against us with its legal demands. This he set aside, nailing it to the cross. He disarmed the rulers and authorities and put them to open shame, by triumphing over them in him."

Jesus is the current reigning King of the universe, and the fact that some are pretending as if this is not reality does not make it any less true. Jesus is Lord; and He has defeated death, the devil, Hell, and the grave once and for all. In a very short time, this will be evident to all in the universe. Everyone will be put underneath the feet of Jesus and made a footstool for Him—everyone, that is, except for those who are part of His body.

IN THE NEW SYSTEM SAVING FAITH PERFECTS THE SAINT

"For by a single offering he has perfected for all time those who are being sanctified" (Heb. 10:14). This is a transition point for the next part of this chapter. Christ's offering has perfected for all time those who are being sanctified; so if you are truly reborn and being sanctified, there is no way to be un-reborn or unsanctified. The death of Jesus removes all sin forever; and in regeneration, it is not us who are sanctifying ourselves—it is Christ the High Priest Who is sanctifying us. The forgiveness is permanent because the sacrifice was permanent.

Ultimately, the sacrifice of Christ is a better sacrifice because it, in fact, fulfills the promise of the New Covenant. Since it brings true and total forgiveness of sins, it makes further sacrifice completely unnecessary.

> "For this is the covenant that I will make with the house of Israel after those days, declares the Lord: I will put my law within them, and I will write it on their hearts. And I will be their God, and they shall be my people. And no longer shall each one teach his neighbor and each his brother, saying, 'Know the Lord,' for they shall all know me, from the least of them to the greatest, declares the Lord. For I will forgive their iniquity, and I will remember their sin no more" (Jer. 31:33-34).

FULL ASSURANCE IN CHRIST ALONE

Therefore, brothers, since we have confidence to enter the holy places by the blood of Jesus, by the new and living way that he opened for us through the curtain, that is, through his flesh, and since we have a great priest over the house of God, let us draw near with a true heart in full assurance of faith, with our hearts sprinkled clean from an evil conscience and our bodies washed with pure water. Let us hold fast the confession of our hope without wavering, for he who promised is faithful. And let us consider how to stir up one another to love and good works (Heb. 10:19-24).

So, in light of what Christ has done for us (Heb. 10:1-18), "let us hold fast the confession of our hope" (Heb. 10:23). What does this really mean? Well, practically, holding fast to something means "we live as if we believe it." This is what biblical faith looks like in practice. Works and actions do not and cannot save us, but they are evidence that our faith and hope are truly in Christ alone. It is living as if the One making the promise is actually able and faithful to keep it.

When we live as if the promise is not trustworthy, we are saying that the One Who made the promise is not trustworthy. A guarantee is only as good as the guarantor. Another way to say it is that a promise is only as good as the person who is making it. Basically, if you reject the promise of God given to us in the Gospel, you are calling God a liar. The author of Hebrews wants to encourage those he is writing to, but he is also drawing a line in the sand as to what it means to have saving faith.

Verses nineteen through twenty-two of chapter ten tell us that if we truly believe that Christ is our Sacrifice for sin, it should fill us with confidence to draw near to God with a true heart and in the full assurance of our faith because our assurance is not found in ourselves but in the all-sufficient work of Christ. The sin that kept us separated from God has been overcome by Christ, so we can now boldly enter the holy place. Those who truly mourn their sin can draw near to God because through Christ, their sins have been forgiven. So, if this is the hope we are holding fast to, why would we not draw near to God? Maybe because you do not really want God or because you still love your sin, and all of this is because you are not truly regenerated.

I have seen people become filled with dread because of statements made here in Hebrews 10. It is meant to fill the unregenerate person with holy fear, but this should not be the case for those whose confidence and hope are in Christ alone. I am not terribly worried about the person who fears the Lord and feels conviction about their sin, as long as they understand the difference between conviction and condemnation. We feel conviction when we sin because this is the work of the Holy Spirit in our lives. We now hate the sin we once loved, and God lovingly convicts us when we fall into it. Conviction is meant to lead us to repentance. Condemnation is what awaits those who are outside of Christ; but for those who are in Christ, "there is therefore now no condemnation" (Rom. 8:1) because Jesus took the penalty of our sin.

A person who fears the Lord is wise, just like a person who trembles at God's Word is wise. These people see the reality of Who God is and the reality of their sins outside of Christ. This should increase our surety because it is the fire of being refined by God. These people have broken hearts, unclogged ears, and open eyes to the realities of God. Some people believe that they are people of faith simply because they are blind to the reality of God's holiness and their own sinfulness. Being blind to these realities is not faith; it is foolishness of the highest order. Do not confess faith with ignorance or arrogance. As Proverbs 9:10 reminds us, "The fear of the Lord is the beginning of wisdom, and the knowledge of the Holy One is insight."

Isaiah 66:1-2 gives us even more insight into Who God is: "Thus says the LORD: 'Heaven is my throne, and the earth is my footstool; what is the house that you would build for me, and what is the place of my rest? All these things my hand has made, and so all these things came to be, declares the Lord. But this is the one to whom I will look: he who is humble and contrite in spirit and trembles at my word.'"

It does not really take much faith to believe you are saved if you do not really know Who God is and how holy and set apart He is. If you do not understand His wrath and burning hatred toward sin and if you do not see that you truly are a hopeless and lost sinner apart from His grace, you will never understand the value of Christ's sacrifice. Do you fear the Lord and tremble at His Word? These questions will produce one of two things in you—dread or gratefulness.

"Let us hold fast the confession of our hope without wavering, for he who promised is faithful. And let us consider how to stir up one another to love and good works, not neglecting to meet together, as is the habit of some, but encouraging one another, and all the more as you see the Day drawing near" (Heb. 10:23-25). This is an indication and evidence that you have saving faith. Not only will you draw confidence from the Word of the Lord and the finished work of Christ in the Gospel; you will also stir others up to do so as well. The evidence of love will be in our lives. We show that we love God by not neglecting the gathering of believers, and we show our love for our fellow believers by encouraging them in the faith. We also show our love for the lost by sharing the true and full Gospel with them as often as possible.

We live a life of holiness, and we call others to do so as well because we believe in the word of the Lord by faith. We believe in a coming judgment; we believe that the same Gospel that is saving us is condemning others; and we believe "'everyone who calls on the name of the Lord will be saved'" (Rom. 10:13). We believe that Jesus Christ will "judge the living and the dead" (2 Tim. 4:1), and we believe that "'everyone who believes in him will not be put to shame'" (Rom. 10:11). We believe, as it says in verse twenty-five, that we will do this even "more as we see the Day drawing near." Do you believe that the Day is approaching? If so, it will change the way you live. The all-consuming fire of the Lord will either refine you or burn you up; it all depends on if you are truly in Christ or not.

REJECTING CHRIST AND FALLING AWAY FROM THE FAITH

"For if we go on sinning deliberately after receiving the knowledge of the truth, there no longer remains a sacrifice for sins, but a fearful expectation of judgment, and a fury of fire that will consume the adversaries" (Heb. 10:26-27). The worst possible state of any human condition is to come into contact with the Gospel of Jesus and then reject it. Some people immediately reject Christ, but the more dangerous place is that of living as if you were a true follower of Christ but then, at some point, rejecting Him—or as the language of Hebrews states, "falling away." Sometimes, this can be after years and years of living externally as if you were a follower.

The apostle John addresses this in his epistle also, where he makes it clear that when people depart from the faith, it shows they were never truly regenerated and reborn in Christ. "Children, it is the last hour, and as you have heard that antichrist is coming, so now many antichrists have come. Therefore we know that it is the last hour. They went out from us, but they were not of us; for if they had been of us, they would have continued with us. But they went out, that it might become plain that they all are not of us" (1 John 2:18-19).

One thing must be made very clear. Falling away into apostasy proves that a person never was truly reborn in the Spirit. I know that this is a contentious subject, but it has to be said. While the Bible does speak about falling away and turning our backs on God, the New Testament is completely absent of any language that makes it seem like one who was born of the Spirit could ever be unborn of the Spirit. It really comes down to this: you can have every single external evidence that you are in Christ, but turning away from Him proves that you never really had an internal transformation.

You might have experienced fellowship with believers, benefited from the Spirit, or even been mentally enlightened about theology and the things of God; but true internal transformation cannot be undone. When you are reborn into Christ, you are born of the Spirit into eternal life; and nothing can separate you from God's love (Rom. 8:39), and nothing can ever snatch you out of His hand (John 10:28).

What causes the true apostasy of someone›s heart to be exposed are different for everyone. But these things do not cause apostasy; they merely expose the true condition of one›s heart. Temptation can cause one to fall away. Everyone is tempted by sin, but the person who is not truly reborn may eventually let that sin draw them all the way out, exposing the true condition of their heart.

First John 2:15-17 admonishes, "Do not love the world or the things in the world. If anyone loves the world, the love of the Father is not in him. For all that is in the world—the desires of the flesh and the desires of the eyes and pride of life—is not from the Father but is from the world. And the world is passing away along with its desires, but whoever does the will of God abides forever."

Ignoring the Gospel is also a means that eventually will expose an apostate heart. The writer of Hebrews asks a very important question regarding this in chapter two: "How shall we escape if we neglect such a great salvation? It was declared at first by the Lord, and it was attested to us by those who heard" (Heb. 2:3).

Another element that often exposes apostasy is that of persecution. Persecution comes in many forms. We see people in different cultures being openly persecuted as they suffer and die for their faith. This has always been a part of the Christian faith. But sometimes, persecution is not clear-cut and severe. People have left the faith in recent years in the West because our culture has shifted in areas of morality and sin. These people claimed Christ when the culture seemed to be in a moral majority; but when the majority shifted and pop culture began to criticize biblical morality, these people's hearts were exposed as not truly belonging to Christ. If persecution causes you to fall away from the faith, you never really had biblical saving faith.

Second Timothy 3:12 says, "Indeed, all who desire to live a godly life in Christ Jesus will be persecuted." In recent years, people have said that for the first time in decades, the Christian church is in decline. But this is simply not true. What is happening is the middle is disappearing. Those who were once lukewarm, social "Christians" are being forced to choose sides; there is no middle ground. And in God's grace, He is making that clearer as we draw closer to the end. Here is something that we can be very sure of: Christ said, "'I will build my church and the gates of hell shall not prevail'" (Matt. 16:18).

False teachers also serve the function of exposing those whose hearts do not truly belong to Christ. Persecution is a means of the devil to scare unbelievers away from following Jesus, whereas false teachers come to entice them away. The reason we must rebuke false teachers, though, is that while they entice away unbelievers, they can also bring much confusion to true believers. False teachers usually create a Christ Who suits the unregenerate person's carnal desires so that a person can have a form of godliness while denying the power of the Gospel.

Second Timothy 4:3-4 reminds us, "For the time is coming when people will not endure sound teaching, but having itching ears they will accumulate for themselves teachers to suit their own passions, and will turn away from listening to the truth and wander off into myths."

Another reason is the unwillingness to let go of the past. This is one of the issues that the author of Hebrews was dealing with—Jews who could let go of the types and shadows of their old religion. We see this today in both extremes—people unwilling to let go of a sinful and destructive past or even people who are unwilling to let go of seemingly good things about their past identity. Rejecting Christ for either reason is still trampling the blood of Christ.

"From now on, therefore, we regard no one according to the flesh. Even though we once regarded Christ according to the flesh, we regard him thus no longer. Therefore, if anyone is in Christ, he is a new creation. The old has passed away; behold, the new has come. All this is from God, who through Christ reconciled us to himself and gave us the ministry of reconciliation" (2 Cor. 5:16-18).

The security of our salvation is promised when we truly become reborn in Christ. This is the transformative power of the Gospel, and this is what the author of Hebrews is urging us to not neglect but instead to anchor ourselves to.

The book of Hebrews is full of the Gospel—the need for the Gospel, the function of the Gospel, and God's method of securing our salvation through the Gospel. One reason people often do not see Christ and the Gospel all throughout the Old and New Testaments and have trouble seeing the continuity of how God is represented in the Old and New Testaments is two-fold:

1. They do not study the Bible exegetically and contextually, and they do not often here it preached this way as well.
2. They do not associate the wrath of God with the Gospel.

There is no way to properly understand the Good News of the Gospel apart from understanding the bad news of what is in store for all outside the saving grace of Christ. It is very sad but also kind of humorous listening to someone trying to communicate a concept like salvation as they desperately try to avoid talking about the wrath of God, sin, Hell, and final judgment. We must belabor these things in order to magnify the grace of God in salvation. It sounds ridiculous to talk about the importance of "being saved" if we do not make it clear what we are being saved from.

This is why the Gospel presentations you hear today in many churches are so very shallow. Where is the seriousness, the urgency, and the honesty? If we do not communicate it like it is important, why are we surprised when they treat it like it is not? If the Gospel is presented like one of many things rather than like it is everything, why are we surprised at the causal and lukewarm nature of many who call themselves Christians?

This is why we, like the author of Hebrews, must make a big deal out of sin. In verses twenty-six and twenty-seven, he highlights what a serious matter sin is and what happens to those who take it lightly. If we want to make much of the Savior and the price He paid for our redemption, we must make much of sin and how damaging and deadly it truly is.

The author of Hebrews is saying if we continue living in open and unrepentant sin after being given the glorious Gospel of grace, there is no other means of salvation beyond that. This is evidence that maybe you have not truly been transformed by the Gospel. If we shrug off the Gospel and all its implications, the only expectation we should have is a fearful expectation of the fiery judgment that awaits the adversaries of God. To reject the Gospel, we really are rejecting the Father, the Son, and the Holy Spirit.

You cannot have true messages about God's grace without the context of wrath and judgment. Treating the sacrifice that Christ made in a causal way is evidence you do not understand the holiness of God and how much He hates sin. I have heard people try to minimize God's posture toward sin and continue in a life of sin by saying, "God hates the sin, but loves the sinner." And while to some degree this is true, let us remember the words of R.C. Sproul: "It has been said that God hates the sin and loves the sinner. But it's the sinner God sends to hell not just the sin."[8]

We must understand that the love of God is charity toward us; we do not have anything of value to give Him. Everything we have is from the Lord. If you give Him your life, you are merely giving Him what already belongs to Him. If you give Him your resources, remember that "all things were created through him and for him" (Col. 1:16). There is literally nothing we can give God that He does not already deserve. So, the love that God extends to us through the cross is the love God has toward us. To reject the Gospel is to reject God's love; and beyond that, there is nothing but the fearful expectation of judgment and the fire reserved for God's enemies and adversaries.

---

8   R.C. Sproul (@RCSproul), "It has been said that God hates the sin and loves the sinner. But it's the sinner God sends to hell not just the sin," X, June 7, 2016, 3:48 p.m., https:// twitter.com/RCSproul/status/740269117698150400.

Anyone who has set aside the law of Moses dies without mercy on the evidence of two or three witnesses. How much worse punishment, do you think, will be deserved by the one who has trampled underfoot the Son of God, and has profaned the blood of the covenant by which he was sanctified, and has outraged the Spirit of grace? For we know him who said, "Vengeance is mine; I will repay." And again, "The Lord will judge his people." It is a fearful thing to fall into the hands of the living God (Heb. 10:28-31).

The author of Hebrews points his audience back to the Law to remind them how swift justice and judgment were under the old system, which was imperfect and flawed. Someone could literally be put to death by the witness testimony of two or three imperfect human witnesses, so he asks, how much more severe do you think it will be when we are talking about the perfect witness, God Himself?

We are rejecting the fullness of the Trinity when we live as if the Gospel is not the most important thing in the world and as if we are not desperate and needy for it. We reject the Father when, as it says in verse twenty-nine, we trample underfoot the Son of God. God owes us wrath and judgment; but out of mercy, He sent His Son to die on our behalf. When we do not accept this precious gift, we gladly trample the Son of God underneath our feet. That is why it will bring the Father great joy one day to put those who trampled the Gospel underneath the feet of Jesus, along with all of God's enemies.

We reject the Son directly by profaning the blood of the covenant. By continuing to live in sin and rejection of Christ's sacrifice, we act as if His precious shed blood is worthless or insufficient. Treating Christ as common and His blood as something other than sacred is blasphemy of the highest order. John 17:19 tells us, "'And for their sake I consecrate myself, that they also may be sanctified in truth.'" Christ not only died for us, but He also consecrated Himself by living a perfect life on our behalf. Then that consecrated blood of immeasurable value was shed for undeserving sinners.

To respond in any other way than with complete humility, thanksgiving, and unconditional surrender is to profane the value of this precious blood.

And finally, we blaspheme the Holy Spirit by rejecting His work of convicting the world of its sin as He lovingly leads us into all truth. This is the Spirit that extends to us God's grace—the same Spirit Who raised Christ from the dead. People sometimes try and make the Spirit of God seem docile and weak. But here in Hebrews 10, we see that when the Father's Son is trampled underfoot and we profane the precious blood of the Lamb meant to sanctify us, this outrages the Spirit. This does not say that Jesus is on bended knee begging us to accept Him into our hearts; this is saying that God made one way of pardon for His enemies to surrender to Him, and those who reject this will incur the full message of the Triune God's wrath and judgment.

The author of Hebrews warns, "For we know him who said, 'Vengeance is mine; I will repay.' And again, 'The Lord will judge his people.' It is a fearful thing to fall into the hands of the living God" (Heb. 10:30-31).

The message of the Gospel is that we had better bow down or be struck down, God has already lavishly shown His love by sending His Son to die while we were yet sinners. If you reject this and continue in your sin, there is no hope for you. The only hope that we have for the lost is the Gospel!

People often say that eternal punishment in Hell seems like an unfair and extreme punishment for those who reject Christ in this life. My response to that statement is that it is because you overvalue yourself and undervalue Christ. The problem is we undervalue the blood that secured a covenant that we did not deserve but was offered as a free gift. So not only are we stained with sin and rebellion; but also, when God drew near to us and offered us salvation from the punishment we deserve, we treat it like it is a casual thing, like we deserve it, or like it is something among other important things in life. Why are we then surprised at God's outrage? The only proper response to the Gospel is falling down on our faces and crying out in gratefulness. If that is not your response, it shows that you do not see Christ as the precious Treasure He is; and because of that, you do not understand the value of His precious and perfect blood shed for you.

According to Matthew, "The kingdom of heaven is like treasure hidden in a field, which a man found and covered up. Then in his joy he goes and sells all that he has and buys that field" (Matt. 13:44). To continue living a life of sin without repentance after hearing the Good News of the Gospel is literally like trampling underfoot God's most precious gift and profaning the covenant secured by His blood! We had better make sure we talk about the vengeance and judgment of God when we talk about the Gospel of grace. I fear for any preacher who preaches the grace of God without laboring to explain what awaits those who reject God's grace.

The stain of sin that produced the need for the cross is everywhere in the Bible, and it is all throughout the book of Hebrews—just like the looming and burning wrath of God is also a thread throughout the book of Hebrews and the entire Bible. It is present in most places we see the grace of God articulated because you cannot have one without the other.

> Therefore we must pay much closer attention to what we have heard, lest we drift away from it. For since the message declared by angels proved to be reliable, and every transgression or disobedience received a just retribution, how shall we escape if we neglect such a great salvation? It was declared at first by the Lord, and it was attested to us by those who heard, while God also bore witness by signs and wonders and various miracles and by gifts of the Holy Spirit distributed according to his will (Heb. 2:1-4).

The author of Hebrews warns us of the foolishness of neglecting this great salvation that has been afforded to us. We must stay anchored in Christ and in His Word because He alone is the Guarantor of the promise of salvation!

For it is impossible, in the case of those who have once been enlightened, who have tasted the heavenly gift, and have shared in the Holy Spirit, and have tasted the goodness of the word of God and the powers of the age to come, and then have fallen away, to restore them again to repentance, since they are crucifying once again the Son of God to their own harm and holding him up to contempt (Heb. 6:4-6).

We must understand that having surety in our salvation is a double-edged sword because the same Gospel that is saving us is condemning others. The radical and unmerited nature of God's grace either makes you grateful or hardens your heart. This is why we must preach and teach the full counsel of God's Word and the Gospel.

Charles Spurgeon once said:

I believe that the gospel makes some men more miserable than they would be. The drunkard could drink and revel in his intoxication with greater joy if he did not hear it said, 'all drunkards will have their place in the lake that burns with fire and brimstone.' How jovial the Sabbath breaker would riot through his Sabbaths if it were not written, 'remember the Sabbath day and keep it holy.' And how happily could the libertine and the licentious man drive on his mad career if it were not told, 'the wages of sin is death and then after death the judgment.' But the truth put the bitter in his cup; the warnings of God freeze the current of his soul. The truth of the gospel and the Scripture shine bright as the midday sun, and let us remember, the same sun which melts the wax also hardens the clay. And the same gospel which melts some persons to repentance hardens others in their sins.[9]

---

9   Charles Spurgeon, *Spurgeon's Sermons: Volume 9* (Peabody: Hendrickson Publishers, 2011).

We find surety in our salvation from the same words that cause fear and dread in those who reject the Gospel and outrage the Spirit of grace. If your view of the Gospel does not include His terrible wrath and judgment, which is a reality for those who reject Christ, you have a terribly unbiblical view of God's grace. We do not get to decide who responds to the message; we have been entrusted to deliver the message with truth and integrity. We cannot—nor should we try—to give someone surety of their salvation. This is something that only the Spirit of God can do. We must hold fast and teach others to hold fast to the message of God's saving grace finding the security of their salvation in the finished work of Christ alone.

> So then, brothers, we are debtors, not to the flesh, to live according to the flesh. For if you live according to the flesh you will die, but if by the Spirit you put to death the deeds of the body, you will live. For all who are led by the Spirit of God are sons of God. For you did not receive the spirit of slavery to fall back into fear, but you have received the Spirit of adoption as sons, by whom we cry, "Abba! Father!" The Spirit himself bears witness with our spirit that we are children of God, and if children, then heirs—heirs of God and fellow heirs with Christ, provided we suffer with him in order that we may also be glorified with him (Rom. 8:12-17).

We have surety in our salvation for two reasons: first, we trust in Christ alone; and second, "the Spirit . . . by whom we cry, 'Abba! Father!' . . . himself bears witness . . . that we are children of God" (Rom. 8:15-16). The promise is that we will be co-heirs of Christ; the evidence in this life is that we are willing to suffer with Him and for Him and His Word!

How we respond to temptation, suffering persecution, false teaching, our pasts, trials, trouble, sin, and everything else is based on how we initially respond to the Gospel. The condition in the Gospel message finds our hearts in determining how we respond to it. Only God can change a heart. We must labor to proclaim the full and true Gospel and the whole counsel of God's Word because it is the only means by which men are saved.

THE AROMA OF CHRIST

There are not many right ways to present Christ and His Gospel. We must present the Jesus of the Bible clearly and correctly to the best of our ability. Anything we do to try and lessen the wrath and judgment of God or the grievous and damning nature of sin does not draw people to God; it merely distorts the narrow path to life.

> But thanks be to God, who in Christ always leads us in triumphal procession, and through us spreads the fragrance of the knowledge of him everywhere. For we are the aroma of Christ to God among those who are being saved and among those who are perishing, to one a fragrance from death to death, to the other a fragrance from life to life. Who is sufficient for these things? For we are not, like so many, peddlers of God›s word, but as men of sincerity, as commissioned by God, in the sight of God we speak in Christ (2 Cor. 2:14-17).

We are merely the fragrance of Christ. We do not get to decide how that fragrance is perceived. It will either melt their heart or harden it; it will either smell like a fragrance that leads to life or a fragrance that leads to death. If we ignore the Gospel of grace, we should expect fiery judgment and the wrath of God. We cannot pretend that the broad road does not lead to destruction (Matt. 7:13-14) just because God's enemies do not like it. We spread the fragrance of Christ, and it will smell differently to those whose hearts are postured differently to God. To one, the blood of Jesus is the ransom for their sin; and to others, it is evidence against them in their indictment.

Let me close this chapter with a story that I believe explains the fragrance of Christ and the surety of faith. It would be like a husband

and wife sitting in their house and enjoying their evening, without a care in the world. They are gathered around the table; and then suddenly, two armed men storm into the house and subdue them. They are being robbed! Very quickly, the men take control of the situation and have both the husband and the wife tied up in a chair. Fear grips the couple as the men quickly begin rummaging through their belongings, looking for things of value that they can steal.

Fear is gripping the husband and wife as they realize they are both completely helpless and at the mercy of these robbers. While they are robbing the couple, the husband and wife can overhear them talking with each other. The men are discussing the fact that since this couple has seen their faces, they are going to have to kill them when they are done robbing them. This raises the fear and anxiety of the couple to a completely new level.

But what the husband does not know is that right before the robbers tied up his wife, she had a brief opportunity to hit the silent panic alarm, which alerted the police that they were in distress. So, off in the distance, you can hear, ever so faintly, the sound of a police siren. It gets closer and closer and louder and louder. But this sound means two different things to two different groups of people, although the sound is exactly the same. To the robbers, the sound of the siren represents doom, condemnation, fear, and judgment. But that same exact sound couple represents help, hope, salvation, and deliverance to the couple.

As it says in 2 Corinthians 2:15-16, "the aroma of Christ" for one is a smell "from death to death"; but for others, it is an aroma "from life to life." We have no control over the condition of someone's heart; all we can do is spread the aroma of Christ to everyone. To those who see God as holy and are repentant for their sins, the Gospel smells like help, hope, and salvation. And to the one who has hardened their heart toward God, the same message sounds as judgment and condemnation because it is.

Those who put their faith in Christ alone for their salvation will not be put to shame. Those who fall away and never return, as the prodigal son did in the parable Jesus told in Luke 15:11-32, were never truly regenerated by the Spirit of God. We will discuss this in much greater detail in the next two chapters, but this all hinges ultimately on what your faith is in and how you view the theological idea of faith. A genuine faith in Christ cannot be taken away by circumstances or external conditions around you; and because of this, genuine faith produces genuine surety because your faith is not in yourself, your performance, your circumstances, or anything else in this world. Your faith is in Christ alone!

CHAPTER 11

WE ARE NOT OF THOSE WHO SHRINK BACK

BY: JOSHUA WEST

"For, 'Yet a little while, and the coming one will come and will not delay;
but my righteous one shall live by faith, and if he shrinks back, my soul has no pleasure
in him.' But we are not of those who shrink back and are destroyed, but of those who
have faith and preserve their souls."

HEBREWS 10:37-39

IN THE LAST EIGHT VERSES of Hebrews 10, the author makes a personal and practical plea to the true believers that made up this small fellowship that apparently was under a great wave of persecution. And while the letter was written to a particular group of people that the author was trying to encourage, the practical picture given here of what genuine faith lived out looks like serves us well to understand as an example of what true faith is.

At the beginning of Hebrews 10, we focused on the once-and-for-all sacrifice of Jesus on the cross; and in the previous chapter of this book, we focused on the middle section of Hebrews 10 and discussed the surety of genuine faith. But before we deal with the last eight verses of Hebrews 10, let's reexamine verses twenty-three through twenty-five as a sort of baseline for what we will be discussing in this chapter: "Let us hold fast the confession of our hope without wavering, for he who promised is faithful. And let us consider how to stir up one another to love and good works, not neglecting to meet together, as is the habit of some, but encouraging one another, and all the more as you see the Day drawing near."

Genuine saving faith has specific markers and characteristics about it. If we truly believe that God, Who promised us salvation through the redemptive work of Christ, is faithful to keep His promise, then we should be able to hold fast to our faith without wavering. Then in verses thirty-two through thirty-six of Hebrews 10, we are given a real-life example of what not wavering from our faith actually looks like in practice.

> But recall the former days when, after you were enlightened, you endured a hard struggle with sufferings, sometimes being publicly exposed to reproach and affliction, and sometimes being partners with those so treated. For you had compassion on those in prison, and you joyfully accepted the plundering of your property, since you knew that you yourselves had a better possession and an abiding one. Therefore do not throw away your confidence, which has a great reward. For you have need of endurance, so that when you have done the will of God you may receive what is promised (Heb. 10:32-36).

The author of Hebrews either personally knew these people to whom he was writing or, at the very least, knew a great deal about them. He was aware of their deep dedication to the Church and to holding fast to their faith. It is apparent that the author knows that this church—like most churches—is made up of true believers and false converts, so he encourages the genuine believers to hold fast and remember that God would see them through. We know this part is written to believers because what he tells them to hold on to is something that would not a false believer would not be encouraged by, the true reward of their faith, which is eternal life in Christ.

This is what biblical faith actually is—believing in the promised outcome of the Gospel of Jesus Christ. The Greek word used most often in the New Testament that is translated as faith is *pistis*. Pistis was a Greek goddess who personified trustworthiness and reliability, someone whose guarantee could not fail. This is why the word we translate into "faith" is something different than the word often means when it uses the term in the modern world and even in the modern Church.

Our faith in God is something completely reliable, completely trustworthy, and completely unfailing. The author of Hebrews is doing what he himself commanded that they do for each other earlier in the letter. He is stirring them toward love and good works as they hold fast to the confession of their faith. The picture being painted here is that of a kind of Christian and a brand of Christianity that cannot be broken by suffering and persecution—willing to suffer for the sake of Christ because their faith in God is true. I believe that the author of Hebrews is making the point that this is the only true brand of Christianity. These people were willing to be publicly embarrassed. They were willing to suffer imprisonment and persecution and be identified with those who were in prison because "you had compassion on those in prison, and you joyfully accepted the plundering of your property, since you knew that you yourselves had a better possession and an abiding one" (Heb. 10:34). Their faith was in the fact that they had a better possession than anything in this world, an abiding one. This is what makes genuine faith.

Biblical faith is knowing that we stand justified before God on the basis of what Christ did on the cross and that God will keep the promises that He has made to us in His Word. Biblical faith is nothing more and nothing less than this. We will dig much deeper into this concept in the next chapter; but for now, remember when we talk about faith in the New Testament, we are talking about saving faith.

This is the better possession that the people in this story were holding on to. It is pretty obvious the first group of people was arrested in the first wave of persecution, and those who were not imprisoned had a choice. They could run and hide and pretend like they did not know those other Christians; or in faith and out of compassion, they could identify themselves with those who were arrested for their faith and risk being arrested themselves and having their property plundered. Why would they do that? Why would they take that risk? The true Christian has already died to the passions and desires of the flesh.

If you trade your cross for comfort, you are not truly in the faith. If suffering can break you, you do not have genuine and saving faith. If Christ is not a treasure to you that was "hidden in a field" that you covered up again and then in your great joy sold all that you have to possess the field, you are not a Christian. If your faith is in anything less than this treasure, you will fall away and be disappointed (Matt. 13:44).

In Romania in the 1950s, there was a pastor by the name of Richard Wurmbrand. During this time, communism was sweeping through Romania, as well as other places. Back in 1948, when many other pastors were, out of fear, bowing the knee to the godless ideology of communism, Wurmbrand publicly said that Christianity and communism were incompatible. He stood for the truth of the Gospel and God's Word. Eventually, in 1959, he was arrested and sentenced to twenty-five years in prison.

He served fourteen years in prison before finally getting amnesty. While in prison, he was severely tortured, mutilated, burned, and even locked for hours in an ice box. His body bore these scars for the rest of his life. While in prison, his release was offered to him several times if only he would publicly denounce Christ as his Savior. He never did.

After receiving amnesty, he started a world missions organization called Voice of the Martyrs, wrote a book called *Tortured for Christ* that was eventually made into a movie, preached all around the world, helped plant churches all over the world, and had a very successful worldwide ministry. One day, a reporter asked him what his greatest accomplishment was or what experience he held most dear. His response was mind-blowing. He said that he was grateful to be counted worthy to suffer for Christ's name in a Romanian prison for fourteen years. The reporter then asked him how it was that the experience of being tortured and imprisoned did not break his faith. His response was, "A faith that can be destroyed by suffering is not faith." And no truer words have ever been spoken. Richard Wurmbrand, like the people in Hebrews 10, had found a treasure of immeasurable value; and there was nothing in this world worth trading it for. This is genuine faith, and this is saving faith.

The treasure of Christianity is not a worldly blessing, comfort, getting something you hope for, having a life of ease, or anything else; the one and only treasure of Christianity is Christ and eternal life in Him and with Him.

What if the church was really like this? What if the members of your small group were willing to suffer, be imprisoned, and even die for you? That would be an attractive church because that is Christ's Church. This is what true Christian discipleship looks like. And although this is rare in the West, in the rest of the world, this is more common. Being a Christian in a Hindu or Muslim context will cost you greatly.

Acts 5:41 says, "Then they left the presence of the council, rejoicing that they were counted worthy to suffer dishonor for the name." This Scripture in Acts is talking about Peter and John as they were arrested for preaching the Gospel in front of the temple in Jerusalem. The Jewish leaders considered killing them, but they did not want to make martyrs of them. So instead, they severely whipped them and warned them that they must stop preaching the Gospel; or else, they would be sorry. It says after they were beaten, they rejoiced that they were considered worthy messengers of the Gospel and were allowed by God to suffer for the name of Christ. It also did not stop them.

In the next verse, we see, "And every day, in the temple and from house to house, they did not cease teaching and preaching that the Christ is Jesus" (Acts 5:42). They had found a treasure that was immensely more valuable than anything else. And this included their own safety, comfort, ease, and even their own lives; and in their great joy, they proclaimed it to anyone and everyone that they could.

They believed in Matthew 13:44: "'The kingdom of heaven is like treasure hidden in a field, which a man found and covered up. Then in his joy he goes and sells all that he has and buys that field.'" The true Christian has found a treasure, an enduring reward, that they are willing to be imprisoned for and joyfully have their stuff plundered. This parable, in which Jesus talks about the Kingdom of Heaven says, "'Then in his joy he goes and sells all that he has and buys the field'"—not murmuringly or begrudgingly but joyfully!

The Christians the author of Hebrews is writing to valued being associated with Christ so much that it brought them joy to lose their possessions on behalf of that association. It was not for nothing, it was on behalf of a better possession, a lasting one, and an enduring one worth losing everything for.

The enduring reward that is worth the loss of all things is the treasure of Christianity; and it is the treasure of the universe in all times past, present, and future. Jesus is the Treasure—the jaw-dropping, all-surpassing beauty and majesty of Jesus! If you do not see Jesus in this way, it is because you do not know Him in a saving way. Because in view of Christ and His mercies toward us, we will offer ourselves to Him "as a living sacrifice, holy and acceptable to God, which is [the] spiritual worship" (Rom. 12:1) of those who actually have been transformed by the beauty and power of Christ and His Gospel.

The apostle Paul understood this as well, and his life is a great example of someone who found the enduring reward of the treasure hidden in a field. Paul was a Pharisee, who was, according to Scripture, moving up the ranks of Judaism quickly; he had authority, prestige, power, and a good life. "For you have heard of my former life in Judaism, how I persecuted the church of God violently and tried to destroy it. And I was advancing in Judaism beyond many of my own age among my people, so extremely zealous was I for the traditions of my fathers" (Gal. 1:13-14).

He describes himself further in his letter to the Philippians:

> Though I myself have reason for confidence in the flesh also. If anyone else thinks he has reason for confidence in the flesh, I have more: circumcised on the eighth day, of the people of Israel, of the tribe of Benjamin, a Hebrew of Hebrews; as to the law, a Pharisee; as to zeal, a persecutor of the church; as to righteousness under the law, blameless (Phil. 3:4-6).

But after Paul met Jesus on the Damascus Road, his life changed— everything about it. The purpose, focus, direction, passion, and everything else changed because he met Christ and was transformed by Him. Paul knew Who Jesus was before; in fact, he was actively persecuting His followers. But when he met Christ on that road, he actually saw Christ for Who He really is— Messiah and King and the beautiful Treasure that nothing else in life could ever come close to comparing to. Listen to what he says about the treasure of Christ in Philippians 3:7-11:

> But whatever gain I had, I counted as loss for the sake of Christ. Indeed, I count everything as loss because of the surpassing worth of knowing Christ Jesus my Lord. For his sake I have suffered the loss of all things and count them as rubbish, in order that I may gain Christ and be found in him, not having a righteousness of my own that comes from the law, but that which comes through faith in Christ, the righteousness from God that depends on faith—that I may know him and the power of his resurrection, and may share his sufferings, becoming like him in his death, that by any means possible I may attain the resurrection from the dead.

Paul saw the value of suffering for the treasure of Christ and for future glory and a future reward. By faith, Moses also saw the value of suffering for Christ over a thousand years before He ever came to earth in human form. "By faith Moses, when he was grown up, refused to be called the son of Pharaoh›s daughter, choosing rather to be mistreated with the people of God than to enjoy the fleeting pleasures of sin. He considered the reproach of Christ greater wealth than the treasures of Egypt, for he was looking to the reward" (Heb. 11:24-26).

This is what genuine and saving faith actually looks like. It is evidenced by our actions and the way we live our lives. Works do not save us; they are evidence that we truly have saving faith. This is the theme that runs from the beginning of the Bible all the way until today. In the next chapter, we are going to look at what biblical faith truly is. But let me say here that this kind of faith we see in Hebrews 10 and in the list of people we will look at in Hebrews 11 are not unique examples of extreme faith; these are pictures and examples of genuine and saving faith.

> Therefore do not throw away your confidence, which has a great reward. For you have need of endurance, so that when you have done the will of God you may receive what is promised. For, "Yet a little while, and the coming one will come and will not delay; but my righteous one shall live by faith, and if he shrinks back, my soul has no pleasure in him." But we are not of those who shrink back and are destroyed, but of those who have faith and preserve their souls (Heb. 10:35-39).

God takes no pleasure in those who "shrink back." Hebrews 11:6 tells us, "Without faith it is impossible to please [God]." It is so important that we understand what faith actually is. Hebrews 10:38 does not mean that God takes no pleasure in you if you "shrink back." And by this, He is a little disappointed in you; but you are still saved. The verse actually means that your faith is not genuine, and you will not inherit the kingdom of God. He is talking about saving faith. Faith is ultimately taking God at His Word.

In verse thirty-nine, the author is boiling down all of humanity into two groups of people: "But we are not of those who shrink back and are destroyed, but of those who have faith and preserve their souls." There are those who have saving faith in Christ, and those people will preserve their souls; and there are "those who shrink back and are destroyed" (Heb. 10:39). There are only two kingdoms, two kinds of people, two paths, two end destinations.

Matthew 16:25 says, "'For whoever would save his life will lose it, but whoever loses his life for my sake will find it.'" Is this the testimony of your life? Does Christ outweigh, outshine, and outrank every other person, place, or thing in your life? There cannot be anything above Him; the only reason there would be is that you do not really see the surpassing worth of knowing Christ Jesus as your Lord.

So very often, people quote Revelation 12:11: "And they have conquered him by the blood of the Lamb and by the word of their testimony, for they loved not their lives even unto death." But they leave out this part of the sentence: "They loved not their lives even unto death." The evidence that you are truly living for a future and enduring reward is that you do not "love this life even unto death." The author of Hebrews is saying that those who truly have saving faith will "shrink back and [be] destroyed" but will, by the power of the Spirit, endure to the end and "preserve their souls" (Heb. 10:39) by faith. We find the end result of both groups of people in Revelation 21:

> And he who was seated on the throne said, "Behold, I am making all things new." Also he said, "Write this down, for these words are trustworthy and true." And he said to me, "It is done! I am the Alpha and the Omega, the beginning and the end. To the thirsty I will give from the spring of the water of life without payment. The one who conquers will have this heritage, and I will be his God and he will be my son. But as for the cowardly, the faithless,

the detestable, as for murderers, the sexually immoral, sorcerers, idolaters, and all liars, their portion will be in the lake that burns with fire and sulfur, which is the second death" (Rev. 21:5-8).

There will not be any good people in Heaven; there will not be any proud people in Heaven; there will not be any cowards in Heaven—only sinners saved by the amazing grace of God as they put their faith wholly in Him and what He accomplished on the cross. Listen to what James the half-brother of Jesus said in his epistle: "Blessed is the man who remains steadfast under trial, for when he has stood the test he will receive the crown of life, which God has promised to those who love him" (James 1:12).

The author of Hebrews encourages those who have suffered so much for the cause of Christ not to let it all be for nothing. Your suffering always has meaning and purpose if your faith is in Jesus. This is why it is so important to understand what faith truly is and understand that, as Christians, our faith is not in something but rather in Someone. To truly see Christ as the Reward for faith actually means to know that while suffering in this life might be long and painful, it will not last forever. But salvation in Christ will. This is what we are actually putting our faith in—that Jesus will keep His Word and His promises and that we will be able, by the power of the Spirit, to endure all things. The only reason we would give in to temptation is because we do not truly believe God and have faith in His Word.

When it is time, God will come without delay and set things right; justice will prevail; and we will be safe and sound in God's loving arms forever. We cannot throw away our confidence in what God has promised without calling God a liar or without saying that what He has promised is not worth it. We can trust the Lord. He has never failed, and He never will.

"Therefore do not throw away your confidence, which has a great reward. For you have need of endurance, so that when you have done the will of God you may receive what is promised" (Heb. 10:35-36).

CHAPTER 12

RECOVERING BIBLICAL FAITH

BY: JOSHUA WEST

"Now faith is the assurance of things hoped for, the conviction of things not seen. For by it the people of old received their commendation. By faith we understand that the universe was created by the word of God, so that what is seen was not made out of things that are visible."

HEBREWS 11:1-3

HEBREWS 11 IS A VERY well-known chapter of Scripture. Some have called it the faith chapter or the hall of faith, but I believe that it is one of the most misused and taken out-of-context chapters in the Bible. It is often a place where preachers pop in and grab an encouraging verse that supports their flawed view of what faith is. So right away, let's talk about what biblical faith actually is.

THE FAITH

It is so important that we define the term "faith" the same way the early church did. The way we often use the term faith in modern Christianity would have been foreign, in my opinion, to how the apostles of the first century would have understood it. Although this is a problem today, it is nothing new. The misuse and application of what faith truly is has come up throughout Church history. It was an issue that was dealt with by the first-century Church, the medieval Church, and throughout Church history. This was at the heart of the Great Reformation—the recovery of the doctrine of salvation by grace alone, through faith alone, in Christ alone, and this, according to the Scripture alone for the glory of God alone. When the first-century Church and the early church fathers of the first several hundred years of the Church used the term "faith" in their writings, it is clear that they were referring to things pertaining to "the faith." It is impossible to properly use the term "faith" in Christianity rightly in any way that can be disjointed from the Gospel and the idea of saving faith.

Biblical faith is knowing that we stand justified before God on the basis of what Christ did for us on the cross and that God will keep the promises that He has made in His Word—nothing more and nothing less. At its worst, we see the most egregious word of faith heretics saying things like, "If you have enough faith, you can command God to do what you ask." Or maybe less egregious is simply the idea that faith itself is a "substance"; and to get God to act upon your behalf, you must be a person of great faith, who has built up a lot of that substance.

I believe part of the problem is the way that the King James Version renders Hebrews 11:1: "Now faith is the substance of things hoped for, the evidence of things not seen." Now, this is merely a poetic way of saying that faith is the substance of something you are hoping for; it is not saying that faith is actually a substance. But Hebrews 11:1 is not talking about believing for whatever your heart wishes for; it is actually talking about a particular thing hoped for, which is "The Blessed Hope." This is referring to the promise of the Gospel. If we look back at Hebrews 10:34: "For you had compassion on those in prison, and you joyfully accepted the plundering of your property, since you knew that you yourselves had a better possession and an abiding one."

The substance of things hoped for, the evidence of what is not yet seen or realized is the better possession, which is an abiding one mentioned in verse thirty-four of chapter ten. The thing we are hoping for and living toward is the promise of eternal life in Christ. We know because of Hebrews 10:34, but we know it even more clearly because this is what the entire chapter of Hebrews 11 is about. It is pointing to a group of people, or "a cloud of witnesses" (Heb. 12:1) that is united by one solitary thing—saving faith in God's promise to save them through a future Messiah.

Let's look very quickly at two pitfalls of misinterpretation we can easily fall into if we are not careful when studying Hebrews 11. These people listed are not necessarily Heroes of Faith. I do not mean to diminish the acts of these people listed in Hebrews 11, but we see that they all made human mistakes and missteps as well as the things we hold in high regard. When reading the Bible, it is very important to remember that there is only one true Hero in the Bible—the God of the Bible.

Hebrews 11 is the tale of people from many different walks of life who made many mistakes and had many shortcomings but are all testament to the faithfulness of God to keep his promises. It is not about having extraordinary faith; it is a matter of whether or not you have genuine faith in God's promises because this is the difference between whether or not you have saving faith.

The other pitfall is believing that if you have enough faith, you can get the same results as the people in biblical stories. God has not promised you that if you build a boat, He will flood the world and save your family. The Bible is not trying to teach you that if you have enough faith, you can definitely have a baby when you are ninety-five years old, as Sarah did; or if you grow your hair long, you will have the strength of Samson. There are promises that are for all people of all times in the Bible, but there are also promises God made to specific people that were only for them.

Biblical faith cannot be disjointed from the Gospel and cannot be disjointed from the promises and the character of God as revealed in His Word. Remember, there are only two kinds of people—those who "shrink back and are destroyed" and "those who have faith and preserve their souls"

(Heb. 10:39). You can "shrink back"—in which case, you will be destroyed—or you can live by faith, which means you are saved by faith, And by this virtue, you will preserve your soul. There is no such thing as a person who is truly saved but does not live a life that is reflective of that saving faith. We all have shortcomings—as all the people in Hebrews 11 did—but we are being saved by faith, not by works. The action and works produced by saving faith are merely evidence of it. A faith that saves, sanctifies, and is genuine will preserve you until the end. Remember that Jesus is the Author of our faith (Heb. 12:2 KJV). He secured salvation; He saved us; He is sanctifying us; He will keep us; and He will finish what He has started if, in fact, our faith is real.

Look more closely at Hebrews 12:2: "Looking to Jesus, the founder and perfecter of our faith, who for the joy that was set before him endured the cross, despising the shame, and is seated at the right hand of the throne of God."

Our faith is based on a promise of something in the future. If that was not true, then what would we need to have faith for? What marks a true life of saving faith? Biblically, it is evidenced by living as if you actually believe the promises and words of God in the Bible are actually true. Although the word "faith" means something in the secular world, we as Christians must make sure how we view faith is rooted in biblical truth. People outside the faith also use terms like "faith, hope, and love." But we do not mean the same things they do when we use these terms. Our faith is in Christ and His Gospel promises to us. Our faith is not in something but rather Someone, and that Someone is the Creator and King of the universe and Someone Whose promises never fail.

We also view the term "hope" much differently than the world at large. Our "hope" is not a vague wish that we hope things might work out. We have a blessed hope that is rooted in the same biblical truth that our view of faith is, so our hope is rock solid. We also do not view the word "love" the way our world does. The Bible tells us that "God is love" (1 John 4:8). So, we define love by Who God is. God's love is perfect, and so is His justice. So for God to be perfect in love, He must also be perfectly just, which means He must condemn sinners. And we know from the Scripture that "the wages of sin is death" (Rom. 6:23).

So just like we must understand love biblically and hope biblically, we must understand faith the same way. We must shed our minds from what the world or bad theology, like the Word of Faith movement, has taught us about faith.

A FAITH THAT PLEASES GOD

"And without faith it is impossible to please him, for whoever would draw near to God must believe that he exists and that he rewards those who seek him" (Heb. 11:6). This Scripture is very often used to rally people to do something, to give to a project at church, or to get involved or to do something that seems less than logical as "an act of faith." But this is talking about saving faith. It is impossible to please God without living as if the God of the Bible actually exists and that He rewards those who seek Him. This is talking about living for God and trusting that He will keep His promises— namely, the promise of a future reward that all who put their faith in Christ will not be put to shame, of a future city from which He will rule the universe, and the promise that nothing will be able to separate us from His love eternally.

The faith that pleases God is our saving faith in Jesus Christ—the faith from which all other things we hope for and believe are rooted in. This is the most important thing to grasp. If you understand this truth, it will correct much of the bad theology you may have been taught. The faith that pleases God is saving faith in His Son. If we try to use this Scripture in any other way than the context here allows, we do damage to the centrality of the Gospel message.

As Martin Luther said, "Faith cannot be inherited or gained by being baptized into a Church. Faith is a matter between the individual and God." Real faith is saving faith, and the book of Hebrews tells us that it has particular attributes. It looks like a life that lives like it believes the Word of God—not because your parents say so, or a denomination says so, or even because I say so in this book but because you have received the Word of God by faith and have put your confidence fully in it. We had better make it our life's mission to know God from His Word and build our lives on the solid Rock that is Christ. Honestly, people do not distort God's Word because it is hard to understand; more often than not, it is because it is hard to accept.

It is not wrong to pray by faith that God would answer your prayers and intervene in your life in other ways; the Bible tells us to do this, but it is foolish to try and tie these requests to the unwavering promises of God in the Bible when they are not clearly connected. In other words, do not put words in God's mouth and hold fast to the things He has promised, pray about everything else, and trust God with outcomes. You will not always get what you want, but God is trustworthy and has your best interest in mind.

A faith that pleases God is obeying His Word at the expense of everything else because your faith is in a future reward. Everything in creation hinges on the power of the Word of the Lord, and the difference between the Christian and everyone else is that we are aware of this truth.

Here in America, the word "faith" has been greatly distorted by the Word of Faith Movement; the soul-damning prosperity gospel; the name-it-and-claim-it theology; the health, wealth, and self-improvement gospel; the pep talk gospel. These false ideologies have done great damage to the biblical doctrine of faith. But as Christians, we cannot let ourselves abandon teaching and preaching about faith; we must reclaim it and proclaim it because people's souls depend on it. We are saved by faith in Christ alone!

Biblical faith is not the thought that God is going to give you a new car, or a promise that you will never get sick, or a guarantee that you will not have trouble or trials in this life. It is the promise that you will never be alone in the trial and that, ultimately, you will overcome and be co-heirs with Christ if you are His co-laborer and persevere to the end by faith.

WHERE DOES BIBLICAL FAITH COME FROM?

So if faith is not rooted in really wanting something or really hoping for something to happen, from where do we get our faith? Our faith is rooted in one thing—the Word of God. God exists, and God has spoken; and the lives of true Christ-followers are utterly and completely dependent on the promises of God. The promises of God's Word are fulfilled by the living embodiment of the Word Himself, Jesus Christ (John 1:1-5). All things regarding prophecy and the Law have been fulfilled in the Person of Jesus Christ, save one—His triumphant return to redeem His bride and judge the world.

You will often hear people speak derogatorily toward the Bible or the importance of studying to show yourself approved (2 Tim. 2:15) in the area of biblical study and say things like, "I don't care about doctrine; I just love Jesus." But without the Bible, you do not know Who Jesus is, what the Gospel is, what the commands of God are, or what the promises of God are. You do not know what pleases Him and what does not. If you believe you are serving Jesus but reject the importance of the Scripture, you are not worshiping Jesus but rather a false version of Jesus that you have invented in your mind. From where does faith come? Romans 10:17 tells us, "So faith comes from hearing, and hearing through the word of Christ." Yes, our faith and hope are in Christ—but only in Christ as revealed in the Scripture. There are many false christs in the world, and the Bible warns us about this. If your affection for Christ is based on anything outside of the Word of God, your faith is not in Christ but in yourself. Matthew 24:24 warns, "'For there shall arise false Christs, and false prophets, and shall shew great signs and wonders; insomuch that, if it were possible, they shall deceive the very elect'" (KJV).

Do not be deceived into thinking that it is legalistic to devote your life to the study of God's Word. It is literally the only way you can know God. We commune with God through His Word and through prayer. Without the

Scripture, you will drift and slip into apostasy. A love for the Word of God is a sign that you are saved.

> How can a young man keep his way pure? By guarding it according to your word. With my whole heart I seek you; let me not wander from your commandments! I have stored up your word in my heart, that I might not sin against you. Blessed are you, O LORD; teach me your statutes! With my lips I declare all the rules of your mouth. In the way of your testimonies I delight as much as in all riches. I will meditate on your precepts and fix my eyes on your ways. I will delight in your statutes; I will not forget your word (Psalm 119:9-16).

LIVES OF FAITH

At the beginning of the list of people in Hebrews 11, we see Abel, Cain, and Enoch compared to one another.

> By faith Abel offered to God a more acceptable sacrifice than Cain, through which he was commended as righteous, God commending him by accepting his gifts. And through his faith, though he died, he still speaks. By faith Enoch was taken up so that he should not see death, and he was not found, because God had taken him. Now before he was taken he was commended as having pleased God (Heb. 11:4-5).

Even right at the beginning of the righteous of God's chosen remnant, Abel made a pleasing sacrifice by faith because he was a man of faith. And although he was killed for his faith, the Bible says that even his blood cried out a better word (Gen. 4:10-11) because his trust was in God.

James Moffatt once said, ""Death is never the last word in the life of a righteous man. When a man leaves the world, be he righteous or unrighteous, he leaves something in the world. He may leave something that will grow and spread like a cancer or a poison, or he may leave something like a fragrance or perfume or a blossom of beauty that permeates the atmosphere with blessing."[10]

The story of Cain and Abel should be a cautionary tale for many who believe that they can worship God in their own way, with offerings of worship that they are satisfied with. They believe because it is pleasing to them that it is also pleasing to God. But the Word of the Lord makes it very clear that we are foolish to think God is like us. Abel chose to please God. And although he was killed, his righteous blood cried out for justice; and God promises he will get it.

The story of Enoch shows that God does what pleases Him. While Abel's story is an example of *worshiping* God by faith, the story of Enoch is an example of *walking* with God by faith. It is important to remember that all mentioned in Hebrews 11 lived lives of faith, and their outcomes in this life were all very different. The point the author is trying to make is that while their earthly outcomes were very different because they are unified by saving faith in God's Word, their eternal outcomes will be the same, as this is true for every person who lives their lives by saving faith.

EVERY TRUE LIFE OF FAITH IS BUILT ON THE WORD OF GOD

> And without faith it is impossible to please him, for whoever would draw near to God must believe that he exists and that he rewards those who seek him. By faith Noah, being warned by God concerning events as yet unseen, in reverent fear constructed an ark for the saving of his household. By this he condemned the world and became an heir of the righteousness that comes by faith (Heb. 11:6-7).

Although there are many different factors that are evidence of saving faith in the life of the believer, there is one that is consistent—the fruit of

---

10   James Moffatt, *The Epistle to the Romans* (London: Forgotten Books, 2012).

obedience. We will not do an exhaustive examination of every character listed in Hebrews 11; but we are going to take time to focus special attention on the stories of Noah, Abraham, Sarah, and Moses. Let's look at Noah and his life of faith and see what we can learn from his example.

It is important to remember that not every Old Testament promise is something that is a promise for you and me. God made specific promises to specific people in order to fulfill His sovereign will on earth. Let us remember the entire Bible is about Jesus, His will, and His kingdom. God did not promise you that if you built an ark God would flood the earth and save your family. This is a type and shadow of the Gospel of Jesus Christ.

The story of Noah is one of the best parallel stories that is a type and shadow of the Gospel of Jesus Christ in the Bible. In the story of Noah, the world was becoming increasingly wicked; and the wrath of God was being stored up to be poured out on humanity. God spoke to Noah to warn him and told him to build an ark that would spare all who heeded this warning and sought safety inside the ark. The same is true today. The wrath of God is being stored up for wicked humanity and will be poured out (Rom. 1:18). But there is a way of escape. The condemnation of God will be avoided by all who heed the warning and hide in Christ for their salvation because "there is therefore now no condemnation for those who are in Christ Jesus" (Rom. 8:1).

God has made promises in the Bible, though, that are for all people in all times who are being saved by faith in Him:

- "And my God will supply every need of yours according to his riches in glory in Christ Jesus" (Phil. 4:19).
- "You prepare a table before me in the presence of my enemies; you anoint my head with oil; my cup overflows. Surely goodness and mercy shall follow me all the days of my life, and I shall dwell in the house of the LORD forever" (Psalm 23:5-6).

- "It is the LORD who goes before you. He will be with you; he will not leave you or forsake you. Do not fear or be dismayed" (Deut. 31:8).
- "I lift up my eyes to the hills. From where does my help come? My help comes from the LORD, who made heaven and earth. He will not let your foot be moved; he who keeps you will not slumber. Behold, he who keeps Israel will neither slumber nor sleep. The LORD is your keeper; the LORD is your shade on your right hand. The sun shall not strike you by day, nor the moon by night. The LORD will keep you from all evil; he will keep your life. The LORD will keep your going out and your coming in from this time forth and forevermore" (Psalm 121:1-8).
- "For 'everyone who calls on the name of the LORD will be saved'" (Rom. 10:13).
- "If you keep my commandments, you will abide in my love, just as I have kept my Father's commandments and abide in his love" (John 15:10).
- "I give them eternal life, and they will never perish, and no one will snatch them out of my hand. My Father, who has given them to me, is greater than all, and no one is able to snatch them out of the Father›s hand" (John 10:28-29).
- "And I am sure of this, that he who began a good work in you will bring it to completion at the day of Jesus Christ" (Phil. 1:6).
- "For I am sure that neither death nor life, nor angels nor rulers, nor things present nor things to come, nor powers, nor height nor depth, nor anything else in all creation, will be able to separate us from the love of God in Christ Jesus our Lord" (Rom. 8:38-39).

And these are just to name a few. Our faith is rooted in the Word of God and the promises He has made to us. If your faith as a Christian is in something other than God's Word, you are standing on very dangerous and shaky ground.

THE OUTWARD RESPONSE OF FAITH IS ALWAYS PRECEDED BY AN INWARD WORKING

So very often, we hear preachers say things like, "It's time to give an offering or do something bold because, remember, it's impossible to please God without faith." This is grossly taking the Bible out of context. The faith described in Hebrews 11 is talking exclusively about saving faith in Christ. It is not about doing something bold or taking action to spark your faith; it is taking God at His Word. Here is what the inward working of saving faith looks like: "By faith Noah, being warned by God concerning events as yet unseen, in reverent fear constructed an ark for the saving of his household. By this he condemned the world and became an heir of the righteousness that comes by faith" (Heb. 11:7).

Here is how true faith is manifest. In the story of Noah, God spoke concerning events yet unseen. He warned Noah about the coming flood and instructed him to build an ark to save his family. In Noah's heart, this produced reverent fear because Noah believed God and took Him at His word. Noah paid very close attention to make sure He obeyed God's detailed instructions on how to build the ark and what steps to follow. We must be very careful that we understand the Word of the Lord because our lives and eternity depend on it. God spoke; Noah believed; and in his heart, it produced reverent fear and, externally, an ark.

Let us remember that this was not a momentary, bold action or a spark of faith. Noah spent decades building the ark day after day, week after week, month after month, and year after year. The word of the Lord produced something that completely consumed and changed the path of Noah's life. Today, we need to ask ourselves if this is true of our lives. This is what true saving faith looks like in the life of a believer.

Many people mishandle the words of Scripture, and this is evidence that it has not produced reverent fear in their hearts, which is evidence of saving faith. One of the marks of someone who has truly heard and perceived God's Word by faith is someone who responds with awe and reverent fear. It is impossible to come into contact with the living God and not tremble. As Proverbs 9:10 says, "The fear of the LORD is the beginning of wisdom and the knowledge of the Holy One is insight. Isaiah 66:1-2 tells us, "Thus says the LORD: 'Heaven is my throne, and the earth is my footstool; what is the house that you would build for me, and what is the place of my rest? All these things my hand has made, and so all these things came to be, declares the Lord. But this is the one to whom I will look: he who is humble and contrite in spirit and trembles at my word.'"

The inward working of faith will always proceed the outward evidence of it; otherwise, it is simply "whitewashed tombs" (Matt. 23:27) and empty works. Outward displays that are not born of an inward working of faith will manifest in one of two ways: you will chase signs and wonders, hoping to get God's attention; or you will strive for legalistic works, hoping to gain God's approval. Both of these extremes are, at their root, basically the same thing. But a true life of faith is born from hearing and believing the Word of God. True faith is produced by the interworking of the Spirit and is evident in a person, who, by faith, trusts in the finished work of Christ. This is why the term "faith" in the New Testament is not usually talking about having a particular outcome when we pray. True saving faith holds fast to God, no matter the outcome in earthly circumstances. We pray by faith that God would heal, help, and move on our behalf; but even when He does not answer our prayers the way we are hoping for, our hope in God is not shaken because our faith is in God, not in ourselves. We trust Him in life and in death. The promise of faith is not that God would perform signs and wonders on your behalf; it is that He "'will never leave [us] nor forsake [us]'" (Heb. 12:5) and that in eternity, we will be with Him forever.

For all who are led by the Spirit of God are sons of God. For you did not receive the spirit of slavery to fall back into fear, but you have received the Spirit of adoption as sons, by whom we cry, "Abba! Father!" The Spirit himself bears witness with our spirit that we are children of God, and if children, then heirs—heirs of God and fellow heirs with Christ, provided we suffer with him in order that we may also be glorified with him (Rom. 8:14-17).

TRUE FAITH WILL ALWAYS PRODUCE OUTWARD EVIDENCE

Jesus said a good tree will bear fruit according to its kind (Matt. 7:17); and James, the half-brother of Jesus, said that "faith apart from works [or evidence] is dead" (James 2:26). Works cannot save you, but they are evidence that you are saved. Noah had faith in God's word, and it produced reverent fear and an ark. This should be the pattern of the life of all true believers. We hear and perceive the Word of the Lord, and it transforms us inside. Because of this, we live in obedience to God's commands. We are not being saved by our obedience; we obey because we are saved.

Noah's faith was not in the ark; it was in the God who had spoken. He had faith in God's Word and was saved by faith. No person in the history of the world in the Old or New Testament has ever been saved by any other means than by faith in God. This is the entire point of Hebrews 11. Salvation is of the Lord, and He is the Author of salvation and will save us in the end. Our faith is in Christ alone.

"And I am sure of this, that he who began a good work in you will bring it to completion at the day of Jesus Christ" (Phil. 1:6). This is why it is so important that we understand the actual promises of God to us in the Bible because these will always come to pass and will never let us down. So often, people are let down because they believe that God has promised them something that He has not. People believe that because they want something or deem it as good, it is promised to them somehow from God. In our day, this has a lot to do with pop culture Christianity, televangelists, and Word of Faith teachers that have taught wicked and deceptive heresy that has had a great and damaging impact on the Church.

Most people believe that if they have enough faith for something they perceive as a good thing, they should expect it to come to pass. I have heard people say things like, "God promised me that my friend would not die"; or "God promised me that my marriage would be healed"; or "God promised me that this business venture would be a success." My question to them is where in the Bible did you read this? Often, they have no good answer; but sometimes, it is because of verses that have been taken out of context and misapplied. God raised the dead in the Bible, so God promised He would raise the dead. God healed in the Bible, so God promised He would heal, etc.

Now do not misunderstand me. I am not saying that God does not heal or raise the dead or do many other marvelous works today on earth because He does. And we should pray for these things by faith. What I am saying is that God has not made a covenant promise to us that if we have enough faith, we should expect these things to always happen. Our faith is in God's eternal promise—not in temporary things. Sometimes, people are confused about this because of simple theological misunderstandings; but other times, it is because of heretical and wicked false teaching.

God tells those who seek His face that they have the privilege to also seek His hand, but we must remember that God is much more concerned with our eternal state than He is with our temporal one. When Jesus taught His disciples to pray, He taught them to pray this way:

> And when you pray, you must not be like the hypocrites. For they love to stand and pray in the synagogues and at the street corners, that they may be seen by others. Truly, I say to you, they have received their reward. But when you pray, go into your room and shut the door and pray to your Father who is in secret. And your Father who sees in secret will reward you. "And when

you pray, do not heap up empty phrases as the Gentiles do, for they think that they will be heard for their many words. Do not be like them, for your Father knows what you need before you ask him. Pray then like this: "Our Father in heaven, hallowed be your name. Your kingdom come, your will be done, on earth as it is in heaven. Give us this day our daily bread, and forgive us our debts, as we also have forgiven our debtors. And lead us not into temptation, but deliver us from evil (Matt. 6:5-13).

We make our needs and requests known to God as our Father, but we do it in light of two things: His kingdom coming and His will being done. So, we ask God to do what we think we need; but we trust that as our good Father, He will do what He knows we need in light of the bigger picture—His kingdom and His will. Even Jesus subjected Himself to this before He died on the cross when He said, "And going a little farther he fell on his face and prayed, saying, 'My Father, if it be possible, let this cup pass from me; nevertheless, not as I will, but as you will'" (Matt. 26:39).

We know that God can, and we hope that He will; but ultimately, we trust in His wisdom, knowing that He knows best, not us. We realize that if we can trust God with our eternity, we can trust Him with our today, realizing that, ultimately, we are not living for this world but for the world to come, and we are not living for an earthly kingdom but a coming kingdom.

THEY WERE LOOKING TOWARD A FUTURE CITY

By faith Abraham obeyed when he was called to go out to a place that he was to receive as an inheritance. And he went out, not knowing where he was going. By faith he went to live in the land of promise, as in a foreign land, living in tents with Isaac and Jacob, heirs with him of the same promise. For he was looking forward to the city that has foundations, whose designer and builder is God (Heb. 11:8-10).

Abraham was called out of the place he was living to go to a place where he was to receive an inheritance, and this was solely based on faith in God's Word. Like Noah, God spoke; it produced belief in Abraham's heart; and he obeyed. It is important to point out that these people who are marked by obedience to God's Word did not live perfect lives of faith; they fell short, messed up, and had moments of doubt. But ultimately, they had faith in God's promise. In fact, these stories are less about the faith of men and more about the faithfulness of God.

We should be encouraged as we look at this group of people to see that those who put their faith in God and His Word will not be put to shame. It is also so very important that we realize that this is not talking about having faith in the sense of hoping for things; it is talking about "the faith" by which we are saved. To use any of the verses talking about faith in Hebrews 10, 11, or 12 in any other way is to take the Scripture out of context. Sarah also believed in a promise that God had made, and this promise was also part of the establishment of the righteous line that would eventually bring forth Christ our Savior. Sarah's promise was attached to the promise of the Gospel that was given to her husband Abraham. "By faith Sarah herself received power to conceive, even when she was past the age, since she considered him faithful who had promised. Therefore from one man, and him as good as dead, were born descendants as many as the stars of heaven and as many as the innumerable grains of sand by the seashore" (Heb. 11:11-12).

This is all connected to the promise made to Abraham by which the Lord said through him all nations would be blessed (Gen. 22:18). It is important to also stop here and correct some more very popular bad theology. The blessing of Abraham has nothing to do with you being blessed financially. The blessing of Abraham was that from his righteousness line would come the promised Seed, Whose heel would be bruised as He crushed the head of the serpent. "The LORD God said to the serpent, 'Because you have done this, cursed are you above all livestock and above all beasts of the field; on your belly you shall go, and dust you shall eat all the days of your life. I will put enmity between you and the woman, and between your offspring and her offspring; he shall bruise your head, and you shall bruise his heel'" (Gen. 3:14-15). The blessing of Abraham is Jesus.

This is about the Gospel and the coming Messiah. Even in the book of Galatians, when Paul is rebuking those who were trying to blend the law of works with the covenant of grace, he explains that God actually preached the Gospel to Abraham hundreds of years before Jesus was even born into the earth.

> O foolish Galatians! Who has bewitched you? It was before your eyes that Jesus Christ was publicly portrayed as crucified. Let me ask you only this: Did you receive the Spirit by works of the law or by hearing with faith? Are you so foolish? Having begun by the Spirit, are you now being perfected by the flesh? Did you suffer so many things in vain—if indeed it was in vain? Does he who supplies the Spirit to you and works miracles among you do so by works of the law, or by hearing with faith—just as Abraham "believed God, and it was counted to him as righteousness"? Know then that it is those of faith who are the sons of Abraham. And the Scripture, foreseeing that God would justify the Gentiles by faith, preached the gospel beforehand to Abraham, saying, "In you shall all the nations be blessed." So then, those who are of faith are blessed along with Abraham, the man of faith (Gal. 3:1-9).

They had faith in a coming Messiah as they looked forward to His appearing; we look back at the work done by that same Messiah as we await His second coming. All people who have been, who are, and who will ever be saved have been saved by one Messiah, one Deliverer, and one Savior—and His name is Jesus. This is faith spoken about in Hebrews 11 and throughout the New Testament and in types and shadows all through the Old Testament— saving faith, the faith given once and for all to the saints.

Noah did not see it in its fulness; Abraham did not see it in its fulness; and neither did Sarah or any of the other people mentioned in the "great cloud of witnesses" (Heb. 12:1). We have the Law, the prophets, Jesus, the Gospel, and the entirety of the New Testament; and we also still do not see in fullness the revelation of God's glory in the Gospel in this life. This is why we must live by faith in the Word of the Lord.

The final mark of someone who has saving faith like those mentioned here is that they are living like foreigners and pilgrims who have abandoned their personal kingdom in this life and are living for a future reward and a future city, "whose designer and builder is God" (Heb. 11:10).

> These all died in faith, not having received the things promised, but having seen them and greeted them from afar, and having acknowledged that they were strangers and exiles on the earth. For people who speak thus make it clear that they are seeking a homeland. If they had been thinking of that land from which they had gone out, they would have had opportunity to return. But as it is, they desire a better country, that is, a heavenly one. Therefore God is not ashamed to be called their God, for he has prepared for them a city (Heb. 11:13-16).

The faith mentioned here has to be talking about something beyond having "the Blessed Life" in the here and now because these examples of lives of faith "all died in faith, not having received the things promised" (v. 11). And this is true of every follower of Jesus. "For me to live is Christ and to die is gain" (Phil. 1:21) because we have acknowledged that we are merely strangers and exiles on the earth. We have received the Word of the Lord; and in our hearts, it has produced reverent fear and true belief. This is evidenced externally by the lives we lead in obedience to the Word of the Lord; and finally, we abandon the things of this world, pick up our tent pegs, and live as strangers and exiles as we move "forward to a city that has foundations whose designer and builder is God" (Heb. 11:10).

"By faith Abraham, when he was tested, offered up Isaac, and he who had received the promises was in the act of offering up his only son, of whom it was said, 'Through Isaac shall your offspring be named.' He considered that God was able even to raise him from the dead, from which, figuratively speaking, he did receive him back" (Heb. 11:17-19).

Finally, in the life of Abraham, we see the faith that has matured to the point of trusting the faithfulness of God unto death. This is what the Christian life looks like, giving God everything even and up to death because, ultimately, our faith is in the promise of eternal life. We see this in a type and shadow in the life of Abraham and his precious son, through whom God would fulfill His promise to make Abraham's descendants as innumerable as the stars in the sky and the grains of sand on the seashore.

In Genesis 15, God told Abraham that although he was an old man and his wife was barren, he would bless the world through his seed; and his descendants would be many. This obviously would take a miracle because of the couple's age and the fact that Sarah could not bear children. God wanted to show His power and Sovereignty by declaring what would be before it happened and through the most unlikely of vessels.

Through everything, God kept His promise; and they had a son named Isaac. I am sure that they loved him deeply and dearly after waiting so long for him to come. This is why when God called Abraham to take Isaac and sacrifice him on the mountaintop that this must have been very difficult. I cannot even imagine what it must have been like for Abraham. But Abraham knew something about God—God always keeps His covenant promises. He was convinced that even if Isaac died, God had the power to raise him from the dead.

This is a foreshadowing of God giving His one and only Son for us in the Gospel, and the life of Isaac and Jesus were tethered to either end of this Gospel promise.

> After these things God tested Abraham and said to him, "Abraham!"
> And he said, "Here I am." He said, "Take your son, your only son

Isaac, whom you love, and go to the land of Moriah, and offer him there as a burnt offering on one of the mountains of which I shall tell you." So Abraham rose early in the morning, saddled his donkey, and took two of his young men with him, and his son Isaac. And he cut the wood for the burnt offering and arose and went to the place of which God had told him. On the third day Abraham lifted up his eyes and saw the place from afar. Then Abraham said to his young men, "Stay here with the donkey; I and the boy will go over there and worship and come again to you." And Abraham took the wood of the burnt offering and laid it on Isaac his son. And he took in his hand the fire and the knife. So they went both of them together. And Isaac said to his father Abraham, "My father!" And he said, "Here I am, my son." He said, "Behold, the fire and the wood, but where is the lamb for a burnt offering?" Abraham said, "God will provide for himself the lamb for a burnt offering, my son." So they went both of them together.

When they came to the place of which God had told him, Abraham built the altar there and laid the wood in order and bound Isaac his son and laid him on the altar, on top of the wood. Then Abraham reached out his hand and took the knife to slaughter his son. But the angel of the LORD called to him from heaven and said, "Abraham, Abraham!" And he said, "Here I am." He said, "Do not lay your hand on the boy or do anything to him, for now I know that you fear God, seeing you have not withheld your son, your only son, from me." And Abraham lifted up his eyes and looked, and behold, behind him was a ram, caught in a thicket by his horns. And Abraham went and took the ram and offered it up as a burnt offering instead of his son. So Abraham called the name of that place, "The LORD will provide"; as it is said to this day, "On the mount of the Lord it shall be provided."

And the angel of the LORD called to Abraham a second time from heaven and said, "By myself I have sworn, declares the LORD, because you have done this and have not withheld your son, your only son, I will surely bless you, and I will surely multiply your offspring as the stars of heaven and as the sand that is on the seashore. And your offspring shall possess the gate of his enemies, and in your offspring shall all the nations of the earth be blessed, because you have obeyed my voice." So Abraham returned to his young men, and they arose and went together to Beersheba. And Abraham lived at Beersheba (Gen. 22:1-19).

A true life of faith has laid everything on the altar, knowing that God will keep His promises and that the best place for the things we love is in the hands of God. God gave the life of His only begotten Son so that through Him, we might have eternal life. This is the fulfillment of the promise God made to Abraham. It was in this act that it was clear that God could trust Abraham with anything, even the heir of the promise. Abraham's faith was not in Isaac or himself; it was in the Lord! "By faith Isaac invoked future blessings on Jacob and Esau. By faith Jacob, when dying, blessed each of the sons of Joseph, bowing in worship over the head of his staff. By faith Joseph, at the end of his life, made mention of the exodus of the Israelites and gave directions concerning his bones" (Heb. 11:20-22).

Here we see the continuation of the righteous line as God faithfully ensured that the Gospel would come to pass through the descendants of Abraham, Isaac, and Jacob, which eventually led the Israelites into Egypt, where they were well-taken care of because of God's favor on Joseph. Joseph lived his entire life in Egypt; but when he died, he commanded that his bones not be buried there but instead be buried in the Land of Promise (Gen. 47:30).

THE TREASURE OF CHRIST

"By faith Moses, when he was born, was hidden for three months by his parents, because they saw that the child was beautiful, and they were not afraid of the king's edict" (Heb. 11:23). Joseph, the son of Jacob, eventually became the second most powerful man in Egypt after interpreting the pharaoh's dreams, which helped Egypt survive a devastating famine that would come upon them. Because of God's favor on the life of Joseph, the Hebrews were very blessed in that land. But when Joseph died and his bones were taken back to the Promised Land, eventually, a new pharaoh came into power; and he had no affection toward Joseph or the Hebrews. So eventually, he enslaved them and caused them to work and mistreated them.

It was in this tough environment that Moses was born. During the time of Moses' birth, the pharaoh had decreed that all male Hebrews under the age of two should be killed. Moses' mother, in an attempt to preserve his life, put him in a basket and sent him down the Nile River. He was found by the daughter of the pharaoh, and she took him in as her son. Although Moses was a Hebrew, he grew up in the palace with all of the privilege and prestige of the royal family.

Moses' Hebrew parents, Amram and Jochebed, were people of faith. The Scripture says that they were not afraid of the king's edict, so they risked their lives to save the life of their beautiful baby. Now it is very important to say something here that might not sit well with some of you. Ultimately, the life of Moses was preserved not only because it was his parents' will but, more importantly, because it was the will of God and God had chosen Moses to be the man who delivered His people from Egypt.

True and biblical faith is not about inviting God into your plans; it is about aligning yourself with the Sovereign and perfect will of God Almighty. Eventually, Moses grew up and realized that serving God in suffering was far better than enjoying life in the palace because he had faith in God.

In the sermon Stephen gives right before he is martyred for his faith, he explains that Moses knew he was called by God and that this calling outweighed the fleeting pleasures of the palace:

> At this time Moses was born; and he was beautiful in God's sight. And he was brought up for three months in his father's house, and when he was exposed, Pharaoh›s daughter adopted him and brought him up as her own son. And Moses

was instructed in all the wisdom of the Egyptians, and he was mighty in his words and deeds.

"When he was forty years old, it came into his heart to visit his brothers, the children of Israel. And seeing one of them being wronged, he defended the oppressed man and avenged him by striking down the Egyptian. He supposed that his brothers would understand that God was giving them salvation by his hand, but they did not understand. And on the following day he appeared to them as they were quarreling and tried to reconcile them, saying, 'Men, you are brothers. Why do you wrong each other?' But the man who was wronging his neighbor thrust him aside, saying, 'Who made you a ruler and a judge over us? Do you want to kill me as you killed the Egyptian yesterday?' At this retort Moses fled and became an exile in the land of Midian, where he became the father of two sons.

"Now when forty years had passed, an angel appeared to him in the wilderness of Mount Sinai, in a flame of fire in a bush. When Moses saw it, he was amazed at the sight, and as he drew near to look, there came the voice of the Lord: 'I am the God of your fathers, the God of Abraham and of Isaac and of Jacob.' And Moses trembled and did not dare to look. Then the Lord said to him, 'Take off the sandals from your feet, for the place where you are standing is holy ground. I have surely seen the affliction of my people who are in Egypt, and have heard their groaning, and I have come down to deliver them. And now come, I will send you to Egypt' (Acts 7:20-34).

Moses had heard the Word of the Lord; it produced reverent fear and a man who walked into the palace of the most powerful man in the world, where he demanded the release of the Israelites on behalf of the Lord. It is very important here to acknowledge that Moses did not have faith in something he wanted; he had faith in something God had declared. This is the same with saving faith in Christ or the faith we have in any of the biblical promises

God has made to His children. We can rest our lives and eternities on them because the word of the Lord never fails (Luke 1:37).

> By faith Moses, when he was grown up, refused to be called the son of Pharaoh›s daughter, choosing rather to be mistreated with the people of God than to enjoy the fleeting pleasures of sin. He considered the reproach of Christ greater wealth than the treasures of Egypt, for he was looking to the reward. By faith he left Egypt, not being afraid of the anger of the king, for he endured as seeing him who is invisible. By faith he kept the Passover and sprinkled the blood, so that the Destroyer of the firstborn might not touch them (Heb. 11:24-28).

Listen to what the author of Hebrews says: he chose to be mistreated with God's people "rather than to enjoy the fleeting pleasures of sin"—the pleasures of this temporal world—because he considered reproach for the sake of Christ greater than the treasures of Egypt. He was living for the reward. Without even knowing Who the Messiah would be, Moses knew that being mistreated and treated with reproach for the sake of the future Messiah was more valuable than the treasures of the world. This is still the case for anyone who is being saved by faith in the Word of the Lord.

Moses was looking toward his reward, just like all the other people mentioned in Hebrews 11 were. Moses lived over a thousand years before Christ, but he still was living by faith in a future salvation and a future reward. And that Reward is Christ. The Reward of our faith is Christ. Jesus is the Gift of the Gospel. If you are looking for your faith to produce something beyond being reconciled to God through Christ, you are living your Christian life in vain.

We may humbly seek the hand of God for temporal things; and sometimes, God, in wisdom, will grant them. Other times, He will not; but rest assured that you can trust Him because He sent His Son to die for your salvation and give you eternal life. If that is not enough, then it is probably because you do not really know Christ as your Treasure and Reward. This is the end result of our faith as spoken of in the Bible.

This is the jaw-dropping beauty of Jesus—that God would die in our place, take our reproach and our eternal shame, and exchange it for eternal life. If your faith in God does not cause you to build a life that pleases God as the world mocks and scorns you, your faith is not in a true revelation of Christ. If it does not cause you to lay your life on the altar because you know that God has the power to raise it up again, your faith is not in a true revelation of Christ. If Christ is not a treasure to you worth rejecting the wealth of Egypt or all the wealth of the world because you see Him as worthy of all loss, all sacrifice and worth giving up anything everything, then your faith is not in a true revelation of Christ. It is in something else, and that something will one day pass away. True saving faith—true biblical faith—is that of a life that is lived as exiles and strangers as we pilgrimage in a future city toward the future reward of Christ.

Look at your life and ask these questions: where are the tents? Where are the arks? Where is the evidence that you are pregnant with a faith that supremely controls your life, expectancy like labor pains, filled with the beauty and violence of something longing to give birth? Where is the evidence of something that is alive and real, changes everything, and will change everything as it gets closer and closer, more and more violent, while we are waiting and longing for His appearing? I am talking about Jesus, and He is everything to me!

Where are the men and women of faith willing to live in tents and spend their lives building arks for the glory of Christ and the salvation of many? Faith is inseparable from the Gospel of Jesus Christ. It is inseparable from the Word of God. The one who puts his faith in the Word of the Lord will not be put to shame because the Word of the Lord cannot and will not return void (Isa. 55:11).

We already stated that biblical faith is knowing that we stand justified before God as righteous because of what Christ accomplished on the cross and that God will keep all the promises that He has made in His Word. But you could sum up the definition of biblical faith with a simple question. Are you convinced?

When the apostle Paul wrote the epistle to the Romans, he was sitting in prison. And from behind the walls of his incarceration, he wrote one of the most powerful promises attached to our faith that has ever been penned. He was living under extreme persecution. Like the people the author of Hebrews was writing to, Paul was facing imprisonment, persecution, and even death for their faith. How is it possible to find strength and joy in this unless death is not the end but merely the beginning of our eternity with Christ? Frankly, most of the promises in the New Testament do not make sense if this is not true.

> What then shall we say to these things? If God is for us, who can be against us? He who did not spare his own Son but gave him up for us all, how will he not also with him graciously give us all things? Who shall bring any charge against God›s elect? It is God who justifies. Who is to condemn? Christ Jesus is the one who died—more than that, who was raised—who is at the right hand of God, who indeed is interceding for us. Who shall separate us from the love of Christ? Shall tribulation, or distress, or persecution, or famine, or nakedness, or danger, or sword? As it is written, "For your sake we are being killed all the day long; we are regarded as sheep to be slaughtered" (Rom. 8:31-36).

When all the trials and trouble of this world come upon you, what do you look to? What do you rely on? See, the Bible tells us that Jesus will judge the living and the dead, but we have been made right with God by the Judge Himself. So, how will the One Who died for our sins judge us? Instead, He will give us all things. Remember, we are His co-heirs if we are His co-laborers. So, what can "separate us from the love of God" (Rom. 8:39)? Paul asks rhetorically, "Shall tribulation, or distress, or persecution, or famine, or nakedness, or danger, or sword?" (Rom. 8:35). He acknowledges that many of them are even being killed because of their faith in Christ to the point where he quotes Psalm 44:22: "'For your sake we are being killed all the day long; we are regarded as sheep to be slaughtered'" (Rom. 8:36).

So, if the faith we are talking about is not a guarantee of protection for trial, trouble, suffering, persecution, or even death, then what is our faith in? Our faith should look to the eternal reward of being with Christ. This is what true saving faith actually is. It is God's promise of restoration and salvation in the Gospel; our faith is in Christ alone, and He is enough! From the depths of his prison cell, the apostle Paul was not feeling sorry for himself or looking for a way to escape, he wanted to encourage his persecuted Christian brothers and sisters in Rome to hold fast to the one things that would never fail them. "No, in all these things we are more than conquerors through him who loved us. For I am sure that neither death nor life, nor angels nor rulers, nor things present nor things to come, nor powers, nor height nor depth, nor anything else in all creation, will be able to separate us from the love of God in Christ Jesus our Lord" (Rom. 8:37-39).

I have been using the English Standard Version for most of my Scripture references in this book, but I really like the way the New American Standard renders the beginning of verse thirty-eight: "For I am convinced." Are you convinced? Being convinced means casting your life away for the glory of God because you have no enduring city here but are already living for that future city.

CHAPTER 13

THOSE OF WHOM THE WORLD WAS NOT WORTHY

BY: JOSHUA WEST

They were stoned, they were sawn in two, they were killed with the sword.

They went about in skins of sheep and goats, destitute, afflicted, mistreated—

of whom the world was not worthy—wandering about in deserts and mountains,

and in dens and caves of the earth.

HEBREWS 11:37-38

ONE OF THE MOST IMPORTANT things we need to understand when reading these Old Testament stories is that it really is just one unfolding story of God's interaction with His creation. The great themes of this story are redemption, grace, judgment, love, and salvation. But the ultimate purpose of this story is the same purpose of everything else in creation—to glorify God! All of these stories build upon themselves and only matter in as much as they are part of God's unfolding story. As Matt Chandler said, "God is not a supporting actor in the story of your life, [sic] you are a supporting actor in God's unfolding story."[11]

---

11   Matt Chandler, "God Is For God," Truth Endures, January 17, 2012, YouTube video, 48:08, https://www.youtube.com/watch?v=9yqQuTT1S40.

Many natural factors tie these stories together. Families—like Abraham, Isaac, and Jacob—all lived their lives in the fulfillment of one promise. All of them became men of faith in their individual lives, thus fulfilling their part in the greater story of God. From the better sacrifice given by Abel to God to the help Rahab the prostitute gave the Israelites that were scouting in Jericho, these are pieces of one unfolding story—the story of God. One interesting fact that always makes me happy to think about is that a Gentile prostitute named Rahab was not only saved by her faith; but she also ended up, by the Sovereign hand of God, in the earthly lineage of Jesus.

There is no way to withhold or stifle the Sovereign will of God in Scripture. He made the promise; and through His mighty hand, all His promises will come to pass. Although all the people talked about in Hebrews 11 are intertwined in different ways, the one thing that unites them is faith in God—genuine and saving faith, which is evidenced in many different ways as we look at each of their individual stories.

Throughout the book of Hebrews, we see that our faith is tied to a future reward, which is more valuable and satisfying than anything in this life—the salvation of our souls and eternity with Christ. But the only people who will inherit this are those who have genuine faith. We know our faith is real when it holds up when it is tested.

ONLY A TESTED FAITH IS A GENUINE FAITH

As we look at Hebrews 11, we realize that although these people were all united by saving faith in God, the outcomes of their earthly lives were not all the same. Some had miraculous stories that ended well; others lived in the wilderness in animal skin or were sawed in half because of that faith. This reality is another reason it is apparent that Hebrews is not talking about faith to get what you want but, rather, saving faith in God.

These all died in faith, not having received the things promised, but having seen them and greeted them from afar, and having acknowledged that they were strangers and exiles on the earth. For people who speak thus make it clear that they are seeking a homeland. If they had been thinking of that land from which they had gone out, they would have had opportunity to return. But as it is, they desire a better country, that is, a heavenly one. Therefore God is not ashamed to be called their God, for he has prepared for them a city (Heb. 11:13-16).

What is most important to Jesus is that we are "complete, lacking nothing" (James 1:4); and the Bible says that God works out the image of His Son in us more often than not through trial and suffering. This is for the saving of our souls and to refine us down into something pure and true.

Blessed be the God and Father of our Lord Jesus Christ! According to his great mercy, he has caused us to be born again to a living hope through the resurrection of Jesus Christ from the dead, to an inheritance that is imperishable, undefiled, and unfading, kept in heaven for you, who by God›s power are being guarded through faith for a salvation ready to be revealed in the last time. In this you rejoice, though now for a little while, if necessary, you have been grieved by various trials, so that the tested genuineness of your faith—more precious than gold that perishes though it is tested by fire—may be found to result in praise and glory and honor at the revelation of Jesus Christ. Though you have not seen him, you love him. Though you do not now see him, you believe in him and rejoice with joy that is inexpressible and filled with glory, obtaining the outcome of your faith, the salvation of your souls (1 Peter 1:3-9).

James, the half-brother of Jesus, also addressed this in his epistle: "Count it all joy, my brothers, when you meet trials of various kinds, for you know that the testing of your faith produces steadfastness. And let steadfastness have its full effect, that you may be perfect and complete, lacking in nothing" (James 1:2-4).

Something we have to realize about the refining process in the testing of our faith is that the test does not change us; it merely exposes who we really are. Remember that "without faith it is impossible to please [God]" (Heb. 11:6); the testing of our faith shows us the state of our hearts—just like when Abraham laid Isaac on the altar because God told him to proved that Abraham's faith in God was genuine, "even to the point of death" (Phil. 2:8). If your faith is not worth dying for, it is not worth living for either.

Saying your faith is in Jesus for salvation when it does not affect your life shows that your confession of faith is just empty words. Only those who truly believe that Jesus is "'the resurrection, and the life'" (John 11:25) are willing to lay down their own lives.

Testing gold does not make it genuine or counterfeit; it merely reveals the truth of the matter. Jesus is the Light that casts out darkness and exposes the truth. If you have true saving faith, God is going to test it and refine it and burn up the dross (Isa. 1:25) until nothing is left but a pure life of faith.

GENUINE FAITH LIVES FOR AN ETERNAL TREASURE, NOT A WORLDLY ONE

"By faith Moses, when he was grown up, refused to be called the son of Pharaoh's daughter, choosing rather to be mistreated with the people of God than to enjoy the fleeting pleasures of sin. He considered the reproach of Christ greater wealth than the treasures of Egypt, for he was looking to the reward" (Heb. 11:24-26). Genuine faith does not chase fortune, fame, prestige, power, wealth, security, or comfort because genuine faith has already found its treasure in Christ; and a life of genuine faith produces a life of faithfulness. Hebrews 11:32-34 tells us, "And what more shall I say? For time would fail me to tell of Gideon, Barak, Samson, Jephthah, of David and Samuel and the prophets—who through faith conquered kingdoms, enforced justice, obtained promises, stopped the mouths of lions, quenched the power of fire, escaped the edge of the sword, were made strong out of weakness, became mighty in war, put foreign armies to flight" (Heb. 11:32-34).

These are the ones we like to talk about when we try to use Hebrews 11 as a narrative of worldly victory and worldly success because it talks about conquering kingdoms and earthly victories, like Daniel in the lion's den and the three Hebrew boys who survived the fiery furnace. But how quickly do we forget the words of those young men as they stood by faith and opposed the king?

If you do not know the story, go and read Daniel 3. In summary, Shadrach, Meshach, and Abednego were young Jewish men who had been exiled to Babylon. While there, King Nebuchadnezzar had a golden idol made and set up to honor him; and it was commanded that when the music played, every person was to bow down and worship the image made in honor of the king.

Because they served God, Shadrach, Meshach, and Abednego refused to bow; and the author of Hebrews references this in his discourse on saving faith in Hebrews 11. This was a tested faith. Anyone who did not bow was to be burned alive in a fiery furnace.

Daniel 3:16-18 says:

> Shadrach, Meshach, and Abednego answered and said to the king, "O Nebuchadnezzar, we have no need to answer you in this matter. If this be so, our God whom we serve is able to deliver us from the burning fiery furnace, and he will deliver us out of your hand, O king. But if not, be it known to you, O king, that we will not serve your gods or worship the golden image that you have set up."

They did not have faith because it was a guarantee that God would preserve their lives; their faith was in something beyond this life because they loved and feared God more than they feared man. They were thrown into the furnace; but God miraculously saved them, and their lives were saved as their faith was tested and proven genuine—not because they were saved from the fiery furnace but because they would not bow either way.

As we look at the last section of Hebrews 11, we see that some of the lives of faith mentioned there ended differently than that of the Hebrews boys mentioned in Daniel. The outcome of many of these lives of faith ended in trial, suffering, and death.

> Women received back their dead by resurrection. Some were tortured, refusing to accept release, so that they might rise again to a better life. Others suffered mocking and flogging, and even chains and imprisonment. They were stoned, they were sawn in two, they were killed with the sword. They went about in skins of sheep and goats, destitute, afflicted, mistreated—of whom the world was not worthy—wandering about in deserts and mountains, and in dens and caves of the earth. And all these, though commended through their faith, did not receive what was promised, since God had provided something better for us, that apart from us they should not be made perfect (Heb. 11:35-40).

These people are mentioned in the same high regard as Moses and Abraham; but these people are commended because they clung to their faith as they were tortured and killed, refusing release because they were living by faith. All things in life are for the glory of God and that "'[His] kingdom come, [His] will be done, on earth as it is in heaven'" (Matt. 6:10). Sometimes, God is most glorified when His children are saved from a fiery furnace or when a woman's child is raised from the dead, like in the case where Elijah brought the child of the widow of Zarephath back to life (1 Kings 17:8-23) or when his successor Elisha did the same for the Shunammite woman's son in 2 Kings 4:18-37. But other times, God is most glorified when His children suffer and even lose their lives for Him. Remember, God did not even spare His own Son, so why would we think we are any different?

This is a concept that Word of Faith types will do anything to avoid acknowledging because their superimposed theology of blessing, health, and wealth will not allow for it. Many have suffered for their faith in the Bible as well throughout the course of church history. Many Christians were tortured and refused release, rather than denying their faith. Others have been mocked, flogged, imprisoned, and chained for the sake of their faith or even stoned to death because of the Gospel.

This was the story of Stephen, who was stoned to death because of his faith. Paul was stoned, beaten, imprisoned, and eventually killed because of Christ. He describes what he endured in his letter to the Philippians: "I want you to know, brothers, that what has happened to me has really served to advance the gospel, so that it has become known throughout the whole imperial guard and to all the rest that my imprisonment is for Christ. And most of the brothers, having become confident in the Lord by my imprisonment, are much more bold to speak the word without fear" (Phil. 1:12-14).

Genuine faith will gladly bear reproach, shame, and suffering for the sake of Christ and to be identified with Christ. If you are ashamed of being identified with Christ to the point of suffering or death, it is because you are not of Christ nor in Christ, and Christ is not in you.

Second Timothy 3:12 even tells us, "Indeed, all who desire to live a godly life in Christ Jesus will be persecuted." Persecution is refining evidence that you are actually living the godly life in Christ, and your faith in God's promise has equipped you for this. If you are truly saved, you will endure and preserve to the end because the Spirit of God living in you will empower you to do so. "He who promised is faithful" (Heb. 10:23). This "so great a cloud of witnesses" mentioned in Hebrews 12:1 is commended not because they are great heroes of the faith or because they did great things for God but because they obeyed God as evidence that they were living by faith, and they did not love their lives even unto death.

They lived by faith as they forwarded the will of the Lord in obedience. Some of them looked victorious in this life, and some did not as they suffered and died. But they all endured the trial and, in the end, were all victorious because they put their faith in God. And they all received the same reward— the crown of righteousness, the crown of life.

The author of Hebrews says that these were men and women "of whom the world was not worthy" (Heb. 11:38) because they were living according to the promises of God by faith. These people did not deserve the pain and suffering that they received, but they gladly accepted it because their great desire was to be identified with Christ. Those who want to identify with Christ in the resurrection must also, by faith, be willing to identify with Him in His sufferings and shame.

> Indeed, I count everything as loss because of the surpassing worth of knowing Christ Jesus my Lord. For his sake I have suffered the loss of all things and count them as rubbish, in order that I may gain Christ and be found in him, not having a righteousness of my own that comes from the law, but that which comes through faith in Christ, the righteousness from God that depends on faith—that I may know him and the power of his resurrection, and may share his sufferings, becoming like him in his death, that by any means possible I may attain the resurrection from the dead (Phil. 3:8-11).

True saving faith is willing to sacrifice any and everything in this life to have salvation in Christ. Salvation is a free gift from God, so we do not earn it by suffering or sacrifice; these things are merely evidence that what we say with our mouths is actually true. If Christ is truly the Treasure of your life, it will be clearly seen as you willfully and joyously lay down everything else in honor of Him. Abraham laid Isaac on the altar because Christ was his Treasure, and Moses suffered alongside the people of God because Christ was his Treasure. Paul and most of the apostles were martyred because Christ was their Treasure. Men and women throughout history have suffered for

Christ, and they will share in the same reward as all the people mentioned in Hebrews 11.

THE GOSPEL-TRANSFORMED LIFE

Jesus gives a clear pathway and understanding of what this faith looks like as it unfolds in the life of the believer in the Beatitudes portion of the Sermon on the Mount. He first explains the condition of what a true life of faith will look like at the heart level in Matthew 5:3-6: "'Blessed are the poor in spirit, for theirs is the kingdom of heaven. Blessed are those who mourn, for they shall be comforted. Blessed are the meek, for they shall inherit the earth. Blessed are those who hunger and thirst for righteousness, for they shall be satisfied.'"

Jesus tells us that those who will inherit the kingdom of Heaven will be those who are "poor in spirit" and realize that they are spiritually bankrupt and hopeless apart from God. They realize that it is only by faith in God that salvation is possible for them. True believers have to first come to the painful understanding that their goodness is not good enough. Seeing that our goodness is not enough, we mourn and repent of our sins. God promises that those who truly mourn will be comforted. Here is where it gets tricky, though. Everyone in life mourns the consequences of their sin, but only the man or woman of faith mourns sin itself. It is these people God will save by faith.

Saving faith also produces meekness. Jesus says, "'Blessed are the meek, for they shall inherit the earth'" (v. 5). It is only those who meekly put their trust in God who will inherit the earth along with Christ. The world despises the idea of meekness. Most people are doing whatever it takes to get what they want to have the best job or the most money or to climb the corporate ladder by any means necessary. The motto of the world is not "the meek will inherit the earth"; it is only the strong who survive, the cream that rises to the top.

We are meek because we believe that no matter what things look like now, in the end, Christ will rule the world; His enemies will be put underneath His feet; and those of us who put our faith in Him will inherit the earth along with Him. This is not because we were cunning, smart, strong, or worldly wise but because we believe that Christ is King. And because we believe, we have bowed the knee to Him in this life so that we can be part of His kingdom in the life to come. Those who recognize they are poor in spirit, mourn over their sin, and meekly put their trust in the Lord will also hunger and thirst to be right with God. And God promises they will be satisfied. "'Blessed are the merciful, for they shall receive mercy. Blessed are the pure in heart, for they shall see God. Blessed are the peacemakers, for they shall be called sons of God. Blessed are those who are persecuted for righteousness' sake, for theirs is the kingdom of heaven'" (Matt. 5:7-10).

These are the ones who walk by saving faith in Christ, and the external evidence of that is that they will be merciful and pure in heart. They will be peacemakers and will be persecuted for it. Because they are right with God, they will suffer persecution. Remember what it said about Noah's obedience to God and the impact it had on those around him in Hebrews 11: "By faith Noah, being warned by God concerning events as yet unseen, in reverent fear constructed an ark for the saving of his household. By this he condemned the world and became an heir of the righteousness that comes by faith" (Heb. 11:7).

His obedience to God's Word not only saved him but also condemned the world around him. A true life of faith will condemn those rejecting Christ all around us as we build the ark of our lives by faith, all the while telling those who mock us and scorn us that there is room on the ark for them, too.

Matthew 5:12 says, "'Blessed are you when others revile you and persecute you and utter all kinds of evil against you falsely on my account. Rejoice and be glad, for your reward is great in heaven, for so they persecuted the prophets who were before you.'" Jesus makes it clear in His sermon—just like the author of Hebrews does—that this has always been the pattern of a true life of faith.

They persecuted the prophets for the same reason that they will persecute us—because we boldly proclaim and live in obedience to the Word of the Lord. The world hates the idea that we obey simply because of the phrase, "Thus saith the Lord." But for the true believer, this is refining us and conforming to the image of Christ; it is making us more and more dependent on Him, and it is growing our faith. This faith says that we are "sealed for the day of redemption" (Eph. 4:30) and that God is continually working "all things . . . together for good of those who are called according to His purpose" (Rom. 8:28).

In this life, our faith will be tested; and storms and trials will come. But if your life is built on the solid Foundation of Christ, His Gospel, and His Word, nothing will ever be able to snatch us from His hand (John 10:28), "separate us from the love of God" (Rom. 8:39), or "put us to shame" (Rom. 5:5). To have a faith that stands up to resting without failing is the desire of every true follower of Christ. And it is my desire to serve well, suffer well, and live well in honor and obedience to the God Who saved me and gave me eternal life. This is what my faith is in—a future reward that will never pass away and that is worth more than all the treasures of this world. Maranatha!

CHAPTER 14

DON'T GROW WEARY

BY: JOSHUA WEST

Therefore, since we are surrounded by so great a cloud of witnesses, let us also lay aside every weight, and sin which clings so closely, and let us run with endurance the race that is set before us, looking to Jesus, the founder and perfecter of our faith, who for the joy that was set before him endured the cross, despising the shame, and is seated at the right hand of the throne of God.

HEBREWS 12:1-2

THE CALLS TO "RUN WITH endurance the race that is set before us" in Hebrews and "not grow weary" in Galatians 6:9 are not calls that are given unaccompanied by the power to do it. First, we have evidence and examples of many who have gone before us. Hebrews 12:1 calls these people "a great cloud of witnesses." We have them in Scripture, but we also have them in our lives—people who have lived their lives by faith as examples for us to follow. There is nothing wrong with looking to an earthly example as long as we understand that they also are merely fallen humans who have been saved by grace and do not follow them at the expense of the Scripture. Paul himself said, "Be imitators of me, as I am of Christ" (1 Cor. 11:1). And so, we follow the example of godly people that God has placed in our lives.

Ultimately, we look to the supreme Example that has been given to us—Jesus Himself. In verse one, the author of Hebrews urges us to focus on the fact that since we do have this "great cloud of witnesses" as an example of what saving faith looks like, we should respond to that by first and foremost laying down all sin, which "clings so closely" (ESV) or "so easily besets us" (KJV) so we can finish this life well.

The call to resist and fight the sin in our life has nothing to do with whether or not we are justified before God; this is assuming that we are believers and that we want to live lives that please God. In order to run the race more effectively, we should mortify, lay down, and actively work at getting rid of the sin in our life. But obvious sin is not the only thing that holds us back in life. The Scripture says, "Let us lay aside every weight, and sin that clings so closely" (v. 1). So, there are some things that might not necessarily be a sin but still are not beneficial for running the race effectively.

Often, we focus on the fact that we need to lay down things in this life, but we do not focus on why. We look at the problem without focusing on the solution. We should look to the "great cloud of witnesses" that show us people have been saved through faith since the beginning because they trusted in God's Word. And because we have witnessed their race, we lay aside anything that is holding us back from the freedom that comes from following Jesus. But ultimately, we must look to Jesus because not only is He our great Example of what a perfect life of obedience to the Father looks like, but He is also "the founder and perfecter of our faith" (v. 2). We are saved by all that Christ did in the past—living a perfect life, dying on the cross, and rising from the grave. But He is also currently perfecting us by the power of His Holy Spirit. He is currently interceding for us and advocating for us at the right hand of the Father. Holding fast to this, we confidently forward His name, His Gospel, His will, and His kingdom on the earth, knowing that He will one day return to redeem us and perfect us physically and permanently.

The people mentioned in Hebrews 11 endured by faith to the saving of their souls—not because they were strong, smart, keen, or special but because they were looking forward to Jesus. Abraham was looking forward to Jesus as he lived in tents and waited on the promise of the Lord. Moses chose to suffer along with the people of God rather than enjoy the riches of the Egyptian palace and the fleeting pleasures of sin because he considered the reproach of Christ greater wealth than the treasures of Egypt.

As we look to Jesus, we see His willingness to suffer for the joy that was set before Him. The people mentioned in Hebrews 11 were looking forward to the reward, to a future city whose builder and maker is God, they were living by faith toward Christ. So, what was Jesus looking forward to? He was looking forward "for the joy that was set before Him" (v. 2). Because of that joy, He "endured the cross" (v. 2); and now, after defeating death, hell, and the grave, "he said, 'It is finished'" (John 19:30) and sat down at the right hand of God. The joy of Christ is the redemption of you and me.

John Owen once said, "The duties God requires of us are not in proportion to the strength we possess in ourselves. Rather, they are proportional to the resources available to us in Christ."[12] We should look at this "great cloud of witnesses" as examples of fragile, sinful, broken human beings, just like you and me, who were justified and imputed with Christ's righteousness by faith. These are examples to help remind us to keep our eyes fixed on Jesus. So, in this, we rest.

DON'T GROW WEARY

> Consider him who endured from sinners such hostility against himself, so that you may not grow weary or fainthearted. In your struggle against sin you have not yet resisted to the point of shedding your blood. And have you forgotten the exhortation

---

12   John Owen, *Exposition of Hebrews, Volume 6* (Seymour: Banner Publishing, republished 1992).

that addresses you as sons? "My son, do not regard lightly the discipline of the Lord, nor be weary when reproved by him. For the Lord disciplines the one he loves, and chastises every son whom he receives" (Heb. 12:3-6).

While it is true to say that we rest in the finished work of Christ, it is also true to say that we wrestle. That is why Paul says in Ephesians 6:12, "For we do not wrestle against flesh and blood, but against the rulers, against the authorities, against the cosmic powers over this present darkness, against the spiritual forces of evil in the heavenly places." We rest, and we strive at the same time. We do not strive in justification. We do not strive to be accepted by God; we do not strive to be saved. We are saved by the finished work of Christ. So we rest in that fact. But because we are justified, we strive to rid ourselves of sin.

I like to say it this way: those who truly rest in Christ will wrestle with their flesh and strive to lay down their sin, and those who rest in their sin will wrestle against their security in Christ. It is because we rest in the surety of the salvation secured by Christ that we wrestle with our sins. Your attitude toward sin says a lot about the condition of your heart, your love for the Savior, and to what degree you truly value Christ as the ultimate Treasure of your life. We do fight and wrestle against our sin and strive toward the mark, but we do not do this in our own power.

May we be able to say with Paul, "I have fought the good fight, I have finished the race, I have kept the faith. Henceforth there is laid up for me the crown of righteousness, which the Lord, the righteous judge, will award to me on that day, and not only to me but also to all who have loved his appearing" (2 Tim. 4:7-8). We strive and wrestle daily, but we find our rest in Christ. We do not find our comfort, our rest, our security, or our joy in money, power, position, relationships, or achievements. We also strive not to rest in our burdens and sin that slow us as we run the race of this life. We find our rest in Christ alone and the promise of the prize that we are running toward.

The aim of our wrestling is rest, and we wrestle against the lies told to us by the devil, our flesh, and this fallen world. They lie and tell us that they have a better rest than that which we find in Christ.

We run the race, fight the good fight, strive, and wrestle from a spiritual place of rest, trusting that Christ has secured our victory. Hebrews is a book that calls for Christian suffering and patient endurance in this life but also offers spiritual rest and, in the end, guarantees victory for those who find their rest in Christ. That is why when the author of Hebrews says, "so that you may not grow weary" (v. 3), he is not saying it from a place of well-wishing hope or vague encouragement but instead with a promise from God Himself. Do not shrink back, hold fast, or grow weary because those who put their trust in Christ will find rest and strength.

Hebrews teaches us that the Christian life is not solely about the here and now, but it is also not escapism. Christianity is not about comfort and has no place for cowardice. It is about faith in suffering, endurance, and ultimately victory. God rarely removes the trial from our life; but instead, He equips us with His all-sufficient grace. And if you are truly saved by grace and reborn in Christ, His grace will be more than enough.

> So to keep me from becoming conceited because of the surpassing greatness of the revelations, a thorn was given me in the flesh, a messenger of Satan to harass me, to keep me from becoming conceited. Three times I pleaded with the Lord about this, that it should leave me. But he said to me, "My grace is sufficient for you, for my power is made perfect in weakness." Therefore I will boast all the more gladly of my weaknesses, so that the power of Christ may rest upon me. For the sake of Christ, then, I am content with weaknesses, insults, hardships, persecutions, and calamities. For when I am weak, then I am strong (2 Cor. 12:7-10).

True freedom comes in the Christian life when you are able to trust in the Providence and Sovereignty of God in suffering, letting Him train and discipline you, as He produces the peaceful fruit of righteousness. "'The Lord disciplines the one he loves'" (Heb. 12:6), those who truly belong to Him. Discipline does not only mean correction of wrongdoing but also training for the sake of development. God has purposed to equip us for every good work and to conform us to the image of His Son, and this is no light matter.

> It is for discipline that you have to endure. God is treating you as sons. For what son is there whom his father does not discipline? If you are left without discipline, in which all have participated, then you are illegitimate children and not sons. Besides this, we have had earthly fathers who disciplined us and we respected them. Shall we not much more be subject to the Father of spirits and live? For they disciplined us for a short time as it seemed best to them, but he disciplines us for our good, that we may share his holiness. For the moment all discipline seems painful rather than pleasant, but later it yields the peaceful fruit of righteousness to those who have been trained by it (Heb. 12:7-11).

When it is happening, all discipline seems painful; but later, it produces fruit. This is true in raising children; this is true in sports; this is true in dieting. God is training us, molding us, and forging us in His refining fire, and all of this is because He loves us and because He knows that it produces the peaceful fruit of righteousness. God disciplines those who belong to Him. True peace comes in the Christian life once you believe and accept that, ultimately, God is in control of all things—the good, the bad, and the ugly. Although this refining process seems painful for a time, we trust that God is using it for our good and to conform us to the image of Christ; and eventually, it will produce the peaceful fruit of righteousness. The heart-examining question you have to ask yourself is do you want to be conformed to the image of Christ by any means possible and any means necessary? Paul tells us why he was willing to endure trials in Philippians 3:10-11: "That I may know him and the power of his resurrection, and may share his sufferings, becoming like him in his death, that by any means possible I may attain the resurrection from the dead."

The same ones who truly hunger and thirst to be right with God are the same ones who want to obtain the resurrection from the dead by any means necessary. These are also the same ones who want to be conformed to the image of Christ, to be free from sin, and to bring glory to their Father in Heaven. These are God's elect! They are at peace in righteousness because their trust is in the Sovereignty of the Lord.

In Exodus 4:11, we read, "Then the LORD said to him, 'Who has made man's mouth? Who makes him mute, or deaf, or seeing, or blind? Is it not I, the Lord?'" It is in the all-knowing, all-powerful, all-sufficient, never-failing Sovereignty of God we put our trust in. Despite what our eyes and feelings tell us, we trust in the Word of the Lord and in His promises to us. The only reason this is not enough for you is if your faith is actually built on something other than the promise of God's eternal grace in the Gospel. You will be let down if your faith is in your hope that God will answer one of your prayers according to your will; that because you are a Christian you will not suffer loss, pain, or suffering; or your faith is in anything other than the finished work of Christ on the cross.

In Hebrews 12:12-13, we read, "Therefore lift your drooping hands and strengthen your weak knees, and make straight paths for your feet, so that what is lame may not be put out of joint but rather be healed." Do not grow weary as you strive toward the mark of faith! Do not grow weary as your loving Father in Heaven disciplines you and conforms you to the image of Christ. We all have trials and shortcomings and things that expose our weaknesses and need for God in this life. So, if you cannot find the grace of God in your trial, it might mean you have not experienced the saving grace of God in the Gospel or that, as a true believer, you have taken your eyes off Jesus as your Source, Power, Purpose, and the Treasure of your faith. If you cannot see the grace of God working in your life in your battle with cancer, the loss of your job, a physical disability, unfair treatment, the loss of a loved one, and all brands of Christian suffering, it means that you do not believe Romans 8:28, which says, "And we know that for those who love God all things work together for good, for those who are called according to his purpose."

This does not mean loss and suffering do not hurt and that we do not mourn or feel the pain; it simply means that we do not suffer and mourn as those without the blessed hope do. We all have a thorn in our flesh (2 Cor. 12:7-10); and for those of us who live by saving faith in Christ, it magnifies the unfailing truth that His grace is sufficient.

God is immensely more concerned with the state of your heart than He is with your level of comfort. God uses trials and suffering to conform us to the image of Christ. He uses thorns in the flesh to keep us from pride and to showcase that "'[His] grace is sufficient for you, for [His] power is made perfect in weakness'" (2 Cor. 12:9). The power of the Gospel is Jesus plus nothing else! Christ is enough. The deeper this knowledge is worked into us, the more we will "walk by faith, not by sight" (2 Cor. 5:7), the flesh, or the worldly wisdom of this fallen world.

Here is the truth—we only grow weary because we are striving in our own power, sometimes in our own direction, and often in our own strength. This is because we have our affection on things other than glorifying Christ. When we believe we are strong apart from God, we expose that we are blind to the reality that it is through the Spirit of God that "*we live and move and have our being*" (Acts 17:28).

BITTER ROOTS

"Strive for peace with everyone, and for the holiness without which no one will see the Lord. See to it that no one fails to obtain the grace of God; that no 'root of bitterness' springs up and causes trouble, and by it many become defiled" (Heb. 12:14-15). Because of the cross, we are now at peace with God and counted as holy and righteous in the sight of God. So because of this, we should strive for peace with everyone—those who are in Christ, those who deny Christ, our friends, our loved ones, even our enemies. This does not mean that to be at peace with others, we disobey God's Word, withhold preaching the truth, or withhold speaking the truth about sin and God's righteous requirements to have peace. That is simply foolish. This means that in areas and with things that do not cause us to sin or condone the sin of others, we strive to be at peace with everyone. As Martin Luther said, "Peace, if possible, truth at all costs."

It is typically when we are focused on ourselves and worldly things—rather than Jesus, His Word, and pointing others toward His grace—that we become defiled. We become bitter, jealous, and angry toward others when we are living for this world and the things we have or want, rather than God. We become entangled in things that have nothing to do with bringing glory to God; drawing others to God; and forwarding His Gospel, His will, and His kingdom.

If we are not at peace with people because we are boldly standing for God's Word, we are not in disobedience. We are commanded to hold fast to the entirety of the Scripture, to preach it boldly and unapologetically, and to keep ourselves free from sin. But let us be honest; often, this is not the reason that we are not at peace with others in our lives. Often, it is because of our flesh and pride. Bitter actions come from bitter roots. These are parts of our life that we have not submitted to the Lordship of Christ.

There is holiness without which no one will see God, and we are only seen as holy in the sight of God if we have been imputed with the righteousness of Christ. We might show ourselves as unholy by how we value our inherence in Christ. Those who are truly saved value saving faith more than anything else in this life and in this world. The author in Hebrews uses Esau as an example of someone who had worldly sorrow because of the reality of their loss but did not truly have godly repentance. "That no one is sexually immoral or unholy like Esau, who sold his birthright for a single meal. For you know that afterward, when he desired to inherit the blessing, he was rejected, for he found no chance to repent, though he sought it with tears" (Heb. 12:16-17).

Paul warned the Corinthian church about worldly grief in 2 Corinthians 7:10: "For godly grief produces a repentance that leads to salvation without regret, whereas worldly grief produces death." This is the epitome of living for the here and now, and this is the opposite of living for a future with God. This is what rejecting the Gospel looks like as an object lesson from the Old Testament. To reject the Gospel for any reason in this life is like trading your birthright and inheritance for a bowl of soup because you are hungry; it is like trading a winning lottery ticket for a dollar so you can buy a soda or trading your house for a blanket because you are cold. This is what it is like when we choose anything over Jesus.

"'For what does it profit a man to gain the whole world and forfeit his soul? For what can a man give in return for his soul? For whoever is ashamed of me and of my words in this adulterous and sinful generation, of him will the Son of Man also be ashamed when he comes in the glory of his Father with the holy angels'" (Mark 8:36-38). There will come a day when people will "seek Christ with tears"; and on this day, it will be too late. On the Day of Judgment, the Lord Jesus Christ will judge the living and the dead; and those who rejected Him in this life will be sent away *"into the outer darkness . . . there will be weeping and gnashing of teeth"* (Matt. 25:30). Although they will seek it with tears, they will find no chance to repent because the time of Christ as Savior will have passed; and now, they stand before Christ the righteous Judge.

We also see this in the parable of the talents in Matthew 25. A certain master was going on a trip; and before he went, he gave three of his servants talents, which was basically a certain amount of money, for each of them to invest based on their ability. To one servant, he gives five talents; to one, he gives two; and to the other servant, he gives one talent. The first two invested the money they had received, and each of them doubled their investment. But the third servant buried his talent instead and did not put it to use. When the master returned, he was pleased with the first two servants, and he responded the same way to both of them: "'His master said to him, *Well done, good and faithful servant. You have been faithful over a little; I will set you over much. Enter into the joy of your master'"* (Matt. 25:23).

But the master was very upset with the third servant because he wasted his talent and did nothing with it. The response of the master was the same response that Jesus will give to those who did not make the most of the opportunity to live for Him in this life: *"And cast the worthless servant into the outer darkness. In that place there will be weeping and gnashing of teeth'"* (Matt. 25:30).

Although many pastors have taken this parable out of context over the years and used it to try and motivate Christians to use their talents for God and for the Church, this is not what the parable is talking about. No one is going to be cast into outer darkness, which is talking about Hell, because they did not meet their full potential in Christian service. If you believe that sort of works-based theology is true, you have serious theological problems in your understanding of justification.

This parable is a warning not to waste your life! The biggest waste of a life is one that does not acknowledge and worship Jesus as King and Lord. So if you hear His voice calling out in the wilderness, "do not harden your [heart]'" in rebellion (Heb. 4:7). Surrender to the Gospel, heed His voice, and be saved. For those who have heeded the heralding of the Gospel call to repent, do not grow weary because you are not running your race in vain.

A KINGDOM THAT CANNOT BE SHAKEN

"Therefore let us be grateful for receiving a kingdom that cannot be shaken, and thus let us offer to God acceptable worship, with reverence and awe, for our God is a consuming fire" (Heb. 12:28-29).

For those of us who have been saved by God's amazing grace, we no longer walk by the flesh; we are no longer under the Law; and we have been grafted by blood into "a kingdom that cannot be shaken" and will never come to an end. We are saved into the eternal family of God, and we share in the birthright of Christ because He made a way for us.

For you have not come to what may be touched, a blazing fire and darkness and gloom and a tempest and the sound of a trumpet and a voice whose words made the hearers beg that no further messages be spoken to them. For they could not endure the order that was given, "If even a beast touches the mountain, it shall be stoned." Indeed, so terrifying was the sight that Moses said, "I tremble with fear" (Heb. 12:18-21).

In the book of Exodus, when Moses went up the mountain to receive the Law of God, the environment was terrifying, as it should have been. When sinful people come in contact with a holy God, it is terrifying. Darkness, gloom, and the tempest-like sound of the voice of God were so terrifying that it made the people who heard it beg that they would not hear it anymore. Even Moses, the man called and chosen by God, said that he himself trembled with fear. This is the relationship of mankind and God apart from the saving work of Christ on the cross. His presence brings fear, judgment, condemnation, and only death. The Law of God means death for sinful mankind. As Romans 6:23 says, "For the wages of sin is death, but the free gift of God is eternal life in Christ Jesus our Lord."

When Moses came down from the mountain with the Ten Commandments, he came with evidence against all of humanity, which exposed God's holy character, man's hopeless nature, and the need for a Savior. There is only one outcome for those who live under the Law, and that is death. Whether you live a good life or a bad life, accomplish many important things or accomplish nothing, attend church or do not, apart from Christ, you are damned because of sin under the Law.

But you have come to Mount Zion and to the city of the living God, the heavenly Jerusalem, and to innumerable angels in festal gathering, and to the assembly of the firstborn who are enrolled in heaven, and to God, the judge of all, and to the spirits of the righteous made perfect, and to Jesus, the mediator of a new covenant, and to the sprinkled blood that speaks a better word than the blood of Abel (Heb. 12:22-24).

For those of us who are in Christ, we have come to a different mountain. We are part of the kingdom of God; we have a blessed hope of eternal life in the heavenly Jerusalem, amongst festal gatherings with angels, in the assembly and presence of "the firstborn of the dead" (Col. 1:18), Who is Jesus Christ. We are under a better covenant because of the blood of Jesus, which the author of Hebrews says speaks a better word than the blood of Abel.

Abel was killed because of the sin of his brother, Cain. Cain and Abel both brought sacrifices to the Lord. Abel's was accepted, and Cain's was rejected. Abel's sacrifice was pleasing to God, and Cain's was not.

> Now Abel was a keeper of sheep, and Cain a worker of the ground. In the course of time Cain brought to the LORD an offering of the fruit of the ground, and Abel also brought of the firstborn of his flock and of their fat portions. And the LORD had regard for Abel and his offering, but for Cain and his offering he had no regard. So Cain was very angry, and his face fell. The LORD said to Cain, "Why are you angry, and why has your face fallen? If you do well, will you not be accepted? And if you do not do well, sin is crouching at the door. Its desire is contrary to you, but you must rule over it" (Gen. 4:2-7).

God did not treat Cain harshly; in fact, He gave him correction and a warning. In this moment, if Cain would have humbled himself and obeyed, he would have been accepted. The correction was that Cain would be accepted if he brought an offering that was in line with what God obviously had commanded and expected. The warning was that if he continued in his anger that "sin is crouching at the door" (v. 7). If he would have humbled himself, he could have taken rule over it. If his heart would have been to please God rather than being jealous of his brother, he would have obeyed.

But instead, he rejected God's counsel and hardened His heart. We know this is true because of what happened next:

> Cain spoke to Abel his brother. And when they were in the field, Cain rose up against his brother Abel and killed him. Then the Lord said to Cain, "Where is Abel your brother?" He said, "I do not know; am I my brother›s keeper?" And the Lord said, "What have you done? The voice of your brother›s blood is crying to me from the ground. And now you are cursed from the ground, which has opened its mouth to receive your brother›s blood from your hand" (Gen. 4:8-11).

This is what the curse of sin produces on every level—death. This was the first record in the Bible of sin actually producing physical death. Going forward, eventually, every person born of a woman would die from murder, accidents, sickness, or old age; but either way, it would be "appointed for man to die once" (Heb. 9:27). The blood of Abel cried out for justice, just like every other sin committed from the Garden of Eden until today does. The blood of every person ever killed, the blood of every baby murdered in the womb, the sin of every evil ever committed in the history of the world, like the innocent blood of Abel, cries out for justice. And that justice is coming for every single sin, big or small, committed by every single person ever born. It is being stored up by God on the mountain of the Law of God, which will be evidence against us all. We will see the righteous wrath and judgment of God as He administers perfect justice.

So, while the blood of Abel cries out for unrequited justice, the blood of Jesus speaks a better word. While Abel's blood cries out for justice, the blood of Jesus cries out *with* justice. This is the mountain of Zion, the mountain of the New Covenant, the mountain of grace. The wrath of God was still satisfied, but it was satisfied with the blood of Christ.

The attributes and character of the Triune God are unchanging. We see God's patience, mercy, and grace all through the Old Testament as He deals with the Israelites as they rebel, harden their hearts, break their vows, worship idols, and repeatedly waver between two opinions.

In fact, it is in the New Testament that we see that greatest display of the wrath and judgment of God anywhere in the Bible. There is one place where we see the judgment of God, the righteous justice of God, the wrath of God, the grace of God, the mercy of God, and the love of God all poured out in full measure, in place, at one time; and that was at the cross. It was because "God so loved the world" (John 3:16), a God full of mercy and grace, that He poured His wrath and judgment upon Himself to satisfy His justice for you and for me.

> See that you do not refuse him who is speaking. For if they did not escape when they refused him who warned them on earth, much less will we escape if we reject him who warns from heaven. At that time his voice shook the earth, but now he has promised, "Yet once more I will shake not only the earth but also the heavens." This phrase, "Yet once more," indicates the removal of things that are shaken—that is, things that have been made—in order that the things that cannot be shaken may remain" (Heb. 12:25-27).

We will answer to God for every sin we ever committed, and the smallest and most insignificant one holds for us a death sentence. We can stand before Christ at the foot of Mount Sinai and be judged according to the perfection of His Law, or we can stand behind Christ at the foot of Mount Zion as a benefactor of His sacrifice and, because of that, also a benefactor of His saving grace.

This is a Gospel call from the author of Hebrews! He is saying to us, "Do not be like Esau or Cain! Do not refuse Who is speaking!" Those who ignored the voice of the Lord and the commands of Scripture in this life did not escape His judgment, and neither will anyone in the life to come. The Word of the Lord is meant to shake all things and eventually consume all things, except for things that cannot be shaken; and the only things that will not be shaken are those that are anchored to the Chief Cornerstone, Jesus Christ.

"Therefore let us be grateful for receiving a kingdom that cannot be shaken, and thus let us offer to God acceptable worship, with reverence and awe, for our God is a consuming fire" (Heb. 12:28-29). Since we are anchored to Christ and our life is unshakeable because it is built on His Word, the author of Hebrews urges us to bring acceptable worship with reverence and awe. If our lives are truly built on Him, our affections are aimed at Him, and our satisfaction is found in Him, we will want to be shaken free of all our burdens and sins. "Our God is a consuming fire"; and He is going to burn up all the dross, all the hay, wood, and stubble, and all broken branches that are not connected to the vine of life.

Unlike Esau, let us see the value of this great inheritance; and unlike Cain, let us heed the words of the God Who has spoken to us. For those of us who are part of the kingdom of God, let us find comfort in the fire of God, knowing that everything He burns up in our lives is meant to refine and conform us to the image of Christ. And everything that is shaken and burned up around us was something opposed to the Lordship and supremacy of Christ.

When it seems like the world is on fire, nothing is stable, and everything around us is shaking, we must not grow weary; we must not faint. We are receiving a kingdom that cannot be shaken, and our faith is in the unbreakable promises of the Lord, the God Who never fails! True saving faith cannot be undone because it is a gift from God, secured by God, maintained by God, and fulfilled by God. Let us bring acceptable worship according to our faith in these promises, with reverence and awe, to the God who is worthy.

Why do you say, O Jacob, and speak, O Israel, "My way is hidden from the LORD, and my right is disregarded by my God"? Have you not known? Have you not heard? The LORD is the everlasting God, the Creator of the ends of the earth. He does not faint or grow weary; his understanding is unsearchable. He gives power to the faint, and to him who has no might he increases strength. Even youths shall faint and be weary, and young men shall fall exhausted; but they who wait for the LORD shall renew their strength; they shall mount up with wings like eagles; they shall run and not be weary; they shall walk and not faint (Isa. 40:27-31).

CHAPTER 15
THE LORD IS MY HELPER

BY: JOSHUA WEST

Let brotherly love continue. Do not neglect to show hospitality to strangers,
for thereby some have entertained angels unaware. Remember those who are in prison,
as though in prison with them, and those who are mistreated, since you also are in the
body. Let marriage be held in honor among all, and let the marriage bed be undefiled,
for God will judge the sexually immoral and adulterous. Keep your life free from love of money,
and be content with what you have, for he has said, "I will never leave you nor forsake you."
So we can confidently say, "The Lord is my helper; I will not fear; what can man do to me?"

HEBREWS 13:1-6

IN THIS CHAPTER, WE LOOK at one of the most powerful promises of God in the Bible to those who belong to Christ: "I will never leave you nor forsake you" (v. 5). Let the gravity of that statement sink in. The God Who is eternal, Who spoke the universe into existence, Who took on flesh to take the punishment for our sins promises us that if we, in fact, are reborn in Christ, He will never abandon us. This statement should put to rest any doubts we have about God's commitment to us as His people.

If the message of Hebrews has worked itself into the depths of your heart and mind and your spiritual eyes have truly been opened to the reality of what it teaches, I believe that nothing in this life will ever be able to break you. That is not because you will never again have trials; but no trial, trouble, or persecution in this life could even come close to comparing to the value and beauty of the reward that awaits us. Paul says something similar in Romans chapter eight: "For I consider that the sufferings of this present time are not worth comparing with the glory that is to be revealed to us" (Rom. 8:18).

One of the practical purposes of Hebrews, in my opinion, is to urge us to take our eyes off the imperfection of this world, ourselves, and our situations and to fix them on something unshakable, something eternal, and something infinitely more beautiful than anything in this life—our risen Messiah and Savior Jesus Christ. We must fix our eyes on our future reward with Him, free from sin and safely secure in Him.

The entire Bible is about Jesus; to see it any other way is to have missed the entire point. Every ceremony, sacrifice, foreshadowing, prophecy, and stream of theological thought is meant to point us toward Christ, His beauty, majesty, glory, and supremacy in all things. As Christians, we must anchor ourselves to the supreme nature of Jesus and take our eyes off living for things like money, worldly success, prestige, power, selfish ambition, and the fleeting pleasure of sin.

After clearly showing the betterness of Christ when compared to every foreshadowing that proceeded Him and urging the believer to anchor oneself to the unshakable Rock, which is Christ, the author of Hebrews gives some practical commands that should flow out of the regenerated heart.

In Hebrews 13:1, we read, "Let brotherly love continue. Do not neglect to show hospitality to strangers, for thereby some have entertained angels unaware." The Bible is an Eastern book that typically speaks in a patriarchal language; so when the author says "brotherly love," this is aimed at Christian men and women alike. Christian brotherhood is not causal, surface-level, or shallow. This is referring to a group of people who have rejected this world and all the things of this world to live for a common treasure, a common life-consuming passion, to which they have completely devoted their lives. As Christians, we are bound together by so many things we share in common. But at the center of it all is a common Savior, Who secured for us salvation and everlasting life by laying down His life. This is why we willingly—gladly, even—lay down our lives for Him and each other. Anything less is not real.

"'Greater love has no one than this, that someone lay down his life for his friends'" (John 15:13). God's love toward us was sacrificial, passionate, and obedient to the Father; and in response, the life of the true believer is sacrificial, passionate, and obedient to Christ, even unto death. But this is also the kind of love that binds us together as believers.

John 13:34-35 says, "A new commandment I give to you, that you love one another: just as I have loved you, you also are to love one another. By this all people will know that you are my disciples, if you have love for one another.'" This brotherly love that is inward to the Christian community is what Christ says bonds us together and testifies to a watching world that we belong to Him.

The author of Hebrews says that in this vein, we should "let brotherly love continue" (v. 1) inwardly to the body and outwardly to the world, showing hospitality to even strangers because this is our nature. It says that sometimes, we might even be showing this hospitality to an angel (v. 2). But I believe that this is a statement of fact and not given as a motivation for showing hospitality to strangers; that would be manipulation. Christians show love and hospitality to strangers and even enemies because they are made in the image of God and because this is the nature of our Father in Heaven.

The Greek word for "hospitality" is where we get the English word "hospital." It literally means to be responsible for the care of someone else's every need. We see this played out in great detail in the story of the Good Samaritan found in Luke 10:25-37. This is what it looks like to show hospitality to a stranger. Our lives belong to Christ. As Paul says in Romans 12:1, our bodies should be "a living sacrifice," which is our true and proper worship to God. We love fellow Christians like brothers, sisters, mothers, fathers, sons, and daughters; and we love everyone else because of the Gospel. This includes the stranger, the foreigner, people of other religions, and even those who consider us enemies.

> "You have heard that it was said, 'You shall love your neighbor and hate your enemy.' But I say to you, Love your enemies and pray for those who persecute you, so that you may be sons of your Father who is in heaven. For he makes his sun rise on the evil and on the good and sends rain on the just and on the unjust. For if you love those who love you, what reward do you have? Do not even the tax collectors do the same? And if you greet only your brothers, what more are you doing than others? Do not even the Gentiles do the same? You therefore must be perfect, as your heavenly Father is perfect" (Matt. 5:43-48).

The true nature of Christianity is radical. There is really no such thing as lukewarm Christianity. In Revelation 3:16, we read that He will spit the lukewarm from His mouth. Jesus is not going to spit true sons and daughters out of His mouth. This is talking about posers, imposters, and false converts. Please remember that the faith spoken of in Hebrews 10 and 11 is not super or extreme Christians; it is the posture and manner of living of every truly genuine believer.

In fact, verse three of Hebrews 13 reminds us of what was said about those of saving faith in chapter 10: "Remember those who are in prison, as though in prison with them, and those who are mistreated, since you also are in the body."

The passage in Hebrews 10:32-34 reads:

> But recall the former days when, after you were enlightened, you endured a hard struggle with sufferings, sometimes being publicly exposed to reproach and affliction, and sometimes being partners with those so treated. For you had compassion

on those in prison, and you joyfully accepted the plundering of your property, since you knew that you yourselves had a better possession and an abiding one.

If we are truly in Christ, then we are all part of the same body. In the end, there will only be two conditions of people on the final day. Christ is King today; but on that final day, He will be recognized and acknowledged by all as King of kings and Lord of lords. On that final day, all people will be made a footstool (Psalm 110:1) and put underneath the feet of Jesus, except for those who are part of His body.

Ephesians 1:21-23 says, "Far above all rule and authority and power and dominion, and above every name that is named, not only in this age but also in the one to come. And he put all things under his feet and gave him as head over all things to the church, which is his body, the fullness of him who fills all in all." All things will be of Him or underneath His feet. This truly is an issue of faith. Loving your brother; being kind to strangers; loving your enemies; suffering with and for other believers; losing your stuff, your freedom, even your life bear witness to or deny your supposed profession of faith. So many people in our culture reject the Word of God, the Gospel, and, ultimately, Jesus because they hate the truth and sound doctrine. But no need to worry—there are hundreds, if not thousands, of ear-tickling preachers and teachers who say exactly what your "itching ears" want to hear.

> I charge you in the presence of God and of Christ Jesus, who is to judge the living and the dead, and by his appearing and his kingdom: preach the word; be ready in season and out of season; reprove, rebuke, and exhort, with complete patience and teaching. For the time is coming when people will not endure sound teaching, but having itching ears they will accumulate for themselves teachers to suit their own passions, and will turn away from listening to the truth and wander off into myths. As

for you, always be sober-minded, endure suffering, do the work of an evangelist, fulfill your ministry (2 Tim. 4:1-5).

And like the apostle Paul is telling Timothy, the author of Hebrews is telling us to stay anchored to Christ as revealed in the Word of God. Reject all things outside of God's written and living Word because, otherwise, you will drift. Drifting from trusting in the Word is a real and present danger, but the author of Hebrews also wants to warn them about external temptation; and in Hebrews 13:4, he focuses on the sanctity of marriage: "Let marriage be held in honor among all, and let the marriage bed be undefiled, for God will judge the sexually immoral and adulterous."

First, marriage is a reflection and example of Christ and His Church. The intimate relationship Christ has with His bride, the Church, is so very important. Two things that God will not tolerate are idolatry and sexual immorality. Second, Paul focuses on three areas we are most often tempted in—sex, power, and money—in Ephesians 5:1-5:

> Therefore be imitators of God, as beloved children. And walk in love, as Christ loved us and gave himself up for us, a fragrant offering and sacrifice to God. But sexual immorality and all impurity or covetousness must not even be named among you, as is proper among saints. Let there be no filthiness nor foolish talk nor crude joking, which are out of place, but instead let there be thanksgiving. For you may be sure of this, that everyone who is sexually immoral or impure, or who is covetous (that is, an idolater), has no inheritance in the kingdom of Christ and God.

Then in Ephesians 5:22-33, Paul compares the sanctity of marriage to our relationship with Christ.

This is why God hates sexual immorality, and this is why homosexuality is the ultimate rebellion against God. It is taking something that is sacred to God and something deemed as very good by God and saying that it is neither good nor special. It degrades the picture and reflection of Christ and His bride, the Church. This is not only to the homosexual but also to the adulterer, the fornicator, and all who are sexually immoral. God will forgive those who repent and turn from these lifestyles; but He will never accept them, nor will He accept any sin, no matter what a wicked culture says.

THE LIE OF THE PROSPERITY GOSPEL

"Keep your life free from love of money, and be content with what you have, for he has said, 'I will never leave you nor forsake you'" (Heb. 13:5). Charles Spurgeon said, ""You say, 'If I had a little more, I should be very satisfied.' You make a mistake. If you are not content with what you have, you would not be satisfied if it were doubled."[13] When it comes to idolatry and immorality, there is no greater idol than the love of money. Of course, in America and in the American Church, we have a theology that teaches us the opposite of this. We hear sermon after sermon about giving so you can receive or that God wants you to be rich so that you can be a blessing. God is rich! He does not need you to be rich for His kingdom to come. Those who teach this are liars or have deceived themselves.

> Those who have believing masters must not be disrespectful on the ground that they are brothers; rather they must serve all the better since those who benefit by their good service are believers and beloved. Teach and urge these things. If anyone teaches a different doctrine and does not agree with the sound words of our Lord Jesus Christ and the teaching that accords with godliness, he is puffed up with conceit and understands nothing. He has an unhealthy craving for controversy and for quarrels about words, which produce envy, dissension, slander, evil suspicions, and constant friction among people who are depraved in mind and deprived of the truth, imagining that godliness is a means of gain. But godliness with contentment

---

13   Charles Spurgeon, *Spurgeon's Sermons: Volume 3*, (Peabody: Hendrickson Publishers, 2011).

is great gain, for we brought nothing into the world, and we cannot take anything out of the world. But if we have food and clothing, with these we will be content. But those who desire to be rich fall into temptation, into a snare, into many senseless and harmful desires that plunge people into ruin and destruction. For the love of money is a root of all kinds of evils. It is through this craving that some have wandered away from the faith and pierced themselves with many pangs (1 Tim. 6:2-10).

These people are depraved in their minds and have been robbed of the truth. "Godliness with contentment" is evidence that you are living for Christ and a future reward by faith. God does not promise to make you rich. God does not promise worldly success in all of your endeavors. God does not promise that you will not suffer, go to jail, get cancer, suffer loss, or endure persecution. God does not promise you your best life now. But He does promise that He will never abandon you; and this is one of the greatest promises in the Bible because if you have God, you have everything.

We can claim Hebrews 13:6: "So we can confidently say, 'The Lord is my helper; I will not fear; what can man do to me?'" Those who do not see this as a treasure and see anything else as more valuable than this promise have been robbed of the truth, and the truth is God's Word. Make sure you are holding fast to the anchor of God's Word because if your faith is in preachers and teachers who tell you what your "itching ears" and wicked heart want to hear, then your faith is worthless.

Those who truly see the value of God's promise to "never leave us nor forsake us" will be able to say with complete faith and confidence, "'The Lord is my helper; I will not fear; what can man do to me?'"

If God promised a worldly victorious, trouble-free, and prosperous life, then why would we be warned not to be tempted by what man might do to us? We see that throughout history, Christians have often suffered to proclaim and live out the message of the Gospel. So either people like John the Baptist, Paul, all the other apostles, and even Jesus Himself were doing something wrong; or things always going well with you is not a promise of the Christian life. But we can find rest in the words of Matthew 10:26-33:

> "So have no fear of them, for nothing is covered that will not be revealed, or hidden that will not be known. What I tell you in the dark, say in the light, and what you hear whispered, proclaim on the housetops. And do not fear those who kill the body but cannot kill the soul. Rather fear him who can destroy both soul and body in hell. Are not two sparrows sold for a penny? And not one of them will fall to the ground apart from your Father. But even the hairs of your head are all numbered. Fear not, therefore; you are of more value than many sparrows. So everyone who acknowledges me before men, I also will acknowledge before my Father who is in heaven, but whoever denies me before men, I also will deny before my Father who is in heaven.

Denying Jesus is not merely uttering the words, "I deny you." Most people do not think they are denying Jesus because their self-invented version of Jesus is here in their minds to give them everything that they want. But Jesus says those who deny His Word deny Him.

> And he said to all, "If anyone would come after me, let him deny himself and take up his cross daily and follow me. For whoever would save his life will lose it, but whoever loses his life for my sake will save it. For what does it profit a man if he gains the whole world and loses or forfeits himself? For whoever is ashamed of me and of my words, of him will the Son of Man be ashamed when he comes in his glory and the glory of the Father and of the holy angels. But I tell you truly, there are some standing here who will not taste death until they see the kingdom of God" (Luke 9:23-27).

DEATH OUTSIDE THE CAMP

For the bodies of those animals whose blood is brought into the holy places by the high priest as a sacrifice for sin are burned outside the camp. So Jesus also suffered outside the gate in order to sanctify the people through his own blood. Therefore let us go to him outside the camp and bear the reproach he endured. For here we have no lasting city, but we seek the city that is to come. Through him then let us continually offer up a sacrifice of praise to God, that is, the fruit of lips that acknowledge his name. Do not neglect to do good and to share what you have, for such sacrifices are pleasing to God (Heb. 13:11-16).

We are exiles, foreigners, and strangers; and we have no enduring city here. It is this mindset that sets us up to be useful, productive in service, and content in the Christian life. We do not wish to suffer or try to suffer, but we must set our minds to the reality that there will be suffering so that we are prepared. This also helps keep us from sin because the mind that has made peace with the reality of suffering will not be tempted to sin in the flesh. This is why the apostle Peter said in his epistle, "Since therefore Christ suffered in the flesh, arm yourselves with the same way of thinking, for whoever has suffered in the flesh has ceased from sin" (1 Peter 4:1).

Therefore, it is so important to look to the example of the apostles and the prophets, the way they lived and the way they viewed God's Word. There is always the temptation to believe that we will somehow be immune to trials and suffering for the glory of Christ; but as we focus on the Scripture, we are forced to prepare ourselves for the realities they faced as well as what Jesus promised in John 15:18-19: "'If the world hates you, know that it has hated me before it hated you. If you were of the world, the world would love you as its own; but because you are not of the world, but I chose you out of the world, therefore the world hates you.'"

IMITATING THE FAITH OF THOSE WHO CAME BEFORE US

"Remember your leaders, those who spoke to you the word of God. Consider the outcome of their way of life, and imitate their faith" (Heb. 13:7). Remember the true followers of Christ who made an impact on your life—pastors, preachers, Sunday school teachers, parents, family friends, youth pastors—those who spoke to you about the Word of God, those who taught you, those who discipled you, and those who lived out their faith in front of you.

What was the outcome of their lives? Well, in a worldly sense, there were probably many different outcomes. But in a spiritual sense, it is always the same—salvation and the heavenly reward of eternal communion and life in Christ. This is why trying to use faith as a formula for worldly success cannot hold its form as we diligently study our way through the book of Hebrews or the rest of the Bible. Just like in Hebrews 11, the outcomes of all their lives were very different; but through saving faith, this cloud of witnesses is eternally united in the end reward of their lives.

Some spent most of their lives building an ark that saved them from the wrath of God. Some lived in tents in a Promised Land that would be inherited and inhabited by future descendants. Some left the treasures of Egypt behind for that same Promised Land and suffered in the wilderness with the people of God, only to die just before they took possession of the land.

> Women received back their dead by resurrection. Some were tortured, refusing to accept release, so that they might rise again to a better life. Others suffered mocking and flogging, and even chains and imprisonment. They were stoned, they were sawn in two, they were killed with the sword. They went about in skins of sheep and goats, destitute, afflicted, mistreated—of whom the world was not worthy—wandering about in deserts and mountains, and in dens and caves of the earth. And all these, though commended through their faith, did not receive what was promised, since God had provided

something better for us, that apart from us they should not be made perfect (Heb. 11:35-40).

But no matter the physical outcome of our life, if our faith is in Christ, we can be sure of the eternal outcome because God has promised; God keeps His promises, and God never changes. As Hebrews 13:8-9 says, "Jesus Christ is the same yesterday and today and forever. Do not be led away by diverse and strange teachings, for it is good for the heart to be strengthened by grace, not by foods, which have not benefited those devoted to them."

This is the character of our Savior—unchanging, dependable, reliable, and unwavering. This is what gives us confidence in the promises that God has made to us in His Word. In verse seven, of Hebrews 13, it says, "Remember your leaders, those who spoke to you the word of God. Consider the outcome of their way of life, and imitate their faith." The apostle Paul was one of these leaders; he was an apostle to the Gentiles and author of sacred Scripture. Listen to what he says in Philippians 3:17-21:

> Brothers, join in imitating me, and keep your eyes on those who walk according to the example you have in us. For many, of whom I have often told you and now tell you even with tears, walk as enemies of the cross of Christ. Their end is destruction, their god is their belly, and they glory in their shame, with minds set on earthly things. But our citizenship is in heaven, and from it we await a Savior, the Lord Jesus Christ, who will transform our lowly body to be like his glorious body, by the power that enables him even to subject all things to himself.

Like the author of Hebrews, Paul is urging us to follow him and the example of himself and the apostles so that we are not led away by strange teachings and theology that are not represented in the Scripture. These strange teachings offer a Christianity without suffering, persecution, sacrifice, reproach, and death. Instead, they promise power, prosperity, worldly success, and a life free from trial. This is not the Christian life. Be sure there are blessings, joys, successes, promises, resurrection power, and ultimate victory in the Christian life; but it comes at the expense of the life of Jesus, and the Scripture tells us that we, too, must lay down our lives to be unified with our Savior.

THE CHRISTIAN CALL TO COME AND DIE

"We have an altar from which those who serve the tent have no right to eat. For the bodies of those animals whose blood is brought into the holy places by the high priest as a sacrifice for sin are burned outside the camp" (Heb. 13:10-11). And here we reach the crescendo of the entire book of Hebrews, a statement of reality to all believers and a charge to unite ourselves with Christ in reproach, suffering, and death. We have something that the world that lives according to their belly and the desires of their flesh does not have. We have an altar that they do not. We have an altar that even the Old Testament priests did not have a right to eat from because this bread of life is only available to those who have died with Christ so that they might be raised with Him.

In the time of the Jewish temple, when a portion of the sacrifices were given to the priests to eat because they were part of the Levitical priesthood, animals were sacrificed for the sin of the people. And then, their bodies were taken outside the city gate and burned. In the temple, the people brought the animals and sacrificed them; their blood was used as an offering for their sins, and then the carcasses were taken outside the gate.

Ancient cities were constructed with city gates and walls that surrounded them to keep the people safe, and Jerusalem was no different. The temple was in the safety of the city; the streets were lit; and there was safety and order just like in the Law of God. Unfortunately, we could not live up to the Law, so the Law could save us. Jerusalem could offer safety but not salvation. This is also true of the Christian life. God is not calling us to seek comfort and safety but rather to follow Jesus and be where He is.

Outside the safety of the Jerusalem walls, where the bodies of the animal sacrifices were burned, was not safe. Out there were lepers, robbers, darkness, and uncertainty. This is also where Jesus was sacrificed for our sins. He left the comfort and glory of Heaven for you and me. The Christian life is about following Jesus and identifying with Jesus in suffering, in dependency on God's Word, in death, and, ultimately, in life through resurrection power. And it is all of it or none of it. We must accept all of Jesus, all of His Word, all of His commands, and all the parts that come with following Him.

Matthew 16:24-25 tells us, "Then Jesus told his disciples, 'If anyone would come after me, let him deny himself and take up his cross and follow me. For whoever would save his life will lose it, but whoever loses his life for my sake will find it'" (Matt. 16:24-25). The idea of denying yourself, taking up an instrument of death, and following Jesus to lose your life only sounds unappealing to those who do not understand the value of having a new life in Christ, the wonder and glory and jaw-dropping beauty of Jesus.

The priest of the Old Covenant lived in the safety of the city and had no power to save or forgive the sin of the people, which meant certain death. But our Great High Priest walked to His death, carrying a cross outside the camp to secure eternal life for all who put their trust in Him by faith. Saving faith brings eternal life and will willingly die to sin, to self, and to the love of this world and all the things in it at the command of Christ because our trust is in a future reward.

"So Jesus also suffered outside the gate in order to sanctify the people through his own blood. Therefore let us go to him outside the camp and bear the reproach he endured. For here we have no lasting city, but we seek the city that is to come" (Heb. 13:12-14). The priests of the Old Covenant could not justify us before God, could not sanctify us to make us free from sin. Only Christ could do this by the power of His own blood. Christianity is a path to a future city and a future reward; and in this life, it is a call to come and die that we might live. Jesus suffered for us outside the camp, so the only proper and reasonable response is to offer ourselves as a living sacrifice and go to Him outside the camp to bear reproach for the One Who bore reproach for us.

It truly is in trial and suffering that we shine the brightest for Christ. It is when the world knows without a doubt that we value Him a thousand times more than any blessing we have in this life. He is more valuable than our homes, our careers, our bank accounts, our place in society, our wives, our husbands, our children, our hopes, our dreams, our safety, our comfort, or anything else in this fallen world that is rapidly fading away.

Remember what Paul said in Philippians 3:17-21. Those who live for comfort, whose "god is their belly," who "glory in their shame" are "enemies of the cross"; and "their end is destruction." But those of us who live as living sacrifices for the glory of Christ do so because "our citizenship is in heaven," and we are waiting for a Savior who will quicken our mortal bodies with "a power that enables him even to subject all things to himself."

Jesus says, "Follow me," or "Come to me outside the camp." This is death to self; but remember that this death equals freedom, peace, power, hope, and eternal life. It is the humbling ourselves to come to Him that is hard because the actual burden of carrying the cross is not because we do it in His power and all for His glory.

Jesus has a better way. He says in Matthew 11:28-30, "'Come to me, all who labor and are heavy laden, and I will give you rest. Take my yoke upon you, and learn from me, for I am gentle and lowly in heart, and you will find rest for your souls. For my yoke is easy, and my burden is light.'"

False teachers often say that the trial is only meant to set you up for a blessing; and by "blessing," they mean worldly wealth or position or something in that vein. They make it seem like that trial is merely a test that if you pass, you get all of your fleshly hopes and dreams. They make it seem like following Jesus is a quick detour to prepare you and equip you to go down the road you really want to go down. But following Jesus means *following* Jesus—obeying His commandments and living to bring Him glory.

It is not a mystery; Jesus is calling us to follow Him down the Calvary Road, carrying a cross outside the camp to suffer scorn and reproach for His name. And those of us whose eyes have been opened to the beauty of Jesus will do so willingly, gladly, and even joyfully.

Noah suffered reproach; Moses believed suffering reproach for Christ was more valuable than all the treasure in Egypt. And many professed Christians could not be bothered to share Christ in a hostile room, or because they might lose their job, or because they are comfortable at home enjoying the safety and comfort they have been blessed with. Many people cannot be inconvenienced to attend church because the wind is blowing too hard, it is cold outside, or they want to sleep in before junior's t-ball game, much less even considering the idea of abandoning the comfort of this country to take the Gospel where there is no comfort. Many would not dream of abandoning a high-paying job to take a low-paying job because they know God has called them there.

I am not saying God has called all of us to do these sorts of things. I am merely saying that the true believer will pray wild and seemingly reckless, faith-saturated prayers like, "God take this life and use it as You will for Your glory. Pour it out like a drink offering to Yourself so that I might die empty for your glory."

"Through him then let us continually offer up a sacrifice of praise to God, that is, the fruit of lips that acknowledge his name. Do not neglect to do good and to share what you have, for such sacrifices are pleasing to God" (Heb. 13:15-16). In our culture, dozens of books are written every year to try to convince us of our worth; and people write songs that fuel a pop culture flame that is bent on convincing us of their worth. Even many deceived preachers will preach that "you›re worth it" and "you›re worthy"; but the book of Hebrews, the entire Bible, every word that I will ever preach, and the sum of creation declare that He alone is worthy! He is worthy of any sacrifice, loss, pain, or reproach. He is worthy of all praise and worthy of all things because He alone is Supreme and Sovereign and the only Savior of the world. Christ is the Treasure, and we are the Reward of His sufferings.

The Lord is our Helper and our strength. He is Love, and He alone is Life. He grants that life more abundantly than we could ever think, dream, or imagine. It is in willfully coming outside the camp to where Jesus is that we will find joy and peace because these things are not found in chasing safety and comfort; they are found where Jesus is. Let us go to Him. Let us abide in Him. Let us see the truth of Christ's beauty so that we might long to live our lives solely for Him.

BIBLIOGRAPHY

Chandler, Matt. "God Is For God." Truth Endures. January 17, 2012. You-Tube video. 48:08. https://www.youtube.com/watch?v=9yqQuTT1S40.

Jones, Martyn Lloyd. *Romans: An Exposition of Chapter 12: Christian Conduct.* Carlisle: Banner of Truth Trust, 2000.

MacArthur, John. *The MacArthur New Testament Commentary: Volume 27 Hebrews.* Chicago: Moody Publishers, 2016.

Moffatt, James. *The Epistle to the Romans.* London: Forgotten Books, 2012.

Owen, John. *An Exposition of the Epistle to the Hebrews.* Carlisle: Banner of Truth Trust, 1991.

Owen, John. *Exposition of Hebrews, 3:7-5:14.* Vol. 4. *Hebrews.* Seymour: Banner Publishing, republished, 1992.

Owen, John. *Exposition of Hebrews, Volume 6.* Seymour: Banner Publishing, republished 1992.

Pink, A.W. *Studies on Saving Faith.* San Francisco: Bottom of the Hill Publishing, 2016.

Sibbes, Richard. "A Breathing After God." *The Complete Works of Richard Sibbes*, ed. Alexander Balloch Grosart. Vol. 2. Edinburgh: James Nichol, 1862.

Sproul, R.C. (@RCSproul). "It has been said that God hates the sin and loves the sinner. But it's the sinner God sends to hell not just the sin." X. June 7, 2016, 3:48 p.m. https://twitter.com/RCSproul/status/740269117698150400.

Spurgeon, Charles. *Spurgeon's Sermons: Volume 3*. Peabody: Hendrickson Publishers, 2011.

Spurgeon, Charles. *Spurgeon's Sermons: Volume 9*. Peabody: Hendrickson Publishers, 2011.

ABOUT THE AUTHORS

JOSHUA WEST IS A PASTOR, evangelist, and author. He currently serves as executive director of the pastors network at World Challenge. He speaks at conferences, crusades, and churches all over the world. The goal and focus of his ministry are biblical preaching and teaching with a high view of God and the Scripture,

centered around the Gospel of Jesus Christ. He partners in life and ministry with his wife and best friend Kiara. Their goal is to preach the Gospel to all people, make disciples, and bring glory to the name of Jesus. They live in Colorado Springs, Colorado, with their son Jameson.

GARY WILKERSON IS A PASTOR, author, and the president of World Challenge, an international ministry that was founded by his father, David Wilkerson, whose mission is spreading the message and mission of Christ all across the world. He has traveled nationally and internationally speaking at conferences and has conducted mission ventures, such as church planting

and starting orphanages, clinics, and feeding programs among the poorest of the poor and the most unreached people on earth. Gary and his wife Kelly have four children and live in Colorado Springs, Colorado.

This book is published in association with World Challenge.

Transforming lives through the message and mission of Jesus Christ.

For more information about
WORLD CHALLENGE
and
The Jaw-Dropping Beauty of Jesus
please visit:

www.worldchallenge.org

Ambassador International's mission is to magnify the Lord Jesus Christ and promote His Gospel through the written word.

We believe through the publication of Christian literature, Jesus Christ and His Word will be exalted, believers will be strengthened in their walk with Him, and the lost will be directed to Jesus Christ as the only way of salvation.

For more information about
AMBASSADOR INTERNATIONAL
please visit:

www.ambassador-international.com
@AmbassadorIntl
www.facebook.com/AmbassadorIntl

AMBASSADOR INTERNATIONAL
GREENVILLE, SOUTH CAROLINA & BELFAST, NORTHERN IRELAND

www.ambassador-international.com
Magnifying Jesus while promoting His gospel through the written word.

Thank you for reading this book!

You make it possible for us to fulfill our mission, and we are grateful for your partnership.

To help further our mission, please consider leaving us a review on your social media, favorite retailer's website, Goodreads or Bookbub, or our website, and check out some of our other books!

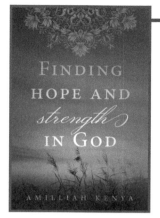

Finding Hope and Strength in God is a twelve-month devotional with different themes for each month focused on pointing you to your all-sufficient Savior, Who will give you strength and hope to face the day and to live a meaningful and fulfilling Christian life. Its practical approach to life will help you navigate real-life situations with tangible solutions to help you find meaning, hope, strength, and courage despite the tumultuous eventualities of life.

God calls us all to live a life of purpose—to live prepared to be on mission and go where He needs us both locally and globally. Through life-shaping stories, *Unseen People* offers encouragement, inspiration and prepares our hearts when it's time to go. Sometimes the hard places He guides us to are next door, not around the world. The call is the same—to see and serve people, to hear and share their stories. You will be different. Their stories will shape you, change you and challenge you to keep going.

For many men, work, relationships, and life in general overwhelm their schedules and keep them from spending time with God. But what they don't realize is that joy is found in those moments spent with their Creator. In *Finding Joy in Every Season*, Chris Corradino provides brief devotionals for every day to help men get in the Word and start their day off right. Spending just ten minutes with God will realign your focus and help you find the joy that comes in the everyday moments.